Wellington's Welsh General

Wellington's Welsh General

A Life of Sir Thomas Picton

by
ROBERT HAVARD

---

*'I found him a rough foul-mouthed
devil as ever lived'*

THE DUKE OF WELLINGTON
ON PICTON

AURUM PRESS

In memory of my father
Gwilym Havard

First published in Great Britain 1996
by Aurum Press Ltd, 25 Bedford Avenue, London WC1B 3AT
© 1996 by Robert Havard

A catalogue record for this book is available
from the British Library.

ISBN 1 85410 402 0
2 4 6 8 10 9 7 5 3 1
1997   1998   2000   1999   1998   1996

Printed and bound in Great Britain by Hartnolls Ltd, Bodmin.

CONTENTS

LIST OF PLATES

LIST OF TEXT FIGURES

PREFACE AND ACKNOWLEDGEMENTS

Thomas Picton, the only Welshman buried in St Paul's Cathedral, is very likely Wales's greatest soldier. Yet he is not the shining paragon of whom a nation can be unreservedly proud. In Cardiff's City Hall, where stand eleven marble statues known as the 'Heroes of Wales', Picton keeps uneasy company with the likes of lawmaker Hywel Dda ('the Good'), love poet Dafydd ap Gwilym, hymn writer William Williams and St David, Wales's patron saint. While they gaze mistily heavenward, the abrasive Picton seems about to draw his sword and shatter the pious calm with his 'voice of twenty trumpets'. A figure of some notoriety, Picton was dubbed 'the Tyrant of Trinidad' long before he was knighted for his exploits in the Iberian Peninsula, and, if many thought him Wellington's best general in the field, others remembered only the ignominy of his trials in London in which he was charged with having sanctioned the torture of a young mulatto woman. It is this contrast that fascinates and, in telling his chequered tale, I have tried to do justice to the different sides of his character.

I became interested in Thomas Picton in a roundabout way. For a long time the only man of that name known to me was a Rhondda miner who went to Spain to fight Fascism and died there in 1939. Tom Picton, mountain fighter, booth fighter and light-heavyweight champion of the Navy in the First World War, was a scrapper the wrong side of forty when the Spanish Civil War started. Probably too addled to find Spain on the map, he went as a volunteer, fought, was taken prisoner, with a right hook – his best punch – he felled a guard for maltreating a comrade, and was put up against a wall and shot. Tom Picton was a legend of my youth, the kind of man yarns breed on. Years later Tom's proud nephew and namesake, Tommy Picton, took me to see family photographs at his brother's house in Llansteffan and, on the way home, suggested that we ought to pay our respects to the most famous Thomas in their family, Sir Thomas Picton, whose pile stood in nearby Carmarthen: 'The nearest thing in Wales to Nelson's column', he said. '*Sir* Thomas?' I asked incredulously, putting the exuberance down to his brother John's hospitality. But I followed his directions dutifully until we came to a great obelisk that pierced the sky. Drawing near the imposing stone plinth, which formed an island in the middle of the road, I read with astonishment a resonant list of Spanish place names: Ciudad Rodrigo, Fuentes de Oñoro, Badajoz, Vitoria.

To a Hispanist, the magic of these names writ large in Carmarthen town proved irresistible. Overhastily perhaps, for my interests up to that point had been exclusively literary, I resolved to look into the life of a soldier who, unbeknownst to me, had achieved fame in Spain. I soon discovered that he had already been the subject of two biographies: H.B. Robinson's nineteenth-century eulogy and Frederick Myatt's recent account, which, though excellent in its way, is a strictly military history. Picton, I also discovered, is centre stage, for a time, in V.S. Naipaul's *The Loss of El Dorado*, but that book covers only his Trinidad years. When, on my doorstep at the National Library of Wales, I found Picton's letters, it seemed to me that there was room for another book, one in which, whenever possible, the man should speak for himself. All dialogue in the text is taken directly from written sources, while scenic description, though necessarily based at times on working assumptions, does not, I trust, compromise veracity. My aim has been to tell Picton's story as straightforwardly as possible, hoping that the perspective of a Hispanist may compensate for my deficiencies as a historian. I had great joy in writing the book, for it took me to a period of time I had never thought to explore and to corners of the Peninsula – also Walcheren and Waterloo – that I might not otherwise have visited. Who could forget the glow of sunlight on the battlements of Ciudad Rodrigo?

I have not written the book Tommy Picton might have hoped for, but there is consolation in knowing that his two namesakes were kindred spirits and, unlike himself, abrasive in both word and action. I am obliged to him for getting me going. I am also indebted to a number of colleagues at the University of Wales, Aberystwyth, who gave me invaluable help and encouragement in their respective areas: Richard Ireland in Law; Gareth Williams in History; Richard Brinkley, a mine of information in the Hugh Owen Library, and the late Fergus Johnson, Professor of History, who made his large Peninsular library available to me. I am especially grateful to two eminent historians, Professor Peter Thomas, an expert in eighteenth-century political history, and Dr Ron Walker, a distinguished Pembroke historian and archivist, both of whom read my typescript and offered much sensible advice. Lastly, I wish to thank Mr Michael George, a most scrupulous and creative editor. Any errors that remain are mine alone.

Robert Havard,
Aberystwyth
October 1995.

ONE

TRINIDAD

El Tío

I

When, on 17 February 1797, an expeditionary force under the command of General Sir Ralph Abercromby sailed through *La Boca del Dragón* into the Gulf of Paria, Spanish rule in Trinidad was effectively at an end. The fleet of 17 warships, 40 transports and 8,000 men signalled British intentions too clearly to leave any doubt in the mind of *Su Excelencia*, Don José María Chacón, the island's governor. Don José was entertaining Admiral Don Sebastián Ruiz de Apodoca at Government House, newly built on the strand of Puerto de España, when he sighted the throng of enemy sails out in the gulf against the blurred backdrop of mainland Venezuela. His sense of imminent catastrophe could have been no less acute than that recorded by Columbus 300 years before when he entered the gulf by the southern *Boca de las Serpientes* and saw a wall of water come charging mast-high out of the Orinoco delta at his tiny band of ships. Columbus, who had just named the island after three contiguous peaks in the Southern Range, promptly invoked the protection of the Trinity and was spared, but the new wave, of gleaming British guns, was likely to be less kind to His Most Catholic Majesty's humble *flotilla*. Four warships and a single frigate, plus a garrison of 600 less than able-bodied men, were all Chacón had to defend his island, a force which left the governor under no illusion about the esteem Trinidad enjoyed in Madrid. To Abercromby it made an equally unambiguous statement about how ragged a power imperial Spain now was.

His fourteen years as governor might have gone unnoticed in Madrid, but Don José, a Knight of the Order of Calatrava, retained a quixotic sense of duty to the Spanish Crown. He dispatched Admiral Apodoca at once, with orders to return to base at Chaguaramas Bay, ten miles west along the cape, from where he was to proceed to destroy the invading ships. Don Sebastián departed, perhaps with warlike purpose, but having taken stock, he resolved to burn rather than sail his meagre fleet. The blaze from the *San Vicente*, the *Gallardo*, the *Arrogante* and the frigate *La Concha* that lit the sky above Puerto de España at 2.00 a.m. the following day was cheered by Abercromby's men out at sea. Before dawn Don Sebastián was back at Government House telling the astonished governor that his act of arson might have cost Spain *La Ysla de la Trinidad* but it would save Spain itself. Henry Nelson Coleridge, who visited Trinidad some years later, learnt how their conversation had gone:

'Only one ship has fallen into the enemy's hands! I have burnt the rest', said the admiral breathlessly.

'Burnt? Burnt!' replied the governor, aghast. 'But have you saved nothing?'

'Sí, Su Excelencia!', Apodoca exclaimed with Castilian verve, 'I have saved Santiago de Compostela!'[1]

At dawn Abercromby instructed Rear-Admiral Henry Harvey to bring the British fleet in to shore. Following the surrender of the *San Dámaso*, which alone had escaped Apodoca's torch, a token exchange of fire ensued with the new forts on Gaspar Grande Island. The latter were quickly evacuated, however, and at noon British troops landed at Mucurapo and marched on Puerto de España virtually unopposed. In a last gesture of defiance a number of French settlers overpowered the arsenal guard, armed themselves and took to the woods. The governor himself briefly retreated to the nearby Laventille Hills, but the message he received within hours from Abercromby convinced him that resistance was futile and his only course was to sign the articles of capitulation, which he duly did at Valsaín shortly after 5.00 p.m. that same day, 18 February 1797.[2] The British had suffered one fatality in the operation, and Spanish losses were also negligible, but when Don José and Don Sebastián were returned to Spain a vindictive Carlos IV overruled his council and held them both guilty of treason. The admiral would be reinstated in 1808, but the ex-governor, denied the right of appeal against the royal decree that banished him from Spanish domains, died penniless in Portugal.

The 62-year-old Sir Ralph Abercromby did not linger to enjoy the island's comforts. He had been sent to suppress the French-assisted Carib revolt in the Windward Islands where there was a volatile mix of populations, French planters, *petits blancs*, black slaves, mulattoes and enclaves of fiercely independent Caribs.

After Trinidad's capitulation he sailed north to Martinique to complete his sweep through the islands before returning home to engage more directly in the effort against France and Spain. Reckoning that Trinidad was vital to British interests, both on account of its size and its proximity to the Spanish Main, Abercromby left behind a force of 1,000 men in Puerto de España, which was all he could spare. To the surprise of many, the man he appointed to their command as captain-general and the island's first British governor was the 39-year-old Thomas Picton, a burly hook-nosed Welshman who was better known for his rough tongue and harsh treatment of his own men than for heroics against the enemy.

Picton's military experience was decidedly limited, but, as Abercromby's aide-de-camp since March the previous year, he had impressed his commanding officer as a strong disciplinarian in the campaigns at St Lucia, Grenada and St Vincent, which saw him promoted to lieutenant-colonel of the 56th Regiment of Foot. Abercromby had more senior officers with him, but they can scarcely have relished the prospect of governing a steamy, disease-ridden, slave island whose shores and interior were rife with all manner of brigands and whose better class of inhabitant spoke only Spanish or French. For brigadiers like John Moore the honourable course lay in Europe. But for Picton this corner of the Caribbean held out hopes he could hardly have entertained just three years before when he arrived in its seas a captain.

He was six-foot-one and he spoke good Spanish. He was governor and he meant to govern.

II

Prior to his arrival in the West Indies Thomas Picton's life had been largely uneventful. The seventh of twelve children, and the fifth son, born to Thomas and Cecil Picton in Haverfordwest on 24 August 1758, he was given the name of an elder brother who had died the previous November at five years of age. The family home was at Poyston, three miles north of the county town, but Cecil Picton was visiting friends in Haverfordwest when labour pains struck with sudden ferocity and she gave birth to the new Thomas in a large house that would later be known as the Dragon Hotel.[3]

His father was a country squire who, in 1749, the year before he married, had been high sheriff of Pembroke. His mother hailed from Llandough, in Glamorgan, and was the daughter of the Revd Edward Powell and half-sister to Richard Turberville, sheriff of Glamorgan in 1740 and, from 1767 to 1768, MP for the county. It was probably through contact with Turberville on county business that Thomas Picton senior had met his future wife. A granddaughter recalled that she 'was a very small woman of great bodily activity' who even in later life 'would sometimes spring up on her son's hunter and trot round the lawn on his saddle'.[4] Married in 1750, she no doubt took the subsequent annual round of childbearing in her stride and counted herself lucky that ten of her children survived infancy. In August 1758, however, with two of her first four sons having died within the last twelve months, she must have been praying for a strong, healthy lad when taken unawares in Haverfordwest. She was not to be disappointed.

At Poyston, the young Thomas enjoyed the busy freedom of a country boyhood with woods, mountains, rivers and sea all close at hand. Attending Haverfordwest Grammar School, he mixed with local lads and had the considerable company of his family: two older brothers, Richard and William, two older sisters, Elizabeth and Frances, plus the steady increment of new arrivals, Charlotte, Edward, John, Jane and Anne. The eldest, Richard, was fond of music and played the flute. Elizabeth, four years Thomas's senior, was his special favourite: tall and devout, she never married. Young Edward was the family scholar; he went up to Oxford, was awarded an MA and took the cloth, his education being rather more rigorous than Thomas's to judge by the latter's always erratic spelling. William was the black sheep who ran away from home at an early age when threatened with a flogging, never to return.[5]

Picton senior was very likely a severe man, and respect for authority would have been a priority in his household. He had standards to maintain in a county where the family name went back to a Norman knight, William de Picton, or Pyketon, whose castle motte on the River Cleddau east of Haverfordwest was built *circa* 1100 and predates nearby Picton Castle by some two hundred years. Military tradition was inbred and it had flourished again recently in the person of young Thomas's uncle, William Picton, who was already a major by the time Thomas could walk. When this genial bachelor came down to Poyston on leave he had brave tales to tell of Minden and Zierenberg in the Seven Years' War when he commanded the 12th Regiment of Foot. Not surprisingly, Thomas, like his younger brother John, was spurred to thoughts of adventure and advancement in the military. In 1771, at the age of thirteen, he was gazetted an ensign in his uncle's regiment.

Before joining his regiment Thomas was sent, on his uncle's advice, to the Military Academy at Little Chelsea, then a hamlet separated by green fields from Westminster. There, under M. Louis Lochée, he studied military theory, a preparation commonly overlooked by better connected officers who simply bought their commissions, and there too he probably learnt some French.[6] After two years, when he was ready for his first posting, he went with high expectations to join his Uncle William in the 12th Foot at Gibraltar, a sensitive spot since its seizure from Spain in 1704. The 'Rock' was going through a quiet time, a lull before the storm, and only the young man's patience was to be tested in more than three years spent at an outpost he could walk round in a morning. He had to content himself with garrison duty, inspecting the tunnelled fortifications, listening to his uncle's stories and, most profitably for his future career, developing a firm grasp of Spanish.

When William was appointed colonel in the 75th or Prince of Wales's Regiment of Foot in 1777 Thomas also transferred and, back in Britain, was promoted captain. But leaving Gibraltar when he did he missed the three-year siege that in 1782 saw the repulse of a combined Spanish and French attack. He also missed involvement in the American War of Independence. In fact, the only opportunity he had to show his mettle was in 1783 on the disbandment of the 75th, then quartered in Bristol. As the senior officer with the regiment he had the unpleasant duty of reading out a disbandment notice to the soldiers assembled at College Green Square, this being consistent with government policy for the reduction of forces after the American war. Once he had paraded the men and read out the notice Picton left the square, and the murmuring discontent grew steadily more ugly until a riot threatened. Recalled to the scene, the 25-year-old captain strode into the midst of the mutineers, on whom his strapping frame and brandished sword had an immediate and sobering effect. Flinging one of the ringleaders into the arms of the provost's constables, Picton proceeded to unleash such a torrent of billingsgate that no man present doubted his best course was to start the long trek home.

Picton was commended for a fearless action that had nipped an ugly situation in the bud, but the promise of promotion on the strength of it did not materialize. On the contrary, the newly formed 75th was among the first to be disbanded on the reduction of British forces in the same year. Like the mob he had so swiftly brought to heel, he was himself obliged to return home to Pembroke, where he spent the next eleven years on half-pay. According to his brother, the Reverend Edward Picton, these years were spent in 'the enjoyment of the sports of the field, in studying the classics, but more particularly in perfecting himself in the art of war'.[7] This was an eloquent attempt to fill a lacuna that has no place in the lives of great men, but in practice Thomas's reading of the classics could have been little more than rudimentary, while his training for war on the Preseli Mountains hardly extended beyond horsemanship, shooting and sharpening his eye for the country. No matter how pleasant such a gentleman's life was, Picton must have grown increasingly impatient as the years went by and each of his requests for active employment met with a negative response from London.

It had been frustrating to learn of his old regiment's exploits in Gibraltar and to be idle in Pembrokeshire while his younger brother John enjoyed active service and overtook him in rank. John Picton had made the luckier transfer from the 75th to the 12th, and was promptly dispatched to Flanders when war broke out with revolutionary France in 1793. Wounded the following year in a sally from Nijmegen, he was promoted to major in 1796 and to major-general by the time he returned home from India only to catch cold and die in his bed at Poyston in 1815. His belligerent role in a scandal in 1798 greatly upset Colonel Arthur Wellesley of the 33rd Foot, the future Duke of Wellington. Renowned in India for his card skills, Major Picton had fought a secret duel with his commanding officer, Colonel Henry Harvey Aston. This proved inconclusive, but a subsequent duel fought between Aston and Picton's close friend, Major Allen, who was suspected of procurement, resulted in Aston's death. Wellesley, who regarded 'affairs of honour' as the curse of the army, had presided over the court of inquiry and fumed at the unnecessary loss of life.

Some time during his stay at Poyston – probably in the year 1793 – it appears that Thomas also fought a duel, at a quarry near Withybush, against a hot-tempered Irishman named Charles Hassall. The cause of the quarrel is unknown, but it may have been a dispute over land, for Hassall was a surveyor-cartographer, newly settled in Eastwood, who would publish important studies of the local agriculture. In the duel Picton suffered a gunshot wound to the throat, which permanently affected his voice and made him sound hoarse.[8] The affair may well have lengthened Picton's stay at home, but by 1794 he was recovered. With war declared and still no sign of an appointment, it was his pride that hurt most. Towards the end of 1794, in desperation, he boarded a merchant ship bound for the West Indies trusting that Lieutenant-General Sir John Vaughan, commander-in-chief of the Leeward Islands and a fellow Welshman, would make him welcome. It was a gamble that paid handsome dividends. For once he would be in the right place at the right time.

When Picton arrived at Britain's West Indian headquarters in Martinique, Vaughan made him deputy quartermaster general with the brevet rank of lieutenant-colonel. Conditions were notoriously unhealthy: in a period of five years, from 1793 to 1798, 35,000 British troops perished in the Caribbean, almost all the 19,000 deaths in the Southern Caribbean caused by yellow fever.[9] Given that sick, discontented troops are notoriously difficult to command, Vaughan was no doubt glad of an officer with Picton's unaffected manner and imposing presence. A bachelor and career soldier himself, who had led the Royal Welsh Volunteers with distinction in the American war, Vaughan had been in the Caribbean since 1779. Rumour had it that in the seizure of St Eustatius from the Dutch in 1781 he had confiscated islanders' goods to line his pockets. Vaughan declared in Parliament, where he sat as member for Berwick, that 'neither directly nor indirectly, by fair means nor foul', had he 'made a single shilling by the business'.[10] The matter had blown over by 1792, when he was created a knight of the Bath for his military services, and there is no reason to doubt Picton respected Vaughan in the eighteen months he spent as his aide-de-camp. As events transpired, Vaughan missed the most critical years in the West Indies for, like so many of his soldiers, he was suddenly taken ill and, in August 1795, he died at Martinique, the island in whose capture from the French thirty-three years before he had fought with great distinction. The consequences could have been dire for Picton, who instantly lost his personal appointment, but just when he was thinking of returning home news came that Britain was to step up its activity in the Caribbean and that Sir Ralph Abercromby, the no-nonsense Scot, would take command.

Abercromby sailed at the head of 27,000 men, the largest expedition ever to have left Britain's shores, but ferocious storms in the Channel forced him back to Portsmouth with considerable loss of life. When his bedraggled fleet finally reached Barbados in March 1796, Picton was among those to be received by the new commander-in-chief and was promptly rewarded with a position as an extra aide-de-camp. This boon may have owed something to the fact that Abercromby knew his Uncle William, who would doubtless have sent Thomas a letter of introduction, but it is equally probable that the Scot took an instant liking to the 36-year-old captain's forceful personality. For one thing, Abercromby had a close knowledge of Prussian

Army practice and he placed a high priority on discipline and *esprit de corps*, both of which he thought had been sorely lacking in the British Army since the demoralizing American war. It was to men like Picton, with his stern look and harsh voice, that he was inclined to turn. His good first impression was confirmed in the fiercely contested campaign in St Lucia, from 26 April to 24 May, which saw the capture of the previously impregnable fortress of Morne Fortunée, an operation in which Picton performed with such distinction that Abercromby recommended him for a lieutenant-colonelcy. Picton then accompanied Abercromby to St Vincent, which fell to the British on 10 June within three days of their landing, after which they returned to headquarters at Martinique. By now a genuine bond had developed between the two men and, when Abercromby sailed home for a brief period of recuperation following the surrender of Grenada in May, Picton went with him.

During this voyage on the cramped forty-four gun frigate *Arethusa* Picton 'lived and even slept in the same cabin with the general', recalled Brigadier General Frederick Maitland,[11] who would supersede Picton as military commissioner of Trinidad in 1803. At such close quarters the younger soldier had ample opportunity to learn from an old warhorse who had risen to the highest rank by sheer dint of effort and who was, besides, very much an independent thinker. Abercromby had refused to fight in the American war, deeming the rebels' cause to be just. Now he was opposed to the political ideology of the French which, with his famously myopic eyes shrouded by bushy white brows, he must have coldly dissected for Picton's benefit. The latter, in turn, would have had the opportunity to impress with his extensive knowledge of the Caribbean, where he had already served longer than most British officers.

It was during their return voyage that Spain entered the war on the French side and Trinidad, a strategic Spanish possession, came to loom large.

III

Abercromby left Trinidad on February 25 1797, barely a week after the Spanish capitulation. Aware of what he called the 'trying and delicate situation' which Picton faced as commandant and military governor of the island, he sought to lighten his task by giving him 'ample powers' and the broadest of civil briefs: 'Execute Spanish law as well as you can. Do justice

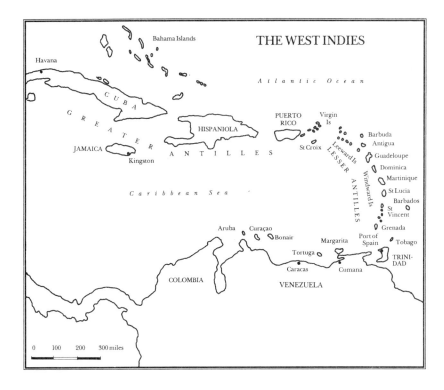

according to your conscience. That is all that can be expected from you.' He likewise informed his chief justice, John Nihell, to 'execute all things in due manner that shall belong to those different offices agreeable to the instructions and powers which shall by my order be given you by lieutenant-colonel Picton'.[12]

It was sensible to retain Spanish law: the islanders were familiar with it and most believed Trinidad would soon be restored to Spain either by force or as a makeweight in a peace treaty. Yet Abercromby, who had studied law without affection as a young man in Edinburgh and Leipzig, also knew that the law of Spain as it was applied in the colonies was chokingly corrupt, a 'den of chicanery', as the inhabitants protested to him. He needed to trim its procedural fat: 'I have received serious complaints of the extortions practised by the exactions of excessive fees, and the mal-applications of useless and unnecessary proceedings in the administration of justice, by the escrivanos, attorneys etc.' Consequently, Abercromby deemed it prudent to dispense with the offices of an assessor and auditor as well as of some lesser legal posts, 'although it may be contrary to the form and spirit of the Spanish laws'. Allowing appeals to the Privy Council only in litigations exceeding £500, he instructed Nihell:

> to shorten and simplify the proceedings, and to terminate all causes in the most expeditious and least expensive manner that the circumstances of them will admit, according to the dictates of your conscience, the best of your abilities, and conformably to the instructions you shall receive from lieutenant-colonel Picton.

By giving Picton the right to interpret without being bound by Spanish law, Abercromby made his position as governor unassailable. In Picton all the offices of government were combined: he was the supreme political, criminal, civil and military authority. He was thus equipped to impose order on an unruly colony, but the privilege of power would exact its retribution.

Order was Picton's immediate challenge. Over the years Trinidad had gained such notoriety for lawlessness that in Grenada they set a 'good behaviour' bond of £1,000 on any immigrant from that island. Lawlessness had much to do with location and size. Extending over 1,863 square miles, the island, as its stretched bull-hide of a map shows, reaches out and almost touches the Spanish Main with its two western extremities. To fugitive *peones* it was a haven from Spanish law, the nearest *audiencia* or tribunal being in Caracas. The densely forested interior also hid runaway slaves and deserting soldiers, neither of whom had come to the island by choice. Proximity to the Main fostered trade, but this had long been subject to the whim of the privateers who hovered along the island's extensive coast.

Picton was little better equipped to break this tradition of plunder than Chacón had been. In his early letters to Abercromby in Martinique he wrote of French privateers in twelve-gun schooners who terrorized and subverted inhabitants along the unprotected north and east coasts. As to the townspeople in what was now Port of Spain, they were unlikely to renounce the old regime and welcome the British if the feeling was that they were only temporary masters. Even with regard to his troops Picton had problems. In an early return he estimated that of the 1,000 soldiers he had been left, only 520 were fit or effective. Of these little more than 300 were British, the remainder consisting, in equal measure, of French Negroes picked up on the island and what was left of a detachment of mostly pressganged Hanoverians who were deserting daily. In short, the situation facing Trinidad's first British governor was so desperate it seemed anarchy would destroy him sooner than the rumoured Venezuelan invasion.

Yet Picton did have 'ample powers', curbed only by his

conscience. He also had support in an unexpected quarter, from the planters. These were mainly French royalists of the *petite noblesse* who had been disaffected by the Revolution. They had come into the island in increasing numbers after the *cédula* of Carlos III in 1783, which opened the doors to all Catholics, Spanish or not, and enticed them with tax-free grants of land.[13] These men had turned their backs on Europe and were out to make or restore their fortunes. Many had come to Trinidad by way of other islands, notably Saint-Domingue, where their enterprises had been ruined by slave rebellions, which they attributed to weak government and to the policies of the French Revolution, which had decreed political equality for mulattoes in 1792 and the total abolition of slavery in French dominions in 1794. In Trinidad, it was the ineptitude of Spanish rule and the neglect of the island that had frustrated them. For such men British rule was the last hope. But it depended crucially on the actions of one man.

The *hidalgos*, Trinidad's upper class of aristocratic Spanish descent, found themselves in much the same situation. For them, too, the old country's alliance with republican France boded ill. Britain, by contrast, offered the prospect of commercial prosperity that had never been realized in generations of Spanish rule. Picton consulted one such Spaniard, Don Cristóbal de Robles, a tough planter with many years' experience in the island's administration. The advice he got, given in Spanish, was simple and to the point. Robles began by dismissing the bulk of the island's population as 'refugees and desperate characters, Spanish peons, or people of colour, a set of vagabonds, who casually come over from the continent, and who are ready to join in any disorder that affords a prospect of plunder; slaves, who have been sent here from the other islands for crimes dangerous to their safety'.[14] He went on to warn Picton:

> If you do not give an imposing character to your government before the climate diminishes the number of your soldiers, your situation will become alarming. If those men do not fear you, they will despise you; and you may easily foresee the consequences. They have been accustomed to a timid and temporising government. A few acts of vigour may disconcert their projects.

Picton did act vigorously. First he showed his own men what to expect if they misbehaved. Typical was the fate of Hugh Gallagher, a sergeant in the Royal Artillery charged with having raped a free Negro woman on the road from St Joseph, seven miles inland from Port of Spain. When Justice Nihell sent

Gallagher to the governor, on 21 May 1797, Picton's examination of the accused was decidedly brief:

'Did you see the sun rise this morning?' he asked gruffly.
'Yes', replied Sergeant Gallagher.
'Then you shall not see it set.'[15]

Whereupon the bewildered Gallagher was hauled away, protesting his innocence and demanding a trial, while Picton's brow darkened as he shouted hoarsely after him:

'Villain! You are going to Hell with lies in your mouth!'[16]

If, for a moment, Justice Nihell thought it would amuse the governor to try a soldier for raping a black woman he was undeceived when he took his after-dinner stroll to the wharf that evening and saw Gallagher's stiff frame swinging from the gallows against the setting sun.

Two days later, having discovered that others had been involved in the incident, Picton ordered 1,500 lashes each for privates Patrick Murphy, Patrick Kenny and Andrew Redman, a punishment they would be lucky to survive. This was too much for Nihell, who soon quarrelled with Picton and was removed from office. But in the governor's defence it must be said that indiscipline among the troops was a menace in an island where the rum ran free and mulatto women walked with voluptuous grace. By making an example of his own men Picton could claim impartiality when dealing firmly and expediently with local delinquents. This he often had to do, as in the case of a man named Celestino, a *peón* from St Joseph, whom he had executed for being drunk and disorderly in the same month of May.

Soldiers who deserted could expect no mercy. Picton offered a reward for their capture, dead or alive, and when fourteen privates in the Hanoverian corps of Baron Hompesch, a Swiss nobleman and British Officer, were brought in he had them executed within hours of taking them into custody. True, it was a capital offence under British law to desert in time of war, but such a mass execution was rare and would have made no little impression. The temptation to desert was great, if only because the Orange Grove Barracks where the men were stationed stood adjacent to the Caroni Swamp on the south side of town, a location that made them prime targets for the mosquitoes spawned in the swamp during the rainy season. Yellow fever was endemic and it is small wonder that many soldiers considered the flesh available in town or on the Main an altogether more pleasant route to damnation. The sole deterrent was Picton's instant justice.

He was no less severe with those who helped deserters, as the

captain of the schooner *Buscaruidos* found when he returned to
Trinidad and was arrested on suspicion of having ferried
Germans to the mainland. Under torture, members of his crew
soon confessed and the captain was promptly shot. A similar fate
awaited those who harboured French privateers. Any wayward
planter could expect a government launch to call, quick transport to Port of Spain, and a dawn rope. The same rope faced
any who had dealings with subversives on the Main. At the end
of 1797 Picton learnt through his intelligence that M. Jean
Baptiste Richard, a mulatto, was corresponding with fugitives
there from Guadaloupe. When Richard attempted to bring
three anti-British conspirators across the gulf, he was intercepted at La Brea Point to the south of the island, brought to
the capital and hanged on the wharf gallows. Suspecting a
degree of complicity on the part of the prisoner's father-in-law,
Mr Moss, Picton invited the latter to watch the execution with
him at his *mirador* on the King's Wharf before sending him off
with some choice words.

In all there were thirty-five executions during Picton's governorship, the majority in his first year. Trinidad's new justice was
rough and ready, but down on Port of Spain's busy waterfront it
was, conspicuously, a justice seen to be done. The *mirador* was
much used since it was well placed for new arrivals to be ushered
through and have the gallows pointed out, ideally when in
service. As they filed past, the governor hailed them from above
and explained the more grisly details of his penal system. This
became a standard harangue when the stability that resulted
from firm rule brought prosperity to the island and more people
of all kinds and colours came in: from planters, shopkeepers and
tradesmen, down to London prostitutes and slaves by the boat-
load.

The slaves felt the full force of Picton's new order. Branding,
ear-clipping and flogging were done at Port of Spain jail, where
those whose offences did not warrant execution were crowded
into steamy cells, the notorious *cachots brûlants*, and staked out
in irons. This correction centre had a salutary effect on the more
liberal masters too, for they disliked paying seven-dollar fines to
bail out a slave whose disability was likely to be rather more
serious now than a hangover. Slave discipline was the backbone
of Picton's order. Rebellions in other islands had shown the
dangers of leniency and it was clear to any literate person in the
age of Adam Smith that a colony's salvation lay in the prosperity of trade, which, in turn, depended on a disciplined and
reliable work force. Soon Picton would publish his own
slave code, saying exactly what slaves could and could not do,

increasing the punishments for those who erred. It was more a directive to the masters than to the slaves.

One of Picton's first measures was to form a militia. The iron hand he had shown in imposing the law ensured no lack of volunteers. He drew mainly on whites, adding a dash of the more reputable Free People of Colour, but resisted all temptation to arm blacks, which had proved fatal elsewhere. Once this part-time body of zealots had been drilled into an effective constabulary his beleaguered soldiers could concentrate on their proper duty, the island's defence. Hand-picked locals who aspired to Picton's favour were decidedly better suited to police Port of Spain's mixed society. To them the town's ills were as visible as the mudbanks in the blue Gulf of Paria. Picton was not blind to them either, nor to the poverty that was the lot of most citizens.

When he took his daily walk from Government House his first paces were pleasant enough. Skirting the strand of soft anchorage along the level parade of La Marina, he came to the busy junction of Cuatro Caminos, where groups of men nodded their respects to him outside Salazar's chandlery and Vicente Sanda's huckster's shop. From there he strode to the impressive masonry quay with its two batteries *en barbette*, where he could trace the rigging of ships against the brilliant bay and the mysterious continent beyond. He watched with satisfaction the colourful coming and going of his troops and the gesticulating commerce of the port. He listened to the roll of drums and to Silvestre, the black town-crier, whose huge voice announced the sale of bankrupt stock or an unexpected prize from the Main.

But if he had a mind to turn inland he at once entered grim streets of low wooden houses that led back in a grid towards the impenetrably wooded mountains behind. As Pierre McCallum, who visited the island in 1803, remarked: 'The town is laid out regularly enough, but the houses are shabby, yet admirably well adapted to roast human beings alive; environed with lofty mountains in a semi-circular manner, as if the founders intended it for an oven.'[17] It was an oven that had always encouraged lethargy and vice, and Picton's militia had no lack of duties to perform.

To confirm the evils his eyes saw, Picton had the evidence of the census done at Abercromby's behest immediately after the capitulation. It made interesting reading. Trinidad's civilian population of 17,718 consisted of 10,009 slaves, 4,476 People of Colour, 2,151 whites and 1,082 native Indians or Arawaks now mostly confined to reserves.[18] Among the whites there were nearly twice as many men as women, but this was offset by a preponderance of women among the People of Colour, especially in Port of Spain. The town's population of 4,525 was roughly a quarter of the island's total. Nearly half the whites lived here, mostly unmarried males, but women of colour outnumbered their male counterparts in town by 771 to 321, and slave women also outnumbered slave men by 856 to 567. The slave women, surplus to requirements on the plantations, were sent to town for domestic service. But the striking disproportion among Free People of Colour points to rampant prostitution, with Port of Spain's numerous taverns being predominantly brothels, plentifully supplied with mulatto women.

Picton was no prude. He knew that a man had sexual needs and indeed he would soon take as his own mistress a *mulata* named Rosetta Smith. He had no wish to monasticize his colony, only to put the lid on its flesh-pots, where trouble invariably started. This meant that the governor's long arm would have to reach into the squalid alleys. But down those same alleys were such lucrative outlets as billiard tables, which could bolster a thirty-bob a day salary. Besides, it would be useful to keep an ear to the ground in places where liquor loosened a man's tongue. Anyone reported as undesirable could look forward to a sharp spell in jail before being deported, as the scholarly agitator Pierre McCallum found when his views on slavery ran him foul of the governor. Picton's simple policy was to have a finger in every pie and run the island like a tight ship: slaves and soldiers, *peones* and planters, tars and tarts all came under his keen eye and his equally harsh law. That his measures were effective is apparent from what he wrote to Abercromby on 4 April 1797: 'A very exact police has been established in the town, and is gradually extending itself over the whole island. The colony is everywhere quiet, and the inhabitants pay prompt obedience to the orders of government.'[19]

It must have been with some satisfaction that Picton put down his pen on finishing this letter. If he then let his gaze drift out to sea he might have indulged in the luxury of more expansive thoughts about his role as governor, even about enjoying some of its perks.

IV

One of the peculiar advantages Trinidad enjoys as the southernmost Caribbean island is that it lies 'without the reach of the hurricanes so destructive in Jamaica and some other islands', wrote Frederick Mallet, captain of Abercromby's surveying

engineers.[20] Another, he added, is the great bay before the Port
of Spain:

> one of the safest and most extensive in the world; ships being able
> to anchor there in a superficial space of above 70 miles, with a
> depth of water from 12 to 5 fathoms one mile off shore, and all
> good holding ground. Should they drive from their anchors they
> go on shore in soft mud, and are got off without damage.

When Picton read this survey and then turned to fix his gaze
on the ultramarine that stretched from Government House to
the cloud-capped mountains of mainland Cumaná, his mind's
eye may well have seen the liquid haven teeming with all manner
of merchant ships bringing cargo from every part of the adjacent continent to the British *entrepôt* of Trinidad. All that was
needed to turn his fancy into fact, to make Port of Spain a new
Venice or Lisbon, was the liberation of the Spanish colonies
from the yoke of imperialism and the dead hand of mercantile
protectionism. As time went on his head turned ever more
frequently from the howlermonkey forests above Port of Spain
to the great slumbering giant across the water. It exercised the
same fascination as it had on Sir Walter Raleigh, who, in 1595,
had caulked his ships at Tierra de Brea's pitch lake in the south
of the island before setting off for 'the large. rich and beautiful
Empire of Guiana'.[21] But whereas Raleigh failed to find El
Dorado in the huge continent, Picton would have its riches
brought to Trinidad.

Irresistible too was the military logic. Now that the colony was
peaceful, now that the island prospered under the code of
British commerce, it only remained to liberate Venezuela. The
junta del gobierno in Caracas had not attacked him because it was
too busy coping with its internal agitators: nationalists, republicans, *americanos*. He would encourage these revolutionaries, fan
their flames. A little assistance might see them unchain
Venezuela. The centuries-old viceroyalties of Spanish America
would collapse like a house of cards. England would prosper and
so would its war effort.

Picton sent spies across the gulf and welcomed *americanos* to
Government House. He dined them well and spoke in their own
language about William Pitt, the Younger, prime minister of
Great Britain and the champion of free trade, and about
Francisco de Miranda, a Creole from Caracas, who even now had
the prime minister's ear in London. And he spoke, with some
embellishment, about his own plans for an invasion that would
spark revolution. The Madeira was palatable, the tobacco fumes
heady, and when Picton's guests took his message back to the

Main it scarcely mattered if some made enough noise for the
governor of Cumaná to hear. Picton wrote to London asking for
a raise in salary: 'I am obliged to spend considerable sums in
gratifications to persons on the Continent', he explained.[22] In
March 1798 he was put on £1,200 a year.

Earnest men were attracted to Port of Spain: Manuel Gual and
José España, who had barely escaped with their lives from an
abortive insurrection in Caracas the previous July. Miranda's
agent, Caro, would come from London. Excited by the endless
possibilities and by the prospect of his backwater island entering mainstream politics, Picton wrote on 25 May to General
Cuyler, commander-in-chief in the West Indies, knowing that he
was about to leave Martinique for London. He began by listing
the geographical advantages of his island, much in the spirit of
Mallet's survey, and went on to describe the 'pitiable state of
misery' suffered by the inhabitants on the continent as a consequence of Spanish rule. Finally he came to the heart of the
matter:

> What I have the honour to propose is not in the nature of a
> conquest, difficult and expensive to be maintained. I have to
> submit to Your Excellency for the consideration of His Majesty's
> Ministers, a plan which has for its object the opening of an
> immense commerce to the industry of His Majesty's subjects, and
> securing them advantages of an incalculable value, to be obtained
> by no other means.
>
> If about three thousand troops could be collected, with a sixty-
> four gun ship, a frigate, and some forty-four Indian transports to
> make an appearance or impression – for a squadron would be no
> otherwise useful – I would propose immediately taking possession
> of Cumaná. The public mind has long been prepared, and the
> people in general look forward to it as the most favourable event
> which can befall them. The prejudices against the English nation,
> which the government had sedulously cultivated by every species
> of misrepresentation and artifice, have happily been dissipated by
> the extensive communication and intercourse they have had with
> this island since the conquest.
>
> A declaration that the intentions of His Majesty's Government
> are to give the inhabitants of South America an opportunity of
> asserting their claim to an independent government and free
> trade will, I am convinced, decide them at once to forsake a
> government which has energy only to oppress them.
>
> The expenses of this expedition I propose would, comparatively,
> be very inconsiderable. It will not be necessary to employ horses
> or pioneers, and the ordnance necessary would be a few light field
> pieces only. The principal objects to be attended to will be arms
> for infantry and cavalry, for the purpose of arming the inhabitants,
> and a liberal supply of ammunition.[23]

Picton then alluded to Miranda, the dandy revolutionary who had peddled his message of Latin American liberation throughout Europe as far as the court of Catherine the Great. Miranda had tried to interest Pitt in an invasion as early as 1790, had tried the same in France two years later when that country was at war with Spain, and was now back in England singing the same revolutionary song:

> There is a native of Caracas, I understand, now in London, who might be useful on this occasion: as a native of the country, who has made himself a good deal talked of, he might fix the attention of those people, and thereby make himself serviceable. For very obvious reasons, I would advise his not being consulted on the business, or acquainted with it, until the moment of execution.
>
> The beginning of November will be the best time for an expedition to that part of the Main; the dry weather sets in much sooner there than in the islands. The expedition should go down immediately to its object, without stopping at Trinidad, which would in a certain degree indicate the point menaced; but it will be necessary to apprise me early of the intention, as the success will in great measure depend upon the previous steps which I may take to secure it.
>
> A subordinate expedition might be undertaken from Trinidad, with five or six hundred men, up the River Guarapiche, which would essentially contribute to the complete success of the undertaking; and this might be performed without any additional expense, as I should be able to provide the vessels necessary for their transport on the spot.

The plan could hardly have failed to interest Pitt and his foreign secretary, Henry Dundas. It had a sound aim: commercial expansion. It was tactically astute: weaken Spain further and divert her ally France. It was cost-effective: the merest nudge from Britain to mobilize an entire continent against the enemy. In London they took Miranda seriously at last. The plan he put to Pitt was similar to Picton's but grander in scale. It called for a joint British–American invasion of Latin America, which, for the British, had the added attraction of bringing the United States into a defensive alliance against France. Their ambassador in London was encouraging. Miranda wrote to Washington, to Alexander Hamilton, a West Indian from whom he could expect a sympathetic hearing, and with government approval he sent Caro, a Cuban exile, to Trinidad. Sir Ralph Abercromby came down from Scotland to see Miranda. Everything pointed to an imminent invasion, large or small, with Picton, 'on the spot', contributing 'essentially' to its success.

But November passed. Miranda got no reply from the United

States and Caro took a year to reach Trinidad after running into a French corsair and being jailed at Algiers. In the meantime, the world moved on: Pitt, having squandered so many lives since 1793 in the forlorn attempt to capture the riches of Saint-Domingue, was now understandably worried about his depleted nation's ability to resist the invasion Napoleon threatened. The Americans, at least some of them, wanted a treaty of their own with France, for the five-headed executive then governing the republic was attempting to isolate the United States by getting Spain to cede the Floridas and Louisiana. Abercromby left for Holland, where the Dutch fleet surrendered to him in late 1799, from where he went on to fight Napoleon in Egypt and die a hero at Aboukir Bay in 1801. Picton's plan went off the boil. The governor cursed his luck and treated Caro shabbily when he finally reached Port of Spain out of sorts and out of date. All that could be done now was to keep the threat of an invasion alive.

At the beginning of 1799, Picton had ordered two small raids across the gulf. The first brought back some cattle. The second fell into an ambush and lost twenty men. The raids were goodwill gestures to the *americanos*, fleabite irritants to mainland *hidalgos*. But Picton kept up appearances and an open table at Government House. To lend urgency to the proceedings, he would occasionally invite Manuel Gual or José España. Lesser men were employed as couriers to distribute pamphlets and incite rumours on the Main. It was bluff and propaganda, about mainland towns that were ready to rise and British warships due in two months time, all the more credible when the courier got caught.

España, tiring of promises and prevarication, left the plantation where Picton kept him and, intent on starting an uprising with slaves from his own estate, returned secretly to the Main. He was betrayed and hanged, his severed head spiked on the town gates of La Guaira. Gual tried to stir things again and became Miranda's agent when Caro, disillusioned, went back to England. Within months he died in St Joseph, poisoned, some said, by a Venezuelan spy. The revolution had come to nothing, but it kept the *hidalgos* on Columbus's 'Tierra Firme' guessing. They put a huge reward on Picton's head. On 25 January 1799 he wrote to the governor of Caracas, Don Pedro Carbonelli, saying his vanity had been flattered by the handsome evaluation: 'Twenty thousand dollars is an offer which would not discredit your royal master's munificence.'

In similar vein he wrote to the governor of Guayana:

> I understand your excellency has done me the honour of valuing
> my head at twenty thousand dollars. I am sorry it is not in my

power to return the compliment. Modesty obliges me to remark that your excellency has far over-rated the trifle; but, as it has found means to recommend itself to your excellency's attention, if you will give yourself the trouble of coming to take it, it will be much at your service.

Your excellency's very devoted humble servant,
Thomas Picton.[24]

The waggish tone suggests Picton was enjoying himself despite the disappointment of his abortive invasion. He had much to enjoy, since he had clapped eyes on Rosetta Smith, a copper-coloured, free *mulata*, half his age and as vivacious as she was unrefined. Rosetta was married, but, having a taste for business as well as pleasure, thought nothing about ditching her insolvent spouse when Picton chose her for his island queen. She bore him four children in as many years and when the polished floors of Government House clattered with wooden toys or an upset vase, its heavy beams rang to the shrieks of Rosetta's patois: *¡Ven acá, Jaime! ¡Pa 'ca, maldito!*

Headstrong and ambitious, Rosetta was as earnest in her demands as the moonstruck governor was in his. It was not enough to be the mistress of *el Tío* ('the Uncle' or 'the Boss'), and take what trinkets she fancied off the counters of Port of Spain shops. It was not enough to be the *Doña Señora*, whose twice weekly levees none of the top brass dared miss. Rosetta wanted property, plantations, slaves of her own. She was a well-shaped woman with a good head for figures: she wanted her cut of Picton's excise duties and of his profits from runaway slaves. Smitten the wrong side of forty, Picton was not about to deny her.

There were scandals. Rosetta duped a widow with two daughters into selling her house on Queen Street at a knock-down price. When the respected Mrs Griffiths had second thoughts about the deal, Rosetta got Picton to send round soldiers to lay siege to the house and starve her out. The house was Rosetta's insurance for a rainy day. In the meantime, it would fetch good rent. Rosetta's eye also caught sight of £4 a month on billiard tables. Soon she was paying tavern women for inside information on their paramours, running her own intelligence network. She took over the fuel contract for the garrison and watched every movement in and out of the jail. Picton, clearing his official £1,200 a year many times over, did not begrudge Rosetta her *bagatelles*.

He was enjoying life. Two-thirds of the British immigrants died within three years of coming to the island, from disease, fever or plain dissipation bred of tropical ennui. But Picton jauntily reported in a letter home that 'I never have enjoyed better health than since my return to this country'.[25]

His daily regime might begin with an early hack that took him along the flamingo-studded coast as far as Chaguaramas Bay. Cooler mornings would see him ride inland to San Juan and St Joseph, or north up river valleys fat with frogs to Maraval, Cántaro and Diego Martín. The roads were now the finest in the West Indies, he boasted, and there was plenty to see on the plantations: slaves cutting cane from January to April, replanting from September to November; *peones* felling trees all year round, shaping cords of timber and clearing bush at £18 a quarrie.

He could be sure of a bowl of coffee if he dropped in on planters like St Hilaire de Begorrat at Diego Martín, or Don Francisco de Farfán at Maracas. Eye to eye on politics, they talked easily about cotton, cocoa, sugar and slaves before the governor made a steady canter back to town to miss the day's heat. He needed to visit his own estates to keep his managers on their toes. His investments were growing steadily and would peak in January 1802 with the purchase from M. Delaforest of a 218-quarrie parcel four miles out on the St Joseph road next to M. Michel de Gourville's plantation. Picton bought the land, buildings and 113 slaves for £50,000 in a deal involving £12,000 down and eight annual payments of £4,687.10s, a measure of his confidence in his own and the island's future.

He was well placed for business operations. When a vessel docked, he would be the first at the harbour to reckon the barrels of shelled corn and, with his inspection officer, Dr Alexander Williams, to run an eye over the latest shipment of slaves from Africa. It was imperative to select only the able-bodied, watching out for signs of smallpox. A good Ibo could fetch $350 while 'refuse people'[26] were more trouble than they were worth.

Afternoons, following a short *siesta*, were reserved for business: letters had to be written on immigration, military and penal matters; interviews had to be held and officials from the *Illustrious cabildo* ('town council') needed priming for the regular Monday meeting. Evenings were for leisure: one of Rosetta's levees or a dinner with *americanos* when some spicy detail about the Caracas Junta's latest atrocity was always worth embellishing. Good for a guffaw was María Luisa, the Spanish queen of legendary ugliness whose frolicking with Godoy while her husband Carlos IV mended his clocks was the stuff of pantomime. Godoy's royal service, they said, had begun in the king's guards and ended in the queen's bed. He was *el príncipe de la paz* ('the Prince of Peace') who saved his best piece for an old hag and told the time by the hairs on her head.

If there was private business to attend to, Picton took his victim to one side for a smoke on the verandah facing the sea, where the fireflies darted. His tall frame, large features and abrasive voice were intimidating enough, but he also had an abrupt manner and a way of turning on his prey with an almost repulsive expression fixed on his brow.

On quiet nights he would walk along the quay at sunset when the Sea Fort gun was fired. On his return, there was fresh fish, plantain and the sweet fruit that Rosetta bullied her maids to prepare. When the moon lit the waters and the mainland mountains went black, there was Rosetta.

V

The island was running as smoothly as one of the King of Spain's beloved clocks. In appreciation, London confirmed Picton's status as civil governor in June 1801. Lord Hobart wrote complimenting him on 'the ability and zeal' he had shown 'in administering the affairs of the island', adding the instruction to 'our trusty and well-beloved Thomas Picton' that he should continue under the laws of Old Spain.[27] In October they promoted him to brigadier-general. This told Picton that his policies were not only expedient but perfectly acceptable. A few stretched necks had paid handsome dividends. No matter what Wilberforce and his friends in the Clapham Sect were saying, London approved his tightening up of the slave code. Nor had they paid heed to a disgruntled British shipowner's claim that island produce had been exported in United States' vessels for the governor's own gain. Dundas wrote accepting Picton's explanation, 'convinced that the charges were without the least foundation', and praising his administration, which, by 1801, had seen the island's population increase by nearly 50 per cent to 24,239 and its sugar exports double in three years to over 14 million pounds weight.

Picton's concern was what he saw as 'the threat of peace'. Commercial success might make Trinidad an item for negotiation in the treaty that was surely coming. In October 1801 he wrote to Dundas about 'the serious apprehensions of their future situation' that the most respectable settlers and planters in the island entertained, warning him about those who 'have their eyes continually fixed on Trinidad, and cannot fail to be affected by its newly acquired opulence and flourishing situation'. He argued that 'it would be extremely impolitic to restore

Trinidad on any terms, or for any equivalent' and implored London not to 'make a sacrifice of us as a peace-offering to a jealous and vindictive government'.[28] His best hopes were realized when Trinidad was not among the dependencies exchanged under the Treaty of Amiens in the following year.

Just when things seemed under control they began to fall apart. Picton's tight ship, unfortunately, did not suit the new British immigrants who had come into the island in increasing numbers after the peace with France. Described by Picton as 'a despicable set of insolvent Liverpool and Manchester shopkeepers',[29] the immigrants had aspirations not only to wealth but to political status, even colonial privilege. They certainly expected more not less freedom than they had enjoyed at home. But they found themselves in an island where power resided in one individual, *el Tío*, a coarse, vengeful man 'bred among the goats on the mountains of Wales',[30] as Pierre McCallum put it, a British governor who lived openly with a mulatto woman, whose friends were mostly Spanish or French and who looked upon immigrants as malcontents, brigands and 'Jacobinal rabble'.

The one constitutional body to which the newcomers had recourse was the weekly *audiencia* of the *cabildo*, a curious Spanish institution – Inquisition some called it – with its *alcaldes* (magistrates) and its *escribanos* (court clerks), which was still held in Spanish. More toothless than 'illustrious', the *cabildo* backed Picton to the hilt. It would do. Each of its twelve members, the *alcaldes*, had been hand-picked by him. They were 'the most respectable proprietors of the Colony', he informed London: Don Cristóbal de Robles, 'a native of Trinidad, a gentleman to whom I am under great obligation for his advice and assistance on many occasions of difficulty in the administration of justice'; M. St Hilaire de Begorrat, 'a French gentleman whose zeal and intelligence and indefatigable industry I have successfully employed in terminating an immense mass of intricate litigation which had been unfinished by the Spanish Tribunals'; Don Francisco de Farfán, Don Bartolomé Portel, M. Michel de Gourville, Don Francisco de Castro, Indave, Bontur and Alcalá.[31] There were British members on the council: Messrs Black, Langton, Nugent and Nihell. But the majority of these were planters too, and, as Nihell, the erstwhile chief justice knew from his experience, if they incurred the *rencor* or disfavour of *Su Excelencia*, they could always be dismissed. The *cabildo*, even in Chacón's day, was a purely advisory body to which the governor could listen or not, as he saw fit. Now that the ultimate court of appeal was in London rather than Caracas there was even less inclination to listen. Indeed, if the members of the *cabildo* wanted to keep their seats on the bench, it was they who did the listening, to Picton.

All of which was too much for the immigrants. They spoke loftily of brotherhood, humanity and the natural 'rights of man', invoking the names of John Wilkes, Thomas Paine and John Locke. They argued the merits of a British constitution, trial by jury, a 'House of Assembly' elected by extended suffrage. They formed an 'English Party', which held meetings at Anthony Walton's tavern. They drew up a petition, signed by 108 British settlers, and, most shocking of all, even proposed addressing the Crown, not through their governor, but through the island's London agent!

Those who *knew* Picton were appalled. For one thing, the London agent, Joseph Marryat, was a slave-holder himself. William Harrison, the chairman, left the meeting much disturbed. Winterflood, the Customs Comptroller, begged to have his name taken off the petition. Others, like Dr Alexander Williams, succeeded in narrowly voting down the proposal to bypass Picton. However, the radicals persisted. They would meet again on 10 December for a grand dinner, ostensibly to celebrate the cessation of hostilities with France, but in fact, and in Picton's reading of it, to announce that the time had come for constitutional change.

Picton acted swiftly. He banned the dinner and informed Walton, the prospective host, that he would be held 'personally responsible for any seditious meeting that might take place on his premises on the 10th'.[32] There was no dinner. Next day Picton summoned Thomas Higham and demanded to see the petition that had been left at his store for people to sign. Higham refused and was thrown in jail. A friend, John Shaw, brought a copy to Government House. Higham was released, but he and Shaw were struck off the militia's roll of officers. Picton began an 'investigation' of every person who had subscribed his name to the petition.

He was incensed. With some justification he spoke of those 'whose pretended humanity frequently resides upon the tongue without ever vexing the heart'. Several of the petitioners owned slaves and their enlightened notion of suffrage did not extend to enfranchising the Free People of Colour. So great was their radicalism they were even averse to anyone who wasn't British signing their petition.

Aware of this contradiction, Picton wrote circumspectly to Lord Hobart, the new secretary of war, with responsibility for the colonies, now that Pitt's resignation had brought a change of government at Westminster. On the democratic issue he began by observing: 'Popular Elective Assemblies have been productive of much ruinous consequences in some of the neighbouring Islands where the elements of society are too different to admit a similar composition to those of the Mother Country'.[33] He went on, more specifically:

> One of the objects, first and most important to determine, will be the right of voting, and it may be thought expedient, as in the old Islands, to exclude the Free People of Colour; here by far the most numerous class in the Colony and of whom many possess considerable property. This distinction will render them at all times dissatisfied with the situation and liable to be affected in their loyalty.

It must have struck Hobart as deeply ironic that the tough-minded ruler of a slave colony could argue against an elected assembly on the ground that it was racially discriminatory. The only practical alternative – that of granting the Free People of Colour voting rights – was, as Picton knew, unthinkable.

Though he had powerful support among the plantation barons, Picton was also caught in a web of contradictions from which the radicals had no intention of letting him escape. The past twelve months had seen him authorize a series of gruesome slave punishments that kept the jail full to overflowing. Many slaves had been indulging in dirt-eating, which produced the fatal *mal à l'estomac*. Nothing horrified planters more than suicide, which simply wiped out their investment in labour. Outbreaks had occurred on the estates of Baron de Montalembert and M. St Hilaire de Begorrat. Picton appointed a 'poisoning commission', led by Begorrat, a recent *alcalde* who had dealt with this kind of thing in Martinique. Those slaves unlucky enough to be apprehended before they died of internal disorders could expect to be hanged, burnt alive or decapitated, their heads displayed as chilling reminders to others at plantations' gates. In response to these atrocities a placard was found posted on the sentry box at the King's Wharf one Sunday morning early in February 1802. It read:

> Sanguinary punishments corrupt mankind. The effect of cruel spectacles on the minds of the populace, is the destruction of all tender emotions. It is more calculated to excite disgust than terror. It creates indifference, rather than dread. It operates on the lower orders of society as an incentive to practices of torture; and for the purposes of revenge, whenever they have the power of exercising the cruelties they have long been instructed in. HUMANITAS.[34]

The author was in fact one William Minchin, a barrister and associate of Higham, Shaw and Sanderson, who would soon be apprehended and banished. His may well have been the only comment published in Trinidad on the executions, for Port of Spain's weekly *Courant* said not a word. Others of Minchin's persuasion must have risked saying a few things in their letters home. There was plenty they could rake up about their governor, not only about slaves, but also about the *mulata*, Luisa Calderón, who had been tortured over a case of housebreaking just before Christmas 1801 and eight months later was still at the jail in leg-irons.

Sensitive to this, Picton complained in his letters home that he was being 'attacked by all that is rascally in the land', that 'these people of bankrupt fortunes were capable of every species of infamy', that there was 'a conspiracy to vilify me in the public opinion by every kind of misrepresentation and calumny'.[35] On 5 February 1802, he issued a proclamation. It was in fact a directive to his supporters and 'every respectable individual who knows how to value the safety of his person and property', which 'property' naturally included slaves. It told them to 'pay strict attention to the conduct of certain well known seditious characters now employing every incendiary means to infuse a spirit of insubordination amongst the Negroes and People of Colour, by infamously representing the wholesome severity of the law'. It finished by calling upon them to use their 'utmost endeavours to bring them forward'. The governor also sent de Gourville, a trusted member of the *cabildo*, to explain things to the island's agent, Marryat, in London. Marryat replied that 'no explanation was necessary'; 'Jacobinism is no longer the rage, and whatever outcry her votaries may raise, they will be able to make no impression to your disadvantage here'.[36]

Joseph Marryat MP, millionaire chairman of Lloyds, could not have been wider of the mark. Soon after receiving this letter Picton read another communication from London that told him his appointment as governor of Trinidad was to be terminated.

The mood in London had changed with the new Addington government and the peace. Notably, the abolitionists had gained ground they would never again lose. Wilberforce had moved the Anti-Slave Trade Bill almost every year since 1791, actually carrying it in 1792 when Pitt made one of his most eloquent speeches to the House, only to see it quagmired in the House of Lords, the stronghold of absentee planters. The execution of Louis XVI, on 21 January 1793, turned people's minds against reform and the declaration of war between Britain and France the following month killed the bill, losing it even the support of Pitt, who didn't want a divisive issue in difficult times.

Yet public opinion remained firmly opposed to what Wilberforce called the 'iniquitous traffic' and 'this greatest of all human evils'.[37] In the new century it was no longer possible to argue as callously as one pro-slaver had in 1791 that dealing in slaves might not be an amiable trade but neither was a butcher's, and a mutton chop was still a good thing! The old rhetoric was trundled out: abolition would help France not Africa; it would lose Britain its 'nursery for seamen'; it would ruin the West Indies. And there was always someone with the view that slaves were 'unfit for freedom'. But Wilberforce chipped away with a succession of restrictive bills: the Slave Carrying Bill, which regulated trade through the Middle Passage, and the Slave Limitation Bill, which confined trade to certain ports on the African coast. Abolition itself would not reach the statute book until 1807, but its momentum was already unstoppable and concessions had to be made. Picton's governorship was one of them.

The decisive point was simple enough: Trinidad was not Jamaica. Its slave population, virtually nil in 1783 when scarcely more than 300 people lived on the island, had only recently passed 10,000, while Jamaica's century and a half of British rule had seen more than 800,000 slaves shipped to that island. From this improbable pairing George Canning, the future prime minister, extrapolated an astonishing statistic for the benefit of MPs: 'If there was a question of suddenly cultivating such an Island as Trinidad', said Canning, 'we must make up our minds to the destruction of about a million of the human species.'[38]

Members who listened to the Trinidad debate in May 1802 were no doubt mesmerized by Canning's ghoulish projection. But his logic was irrefutable: Trinidad had missed the slave boat. In the present climate the only permissible large-scale influx of labour would have to be from Britain and Europe, or possibly Asia. That meant free labour. Influenced by the thinking of Adam Smith, the abolitionist James Stephen, a member of Wilberforce's Clapham Sect, had argued in his recent book, *The Crisis of the Sugar Colonies*, that free labour was, in the long run, more economical than slave labour. Colonial development wasn't just a question of muscle and bone: the whole baggage of wives and children had to be catered for if slaves were to thrive. And did the black man pull his weight? Not like a white working his own land. Much simpler to export British yeomen, with a generous helping of London tarts, so long as they could be kept from dying. Politically too, white immigration was preferable. It freed the colony from fear of revolution and it made constitutional reform possible, the latter being out of the question under a Spanish–French barony.

When it came down to it, this change of tack from slave colony to a policy of settlement was more in line with the view Westminster had always taken of Trinidad. The importance of the island did not lie in its internal resources. The crucial factor and the island's main asset was its location and consequent potential as a trading port with Latin America. What needed development was Port of Spain and the mercantile class, not plantations in the backwoods. Picton had made the island efficient, but only in terms of sugar and slaves. As governor he was not the kind of man egalitarian revolutionaries on the Main could have faith in. It was outrageous in such enlightened times that he had doubled Trinidad's slave population from 10,009 in 1797 to 19,709 in 1802. Slavery was out of style and so was he.

On 9 July 1802, Hobart wrote to Picton explaining the new government's plans for the island. It would remain a rare species of Crown Colony with no self-government or elected assembly. But as a concession to the constitutionalists, perhaps also to the abolitionists, there would be a triumvirate commission, since three men offered advantages 'which cannot be expected from the labours of any one individual'. Hobart went on to praise Picton: 'your conduct from the time when the island was first placed under your charge has induced his Majesty to select you as one of the persons to whom this important trust shall be confided'.[39]

None of which disguised the fact that Picton's new assignment as military commissioner effectively demoted him. Outranking him was the naval commissioner, Commodore Samuel Hood, who had recently fought with Nelson on the Nile, and above both Hood and himself, on £3,000 a year as opposed to their £2,000, would be the civil or first commissioner, Colonel William Fullarton, of the Indian Army and MP for Ayrshire, who had not been a serving officer since the 1780s.

Picton felt 'degraded in the eyes of the world' and considered his new position 'humiliating'.[40] As governor he had served the Crown 'zealously and honestly', he reflected, 'probably as well as any man could have done in my situation'. Indeed, he had been 'in a most extraordinary situation' since the conquest, having to bear a terrible responsibility on being 'left nearly six years, solely to my own judgement and discretion'. To London Trinidad was an 'embarrassment', which they had got rid of 'by throwing it upon me'. Yet under his administration the colony had flourished as never before. He had turned it from an assassin's hideaway into a planter's paradise, and on the island they considered him the colony's saviour. The pity of it was that if Westminster had listened to him, Latin America would very likely be free. All they had done was deceive him with fine words:

> Amidst the strongest official assurances of the fullest confidence and approbation of the measures I pursued in this high station, without any previous communication, I was suddenly superseded, and appointed to a subordinate situation in the same government, without my consent, or even knowledge.

Picton smelt a rat. He thought about resigning. However, the prospect of half-pay was not alluring. He was still *el Tío* – at least for the time being – and there were things he had to tidy up. There were also things no first commissioner could take from him.

VI

Colonel William Fullarton of Fullarton, Ayrshire, was one of the old school, refined, punctilious, pernickety in his speech, prolific in his correspondence. He took snuff, wore red cuffs and huge shoe-buckles, carried a cane in his right hand and steadied a dress sword with his left. Well connected through his marriage to Marianne McKay, the daughter of George, the fifth Lord Reay, he knew the colonial ropes from his service in India twenty years before. As the Honourable Member for Ayrshire until his recent commission, he also knew which way the liberal wind was blowing and, nearing fifty, was resolved to sail with it.

His brief was to recommend a 'system of Government applicable to the peculiar circumstances' of Trinidad, report on its military and naval security and undertake a topographical survey that would determine those 'local situations most favourable for European constitution'. Among the Colonel's credentials were his fellowship of the Royal Societies of London and Edinburgh and his authorship of a book on agriculture in Ayrshire. However, he had probably been chosen more for his political savvy, since he faced the 'delicate and arduous'[41] challenge of pointing a three-cornered hat in a colony of mixed races and factional interests. There had been talk of his being sent out to discredit Picton, a certain Dr John Lynch, an Irishman, having heard words to this effect when interviewed for immigration in London by the Colonial Under-Secretary, Mr Sullivan. That was an unfortunate impression, which Fullarton would have to erase.

Receiving his instructions in September 1802, Fullarton left Portsmouth on 26 October sailing under Captain Columbine on the *Ulysses*, which was accompanied by two armed brigs. He took with him his wife, his wife's sister, Miss McKay, and a vast retinue of secretaries, assistants, surveyors and surveyors' assistants. This was partly a matter of style, for Fullarton was inclined to be liberal with government expenses as he showed in 1799 when raising a large body of soldiers for Ireland, known as Fullarton's Foot. At the same time he was shrewd enough to know he would need a strong contingent of his own appointees in Trinidad. Regrettably, Commodore Hood, a bachelor not yet forty, who had performed so brilliantly in the Battle of Abu Qir, had been unable to sail with him on account of the hostile turn of affairs with France. It was only with 'extreme reluctance' that Fullarton proceeded without the third commissioner. No doubt he reckoned on the latter's support should any difference of opinion arise with ex-governor Picton whom he saw, not incorrectly, as one 'possessing all the influence arising from six years of absolute and undivided authority, during which period he had nominated to their situations almost all the official persons in the island'.

When Fullarton reached Barbados he was surprised to find Hood already there enjoying the hospitality of General Grinfield, commander-in-chief in the West Indies. His elation was short-lived when Hood explained that his duties would not permit him to sail on to Port of Spain for a while yet. Grinfield informed Fullarton that should any disagreement arise between him and Picton, he, for his part, would 'take care to steer clear of all disputes not military'.[42] Fullarton left Bridgetown wondering if there was a conspiracy against him, and whether the cause of Hood's delay was naval duties or Grinfield's eldest daughter.

The *Ulysses* anchored in the Gulf of Paria on Monday 3 January 1803, and next day Fullarton went ashore to be received 'with great politeness and attention' by Picton and all the dignitaries of the colony. At Government House he immediately took the oaths of office and assumed his seat on the *cabildo* and the council. Addressing these bodies he expressed his 'earnest desire to co-operate with Brigadier-General Picton and with Commodore Hood', adding, not merely for form's sake, 'and with all classes of the community, in order to carry into full effect the wise, liberal and enlightened instructions under which the Commissioners were directed to act for the future welfare and prosperity of the Colony'. He approved the continuation of the Monday meetings of the *cabildo* and suggested Thursday meetings of the council, which would now be attended by Colonel Rutherford, the surveyor-general, Mr Archibald Gloster, the attorney-general, Mr Adderley, the police superintendent, and Mr Joseph Woodyear, the public secretary, as well as by the commissioners themselves. He then retired to the house Picton had chosen for him, Government House, with its 'one habitable bedroom', being unsuitable. Fullarton also found this second dwelling too small and badly situated, by no means 'the best in town' as he had been promised. He promptly made arrangements for work to start on the restoration of a large, run-down government property on the strand, work that would eventually cost the island's coffers $6,000.

On Wednesday 5 January Fullarton was astonished to read in a special issue of the *Courant* that in his inaugural address of the day before he had 'bestowed unqualified praise and approbation on all the proceedings under General Picton's government'. This he regarded as a 'gross mis-statement' and he immediately instructed Adderley, a witness to his speech, to write to Hobart denying the report and affirming that he had spoken only of conciliation and cooperation. This was Fullarton's legalistic way of avoiding the snares he felt sure Picton was setting him through cronies like Matthew Gallagher, the printer.

The following day, Thursday, he was further tested when visited, in the evening, by Messrs Gloster and Woodyear, two Pictonites on the council, who urged him to 'concur in a Proclamation, declaring that all laws, usages and employments should continue in full force'. Since the object of this, they explained, was to remove apprehensions which members of the community had about 'innovations and supersessions', Fullarton felt obliged to sanction it. Later, however, when he had had time to reflect on the matter with his wife, he realized that much might be read into this his first public act. Putting his name to such a proclamation might not only tie his hands with regard to future appointments but, more seriously, could be construed as his having condoned the previous laws and even their implementation under Picton.

At 6.00 a.m. the next morning he sent Mr Burke, the commission's assistant secretary, round to Gallagher's to say that he did not want the proclamation printed. Without Commodore Hood's approval it would not be a proper document. In the meantime he would be pleased to read the proof-sheet. Gallagher replied that it would be ready for the first commissioner by 8.00 a.m. Before that hour arrived Fullarton heard that the proclamation was placarded all over town. A furious first commissioner summoned Gallagher and reprimanded him for disobeying an order. In apparent bewilderment, Gallagher blubbered that he had received a counter-order to print the proclamation from Woodyear, who, as public secretary, controlled all payments for publications. At Fullarton's instruction Gallagher went off to tear down all the proclamations and bring them to the first commissioner. No doubt he had to force his way through throngs of curious readers to accomplish this task. Others must have stood back smiling in the morning sun.

This second mischief could not be explained away with a letter to London. Fullarton's authority had been challenged by an underling, and the sprat had been properly admonished. The rest were not so easy to get at. Woodyear was as slippery as an eel and, if pressed, would doubtless claim some unfortunate misunderstanding, probably with the collusion of Gallagher. Gloster, his other visitor of the night before, was a fawning toad, calling at his house every whip stitch. Why, he'd even offered his services as an aide-de-camp, which Fullarton had politely declined, saying such a position was incompatible with Gloster's station as attorney-general. In point of fact he had thought the offer an affront: was the man unaware that Fullarton had his own people who were seeking preferment?

As for Picton, he was cordiality itself. He had invited the first commissioner, his wife, his wife's sister and the entire Fullarton entourage to a grand ball on 19 January in honour of the Queen's birthday. That was all for show, Fullarton suspected: to show how a planter entertained, and to show who still called the tune at Government House. But Fullarton resolved to play Picton's game. It was too soon to seek a confrontation, and he had heard from Hood, who assured him of his intention to sail for Trinidad soon. The first commissioner would go to Picton's ball and avoid trouble until Hood arrived. Meanwhile, the trusted Adderley, 'a young man of abilities, urbanity and inflexible integrity', could go about his business as the new provost marshal and inspect the jail.

It turned out to be 'a splendid ball and entertainment', though it is doubtful whether Fullarton would have relished having his ladies introduced to Picton's vivacious partner. There was a certain line below which even liberal thinkers did not go. It is even less likely that Marianne Fullarton would have been amused by the strange coincidence that the mistress of Government House bore the same name, Rosetta, as her own daughter, though the two women may well have exchanged a stiff pleasantry on the point.

In the meantime, the jail made a different impression. Adderley found it deplorable, inhuman, a place where persons were committed without their offence having been specified, 'jusqu'à nouvel ordre'. Worse, the jailor, M. Jean Baptiste Vallot, seemed to have a highly irregular degree of discretion when it came to inflicting punishments. Fullarton instructed Adderley to 'rectify this illegality'. Offences would henceforth be specified in writing. M. Vallot would report to the provost-marshal and to the first commissioner before any punishments were inflicted.

This caused an uproar. The *alcaldes* John Black and Nicholas St Pé petitioned Fullarton: if people of colour could not be thrown in jail to cool off, if slaves could not be punished without putting pen to paper, what was the world coming to? Picton articulated their fears more rationally in council:

> The laws in all countries where slavery is established or tolerated allowed the master to secure the obedience of the slave by reasonable and moderate punishment. But the First Commissioner, by ordering that no punishment should be inflicted without his order, has superseded the power of masters and magistrates; and in a certain degree rendered the slave independent of both.[43]

In short, Fullarton's order threatened to undermine the whole system of the slave colony and the planters would not wear it. Didn't he know that the jail was not so much a jail as a correction centre?

On the last Monday in January Fullarton attended the *cabildo* and urged the fitting up of a new jail. Black, Begorrat and St Pé objected strongly to such a waste of public funds. Finally, the official body grudgingly agreed to accompany Fullarton and Adderley to inspect a piece of ground where a new jail might be built. After this they visited the existing jail, where the decrepit Vallot, 'one of the most dismal ill-looking monsters of the human species', as McCallum would describe him, was mightily surprised at their request to be given a tour.

As he had been led to expect, Fullarton found 'such a scene of wretchedness, disease, famine, and exquisite misery, tantamount to torture, as had never been witnessed under a British Government'. With incredulous horror he expressed his entire disapprobation to the *alcaldes* and the *cabildo*, pointing out that the jail was, in practice, inflicting punishment on its inmates before sentence had been passed. Most disturbing was the sight of 'five of Baron Montalambert's [sic] slaves on hard boards, without light or air, in noxious cells, with their feet morticed in fixed fetters, in positions of prolonged suffering; although the proceedings had not extended farther than to the preliminary information, or *procès verbal.*'

Begorrat, much offended, argued that there was no mode of extorting truth out of such villains except by torture. But Fullarton had seen all he wanted and, on leaving, had the unexpected bonus of a submission from William Payne, Vallot's assistant. Payne, who was clearly in a sour mood, thrust a paper into Fullarton's hand. It was a list of sixteen persons on whom he had done work, mostly floggings, pillories and ear-clippings, but it included one he had hanged, decapitated and burnt at St Joseph. Payne was aggrieved because he had only got two joes, or Portugal pieces – less than £1 – out of Vallot and Picton for all his sweat.

Fullarton had his written evidence. Encouraged, he took them all back to the jail next evening together with Captain Columbine, commander of the *Ulysses*. If they didn't agree to build a new jail, he said, he would put the prisoners on a hulk and have Columbine anchor them in the bay. Were they completely oblivious, he wondered, of the enlightened measures towards slaves that his good friend Lord Seaforth had introduced in Barbados, an island that had enjoyed his vigorous and benign governorship for more than two years.

On Wednesday 2 February an anxious Picton visited Fullarton to complain about his attending meetings of the *cabildo*, something he, as governor, had never done. Nor was it proper to impose upon 'gentlemen' to accompany him to the jail. His visits could only convey an impression that the royal jail had been neglected and its prisoners maltreated. Fullarton replied that Picton, with such an intimate knowledge of the colony, had no need to attend the *cabildo*, whereas he, the recently appointed first commissioner, needed to observe everything at first hand. He would continue to attend the *cabildo*, as was his right and duty. There would have to be a new jail, with better conditions for the prisoners, he added. Then he took his leave of Picton by thanking him for expressing his views so frankly. Next day, in council, the purchase of a house 'proper for a jail' was approved by all members, including Picton, and the matter seemed to have been cordially settled.

In the following week two new arrivals provoked disagreement between the commissioners. The first to arrive, from New York, on Sunday 6 February, was Pierre McCallum. He was a sort of peripatetic agitator, a political agent-cum-journalist whose purpose was to activate libertarian issues and discredit Picton. Passing unhindered through the relaxed immigration controls, he went to pay his respects to Fullarton – 'I spent an hour with this excellent man in his study'[44] – and then retired to a hotel where he set about organizing an action group called the Ugly Club and researching a book intended to expose the ex-governor. Within a few days one of the town's shopkeepers, a Mr Rigby, put out an advertisement for a meeting at which it was proposed to consider the proper application of British laws. Picton responded as of old: there would be no meeting; he would have Hargraves the printer's licence off him. Fullarton thought otherwise: there was nothing in the advertisement deserving of censure. The 'inoffensive' Hargraves kept his licence, but Picton railed so furiously against Rigby and the other merchants they gave up their meeting and contented themselves with Saturday night 'literary' gatherings at McCallum's hotel.

The second arrival to cause a stir was a coloured woman, Mme Duval, who came from the Main on Saturday 12 February. Fullarton had granted her a week's stay to sort out family affairs and collect her lately deceased brother's property. This was less than the three years she was entitled to under the terms of the Treaty of Amiens, but more than anyone of her kind had been allowed of late owing to the concern about persons returning to British colonies they had left during the war with France.

Picton was prickly. Seeing her at the harbour, he told her in no uncertain terms to re-embark at once, and put her in the charge of a constable. When Mme Duval produced the document signed by Fullarton allowing her a week's stay the constable took her to see the first commissioner, who confirmed his original order and, at about 3.00 p.m., released her. He then sent the commissioner's assistant, secretary Burke, to explain the matter to the public secretary, Woodyear, whom he had previously instructed to inform Picton of the special dispensation he had given Mme Duval on compassionate grounds. Woodyear, he said, could have the whole thing out with Picton.

At 8.00 p.m. that same day Picton stormed into the first commissioner's house and found him 'sitting there at coffee' in the drawing room with his ladies and a large company of adherents. Seeing Picton's dark mood, Fullarton quickly ushered him to the verandah, but this proved to be insufficiently removed from the genteel gathering for them to avoid hearing the ex-governor's 'torrent of Billingsgate' as he complained in vociferous tones about the Duval woman being given a week. He, in consultation with the public secretary, had determined to have the woman quit the island forthwith, said Picton, his voice growing steadily hoarser as his hands struck the balustrade violently. He had sent her packing once before and was not going to give her another hour on British soil!

But had not Picton heard of the 'dispensation'?, Fullarton rapped back. Had not he heard of the word 'compassion'?

You could not make exceptions and you could not have compassion with 'reptiles' like these, Picton bellowed. The whole island would be flooded with French sympathizers and Republicans inside a fortnight. God knows, he added as he stormed through the drawing room, they had enough subversives amongst their own![45]

Once Picton had left, Fullarton sent for Woodyear. He was going to get to the bottom of this. That the third commissioner should have caused 'a public disturbance' in his own house, 'in the presence of Mrs Fullarton' and his guests, was, as he told them, an unspeakable outrage. While they waited for Woodyear to appear, Fullarton, true to form, prepared a statement on Picton's amazing conduct, which his guests promptly signed. Woodyear, it turned out, could not be found that night, but on Sunday morning he came fully prepared to make an abject confession, in writing. He had failed to represent the case of Mme Duval properly to the ex-governor. Picton retaliated with a show of power: as military commissioner he withdrew all guards and sentries from Port of Spain. This threatened mayhem because, as everyone knew, the police could not cope on their own.

On Monday 14 February, a special meeting of the council was called and in it the first commissioner read out his prepared statement. Then, item by item, he recited the list he had received from Payne, the executioner. Picton seethed. This was too much, and he told Fullarton so in language that 'was, if possible, more outrageous than on the previous Saturday'.[46] The council was astounded. They urged a reconciliation between the two commissioners 'for the welfare of the colony'. Fullarton could not dissent to this unanimous request, but Picton would have to pay a price: a written apology to Mrs Fullarton, and Woodyear would have to go.

That same day Mrs Fullarton received a brief letter in which Picton apologized for 'the high tone of voice' he had used that evening, having 'entirely ceased to recollect that Mrs Fullarton and the family were within hearing'.[47] At the regular meeting of the council on Thursday Fullarton formally moved the suspension of Woodyear for his failure to communicate to Picton the first commissioner's instructions about Mme Duval. This, Fullarton logically insisted, was the only honourable way he could agree to the reconciliation that the council so strenuously urged and which he too considered imperative, inclined as he was 'to sacrifice personal feelings to public duty'. Picton spoke strongly against the suspension and even had his protest entered in the minutes. This was no more than a gesture on behalf of his crony, Joe Woodyear; in actuality, by offering to replace the town guards, Picton had conceded.

Still Fullarton was not satisfied. He wanted Adderley to take over as secretary to the commission. He wanted Don Pedro Vargas appointed to the new post of interpreter, and he wanted others of his young men – who had daily been growing more impatient – put on the official payroll as assistants. Last of all, said Fullarton, dropping a bombshell, he wanted:

> certified statements of all the criminal proceedings which have taken place since the commencement of the late Government, together with a list, specifying every individual of whatever country, colour or condition, who has been imprisoned, banished, fettered, flogged, burned or otherwise punished; also specifying the dates of their respective commitments, trials, sentence, period of confinement, punishments; and of all those who have died in prison.[48]

Next day, Friday 18 February 1803, the sixth anniversary of the conquest, Picton resigned.

VII

Until such time as London received and accepted his resignation Picton was obliged to discharge his duties as third commissioner. Meanwhile, events moved on.

Four days after Picton tendered his resignation Commodore Samuel Hood arrived from Barbados with General Grinfield, commander-in-chief in the West Indies. Fullarton, who had been waiting nearly two months for his colleague, was determined to make the most of the occasion. He resolved to board the flagship without Picton and be the first to greet this hero of the Nile. To lend an air to the proceedings he took with him Sir James Bontein, the only titled Englishman on the island, who had come out looking for an appointment some time ago, got nothing from Picton, and had thrown in his lot with the first commissioner.

As soon as the flagship cast anchor in the bay Fullarton and Bontein went out in a launch, leaving Picton and his soldiers broiling on parade at the wharf. In his blue Windsor uniform, dress sword and cane, Fullarton cut a fine if slightly stooped and old-fashioned figure on the quarterdeck of the newly arrived ship. Revelling in the pageantry and ceremonious salutations, which he protracted with decorous tittle-tattle, Fullarton eventually brought the company ashore to a rather less formal reception from a bristling Picton. The latter greeted General Grinfield with all due respect, but then, ignoring Hood, went on to address Sir James Bontein mischievously: 'I hope your

Excellency has arrived in good health. I beg leave to congratulate you on your landing safely in Trinidad.'[49]

To Sir James's evident consternation Picton added, 'I understand you have been appointed Commissioner.'

Joe Woodyear, the deposed public secretary, now stepped forward and assured a gaping Bontein he had no intention of applying to him to be reinstated. By the time Bontein realized he was the butt of Picton's ridicule no one on King's Wharf doubted that the island's ex-governor had taken grave offence at his demotion on the reception committee.

What Fullarton described as an 'indecorous scene in front of a large gathering on the Mole' might have turned decidedly sour had Bontein been a more forceful man or had the first commissioner come to his defence. Whether out of respect for the occasion or fear of Picton's tongue, Fullarton said nothing. Surprisingly, neither Hood nor Grinfield remarked on Picton's bludgeoning irony.

Later, Fullarton claimed that Grinfield commented to him on the troops' presentation of arms and ceremonial evolutions as being 'so awkwardly executed'. It appears that 'part of a Black regiment wheeled by sections instead of divisions', which mistake, according to Major Draper, Picton immediately corrected.[50] But the criticism that Fullarton claimed Grinfield made, that 'these troops are twenty years behind', is unconfirmed and seems more likely to be an invention attributable to Fullarton's pique. In his correspondence, Grinfield, who was soon to die of fever in Bridgetown, spoke highly of Picton as an 'excellent man' and a commander of soldiers with whom he had not 'the smallest occasion to be dissatisfied'.[51] What is certain is that Fullarton never again attended military parades with Picton and Grinfield, and that his absence on these occasions did little to endear him to the commander-in-chief. As for Sir James Bontein, he soon went quietly home to England.

After the welcoming ceremony Hood was taken to the house Fullarton had found him. It was, said the first commissioner, 'not only commodious, but very pleasantly situated, having a fine view of the Gulf of Paria and of the shipping'. But Hood thought it too grand for a bachelor and complained that Fullarton had hired it without consulting him. He also declined the services pressed on him by the prissy Mr Vint, one of Fullarton's preferment-seekers at the secretary's office.

Grinfield, for his part, was invited to lodge at Fullarton's house for the three weeks of his stay on the island. Inside a week he had so tired of the sniping against Picton by Fullarton, his wife and sister-in-law that he moved to the same hotel in which

Pierre McCallum was staying, near the Orange Grove Barracks. Grinfield found nightly tales about the ex-governor irksome when his days were spent with Picton examining the island's fortifications. He was a soldier and he cared nothing for the first commissioner's fussy papers on such altercations as occurred over the Duval woman. Grinfield disliked tale-bearers and 'affidavit men'.

So did Samuel Hood, who later called Fullarton 'an old intriguing politician'.[52] Hood, from Kingsland, Dorset, had seen action in the Caribbean twenty years before when he was just eighteen, having taken part in the epochal naval victory of the Saintes achieved by Admiral Rodney in April 1782. Though he was now between wars, Hood gravitated naturally towards the soldier in Picton. Rather than the tiresomely proper conversation at the Fullartons', he preferred the rumpus of Government House: Picton swearing at the top of his lungs when one of his brats ran amok; Rosetta, gossipy and tyrannical in her mongrel tongue, nursing her youngest and making dark eyes at the Commodore.

Hood could talk to Picton. About war and soldiering, about money and women, especially women: gentlewomen, tavern or serving women, white, black or brown. When Rosetta retired, the two men filled their cups and talked into the night. They talked about Pitt, deposed and sickly, mortgaged to the hilt. About Henry Addington, 'the Doctor', Pitt's *locum tenens*, so concerned for the nation's health he would put British forces on a peace footing when a war with France was staring him right in the face. 'Pitt is to Addington as London is to Paddington' went the rhyme, to which Hood added that the Treaty of Amiens was an offence to patriots: the first consul kept his conquests while all John Bull had to show for his pains were Ceylon and Trinidad. It was abject submission, *grovelling* to the French. But at least they had Trinidad to raise a glass to.

They talked about the evangelical Wilberforce, skeletal on laudanum; mad King George, conversing with an oak in Windsor Great Park while his gluttonous son and heir was such a burden on society ladies; only the sturdiest dared cross the threshold of Carlton House. They talked about Nelson, who had left Hood three ships to blockade all Egypt while he went swanning off to Emma at Naples. 'Oh, it was a grand life in the Mediterranean!' said the naval officer, laughing: hadn't he proved it when he was governor of Castel Nuovo?

There was a lot to talk about, a lot Picton had to catch up on if he was going to enter the new century. He needed to know the mood in Westminster, what pretentious liberalism people like Canning were popularizing, *easy on the tongue, never vexing the heart.* Picton explained why he had resigned, how he felt on being demoted, what he felt about slavery. Were not officers entitled to a plantation or two as reward for hard service? There were good pickings in Trinidad, if Hood knew where to look. As for Fullarton, he had the neck to have blacks build him a palace on the strand! London had misunderstood Picton, treated him abominably. That's why he'd resigned. Fullarton was a fop, a petticoated pen-pusher, 'an artful cunning man', said Picton, 'under the absolute direction of an intriguing woman'.

Within a short while, to his shattering disappointment, the first commissioner found himself isolated. So long as Grinfield remained in Trinidad 'affairs were conducted on a footing of apparent civility', but as soon as he left, on Sunday 13 March, Fullarton felt exposed. Picton and Hood, he claimed, held 'secret meetings' at Government House prior to joining him in commission. Hood's behaviour was 'perfectly unaccountable', his mind 'poisoned by misrepresentations sent to him at Barbadoes', the 'grand object' of which was to overthrow the commission and have power vested once again in the former governor.[53] The military, at Picton's behest, neglected its policing of the town. Fullarton could not rely on proper records of *cabildo* meetings and was unsure of the safe passage of his mail by sea. Tired of the constant acrimony, he told his fellow commissioners he would leave Port of Spain to embark on his island survey.

He changed his mind after the council on the Thursday following Grinfield's departure. In it Picton read out a minute that, Fullarton said, not only contained 'expressions highly unbecoming and inadmissible' towards him as first commissioner but which also sought to make him 'concur in supporting a system of severity' repugnant to his sentiments. Not to be caught out in viva voce, Fullarton responded by asking Mr Unwin, clerk of the council, to furnish him with an exact copy of Picton's words so that in due course he 'might answer the statement as it deserved'.

In the six days before council met again Fullarton busied himself. He wrote to Hobart and, leaving nothing to chance, sent one of his surveyors, Major Williamson, to explain things in person. It was open warfare now and Fullarton set about gathering evidence against Picton. He named two of his men, Hayes and Proby, 'to take these informations in proper legal form', and he appointed Don Pedro Vargas as assessor. They knew exactly where the 'mass of criminal information' was to be found.

By 24 March, Fullarton was ready. In council that day, after referring to the conniving that had gone on between the two junior commissioners and to the 'series of transactions' they had engaged in together, he read out thirty-six charges against Picton: torture, false imprisonment, execution without trial and one burning.[54]

Picton, a terrible frown fixed on his brow, seethed as never before. Then, striving to overcome his habitual hoarseness and to keep his words within accepted bounds of decorum, he asked Hood in front of the members of the assembled council if there was a single grain of truth in Fullarton's remark that they had discussed matters privately before meetings.

Samuel Hood erupted, as if on cue. The accusations were 'a libel on His Majesty's Ministers', he said, addressing the first commissioner in ringing tones: 'I am ashamed of you; ashamed to be seen in the same company. Nothing but the paramount obligation of His Majesty's Commission could seat us at the same board. I shall however request to be relieved as soon as possible from so disagreeable a situation, with a colleague with whom I can have no further confidence.'[55]

Having nailed his colours to the mast, Hood proceeded to sweep the deck. He had 'never had any conversation with General Picton respecting the disagreements' over Woodyear. Picton had always let him see his own way. Fullarton, by contrast, had taken advantage of his absence in Barbados 'in the most arbitrary and indecent manner to suspend the Public Secretary, contrary to the opinion of the Council', and indeed of his colleague. Hood thundered his last remarks at a visibly distressed Fullarton: 'You are doing everything you can to ruin the country; but you shall not effect it; we will not allow you.'[56]

If Picton's resignation had been a blessing, Hood's was an embarrassment. Losing one commissioner was acceptable, losing a second who had been in office no more than thirty days was tantamount to a vote of no confidence. It made Fullarton look autocratic and suggested that he had no concern for the collaborative spirit of a commission. Having done his duty in the fight with Buonaparte, Hood was highly regarded in London, as everyone kept reminding Fullarton. They would surely ask why the first commissioner could not get on with him. Was he incapable of leadership and high office? What had he done in his short time in Trinidad but foster disharmony?

These musings gave Fullarton cause for anxiety. It was time to start making positive gains. He resolved to embark on the survey that was such an important part of his brief. He would leave the two junior commissioners to stew in their own juice. He had all the information he needed against Picton. True, the Welshman had nearly duped him. His request on 17 March for certified statements of all the criminal proceedings under the late government was countered by Picton's minute that the records be sent direct to England. But he had not fallen into that trap. Noting that Picton made no mention of copies, he realized instantly what a simple matter it would be to lose the originals in the Atlantic brine. He outfoxed Picton by having all the proceedings sent to Don Francisco de Castro, the keeper of the archives and government *escribano*, from whom he then obtained them himself for purposes of inspection and for his young men to copy. He had evidence on *el Tío* now, in triplicate. There was no need for him to stay in Port of Spain.

Fullarton's insistence on certified statements of past criminal proceedings alarmed no one more than St Hilaire de Begorrat, Picton's steadfast friend and one-time leader of the commission that investigated dirt-eating. The *alcalde* was uneasy about what had happened in jail to Luisa Calderón, a *mulata* of no account. On the Monday after the commissioners' last row in council Begorrat visited the *escribano* and asked to see the process against Carlos González, a case of theft over which, as *alcalde*, he had presided some two years earlier and in which he had found it necessary to authorize the torture of González's young lover and accomplice, Luisa Calderón. Begorrat told Castro that he wished to check a detail in the report, a trifling matter about the age attributed to Luisa Calderón at the time of her imprisonment. When Don Francisco explained that the report was now with the first commissioner a troubled Begorrat went off to tell Picton the bad news.

Picton and Hood immediately put their heads together, forming what Fullarton described as 'an extraordinary meeting of the Commission', which, he said, 'carried nullity on the face of the proceedings' since they had given no notice of the meeting to him as first commissioner even though he was in Port of Spain at the time. The two junior commissioners summoned Castro and, after abusing the *escribano* for allowing Fullarton access to the archives, stripped him of his office and placed him under house arrest in the charge of *alcalde* Black, deeming it improper to send a government official to jail.

Fullarton got news of Castro's arrest at about 6.00 p.m. when at table in his own house with a large company. In agitated mood, he resolved to go immediately to see the *alcalde*, taking with him for support Messrs Adderley, Burke, Hill, McKenzie and Vint. The dinner had been a formal occasion on the eve of his embarkation, hence Fullarton was in full dress uniform and carried both sword and cane. The impression made by the first commissioner, thus armed and accompanied by his posse of young adherents, was altogether intimidating to Black and his fellow *alcalde*, the 54-year-old Nicholas St Pé, who, jointly, were to claim that Fullarton burst in on them and threatened them with the gallows.

To Fullarton's furious questions Black replied that Castro was indeed under house arrest, by order of the council, that he had been arrested for releasing papers from the archives. Retaining a degree of circumspection, Fullarton retorted that Castro would have been in breach of duty only if he had refused to release papers to him as first commissioner. His arrest was totally illegal, as were the instructions from the junior commissioners whose sole intention was to discourage foreigners like Castro from giving evidence against Picton.

It was a hanging matter, said Fullarton raising his cane, and though he could not call out the militia to free the *escribano*, the *alcaldes* had better mind how they conducted themselves. He held Black personally responsible for the well-being of Castro, whom he there and then made commissioner of population for his added protection. Fullarton's voice could be heard across the street when he said he would hang everybody, 'Pend tous', if harm came to Castro. The *alcaldes* agreed to take good care of their charge.

Next morning the first commissioner was down at the harbour with Messrs Vint, Vargas and Hill ready to embark with Captain Marsden on the schooner *Start*. His sole wish was to get away, this being as much an issue of personal safety, he felt, as of following the instructions of His Majesty's ministers. At Barbados he would explain things to Grinfield and intercept the Trinidad mail. Once he had possession of the letter accepting Picton's resignation he would return to Port of Spain and govern in the enlightened manner he had always intended.

One last trial awaited Fullarton before he sailed. Hood roundly informed him that, as naval commissioner, he would seize or sink the vessel if it ventured to stir without the signatures of the other two commissioners on the register. They in turn would sign the register only if they were given access to the criminal records that, they claimed, were now being illegally removed from the island.

For two days messages went to and from the schooner as it stood in Port of Spain harbour. The townspeople looked on incredulously at this virtual imprisonment of their first commissioner by two junior commissioners, both of whom, in fact, had resigned.

Fullarton wrote that he had informed his fellow commissioners of his intention to sail on two previous occasions in council and they had made no objection. Captain Marsden entered a protest against them for detaining his vessel unlawfully. Marianne Fullarton went dutifully aboard to visit her husband. Just when a resolution condemning the first commissioner's flight was being read out in council a message came from the *Start* via Adderley, the provost-marshal, that Fullarton had deposited all criminal records safely on shore. He would not, however, say where.

Hood and Picton were powerless to stop Fullarton's departure, and, on 1 April, he sailed.

VIII

On 2 April 1803 Picton and Hood wrote jointly to Hobart informing him of what they termed Fullarton's precipitate departure from Port of Spain, and charging the first commissioner with 'direct and serious derangement of intellect'.[57] This was followed, on 13 April, by an address from the *cabildo* to the Crown that spoke of 'the vexatious and reprehensible conduct of your Majesty's First Commissioner in this government'. They censured Fullarton on three counts: for arresting Black, an elected *alcalde*; for releasing the *escribano* Castro, who had been placed under arrest by the *cabildo*; and for taking possession of public records without the permission of the *cabildo* and the other commissioners.

The last count was substantive. When the *cabildo* met on 31 March, with Fullarton 'cabin'd, cribb'd, confin'd' out in the bay, it resolved that the first commissioner had 'treated the Council with contempt and insult' by ordering the *alcaldes* to produce copies of all criminal proceedings since 1797; that he had thereby made himself a 'public informer and denouncer against the whole military and civil authority of the late government of this colony'; that his '*enlèvement* of the public records' had wrested the strongest means of defence out of the hands of the persons he accused of misgovernment and had vested them exclusively in his own.[58]

The resolutions ended with broader charges: Fullarton had connected himself with 'disaffected characters and classes of inhabitants' and had kindled 'a spirit of party and faction among the white inhabitants of all nations and languages'; he had weakened 'the legal authority of the master over the slave' and reduced the efficacy of the Commandants and of the police. Taking particular note of 'the present desertion of his post', the *cabildo* roundly declared that 'the First Commissioner has lost the confidence of this Board'.[59]

On 16 April, an advertisement was published by *alcaldes* Black and Saint Pé concerning the illegal removal of criminal processes from the archives. It gave public notice that:

> one hundred dollars will be paid to the person or persons, who will deliver us, or either of us, the said thirty-six original criminal processes, or will give such information that will lead to a discovery thereof; and if any person or persons are hereafter convicted of having concealed the same, after this notice, he or they will be prosecuted according to law.

Fullarton's supporters saw this as a stratagem to incriminate the first commissioner and provide for his immediate arrest upon his return to the island after completing the survey.

On 27 April, Picton and Hood went the whole hog. They issued a proclamation that stated:

> Whereas it now appears that Colonel William Fullarton, his Majesty's First Commissioner for this Government, hath withdrawn himself therefrom, and from the duties thereof, without his Majesty's leave, and without permission from us, or any consultation with his Majesty's Council of this Island: We do, therefore, by and with the advice of his Majesty's said Council, hereby proclaim and declare, that we consider and deem the said William Fullarton no longer officiating as one of his Majesty's Commissioners in the government of this Island; and we require all persons, civil and military, to govern themselves accordingly.[60]

Shortly after signing this proclamation Hood left Trinidad for good. He had effectively opted to reinvest power in the hands of one man, ex-governor Picton. The first commissioner, it seemed, no longer had any official capacity in which to return to the island.

Fullarton would later argue that his absence was justified and that he had twice given the *cabildo* notice of his intention to embark on the survey. Besides, if Hood could choose to remain in Barbados for 'as long as he judged expedient, without offering any explanation', surely he, as first commissioner, could absent himself on official government business. Fullarton made his point well, but it is also true that he was away two and a half months, only a small part of which was spent surveying Trinidad.

After leaving Port of Spain a jittery Fullarton visited six islands in quick succession, his first port of call being Clifton Harbour in Union Island, the southernmost of the Grenadines. This was a safe haven from which Adderley was dispatched to London on the *Lemlair* with instructions to give Hobart a full account of the recent 'disgraceful events'. The first commissioner then sailed to St Vincent, hoping to meet there, but in fact just missing, Commander-in-Chief Grinfield. On he went to Martinique, Dominica and Guadaloupe, before returning to St Vincent, where he took on board Dr Anderson, the 'celebrated naturalist'. Only then did Fullarton make a circuit of Trinidad, and brief it was for he was back in Bridgetown before the end of May.

His primary purpose in visiting Barbados and the other islands was to intercept the dispatches expected from Hobart. His fear was that these would be withheld from him in Trinidad, where, he claimed, 'the Post-office was in the hands of Picton's emissaries'. He was lucky enough to find the mailboat at Bridgetown, and, obtaining permission from his old friend Lord Seaforth to have the dispatches opened, he gained possession of the letter that he must have read with undisguised joy: the King was graciously pleased to accept Picton's resignation.

Fullarton set about bringing this news to the attention of those who mattered. He sent copies to Seaforth, Grinfield, Hood, Colonel Hope, commander of the regular troops in Trinidad, and to Colonel Grant, commander of the militia. Naturally, the original was resealed and forwarded to Picton. Enclosed with the copy to Grinfield went a letter in which Fullarton took the trouble to explain that in the event of Picton's offering resistance when he returned to his seat of government in Trinidad, he was resolved not 'to hazard the tranquillity of the Colony, by attempting to enforce a landing'. He would leave the question of any such resistance to be adjusted by General Grinfield, 'as a mere point of military power and aggression'.[61] Fullarton then departed Bridgetown on 1 June, going by way of the east coast of Trinidad, where, in the spirit of the ongoing survey, he inspected various settlements, and, on 6 June, 'under the immediate protection of Captain Columbine of His Majesty's ship *Ulysses*', he anchored off Port of Spain.

During Fullarton's absence from the island Trinidad had reverted to a state of calm under Picton law. Joseph Woodyear had been reappointed public secretary as a matter of course, but others felt the backlash of the new order. Among them was the agent Pierre McCallum, whom Picton had long suspected of being engaged by Fullarton – or London – to rake up 'a kennel of information' with which to defame him.

At 2.00 p.m. on 11 April, McCallum was arrested and taken before Picton and Hood at the latter's house. He denied that he was, in Picton's words, 'a common disturber of the public peace',[62] and rejected the charge that he had failed to enlist in the militia, which, he pointed out, was a voluntary corps. Nonetheless, McCallum found himself committed to the custody of the sinister Vallot. He later claimed that during the eight days that he spent in jail an attempt was made to poison him. His trunks at the hotel were searched and the minutes of the Ugly Club's meetings found. The Club was declared unlawful, but neither an inspection of its minutes nor a further interrogation of McCallum uncovered sufficient evidence to warrant prosecution. Frustrated, the two commissioners put McCallum on board an American schooner bound for New York and no more was heard of him until 1805, the year of publication, in London, of his damaging pro-Fullarton, *Travels in Trinidad*.

Several others suffered similar misfortune. Mr Tumbrill, surgeon in the Royal Artillery, was arrested and interrogated on 15 April for having had the temerity to vouch that Sergeant Gallagher had been executed without trial. Among those banished were a M. Dubois and Mme Sophie Ventouse, and when Picton remarked testily of the latter, 'I banished that woman before, and now she has returned!', the bold Mme Ventouse is said to have replied: 'Non, mon General, c'est faux; vous ne m'avez pas bannie mais vous m'avez si maltraité, que je me suis bannie moi-même.'[63]

Another to feel Picton's wrath was, not surprisingly, the steadfast Mrs Fullarton. Picton tried to isolate her by threatening to banish anyone known to be hospitable towards her. Warming to his role as *el Tío*, Picton held that the proclamation that had stripped Colonel Fullarton of his commission had also stripped the commissioner's wife of her privileges and left her with no more standing than any other white citizen. Consequently, on 28 April, he withdrew the guard from her house. Indeed, according to his detractors, he instructed men who were working on the house at the time to unload their carts of earth in sight of the front gallery, and while they were engaged in this he took care to attract the attention of Mrs Fullarton and Miss McKay, who were inside, with his raucous vociferations. Clearly, had these gentlewomen wished to leave the island, the ex-governor would not have stood in their way.

Depending on where one's sympathies lay, Picton's actions during Fullarton's absence from the island were seen as either confirmation of a power-crazed, vindictive spirit or principled adherence to law and order. The situation on the island had undoubtedly deteriorated under the triumvirate and was threatening to undo what Picton very likely considered six years' good work. Irreconcilable as were the differences between him and Fullarton, their conflict had been exacerbated by the naval commissioner's having thrown in his lot with the military commissioner, thereby raising the latter's rank by aggregate. Fullarton's 'desertion' on the pretext of a geographical survey, which stood low in Picton's order of priorities, confirmed, to his way of thinking, the first commissioner's lack of mettle if not his complete instability. From a soldier's point of view, he was simply unsuited to the high office to which he had been appointed.

Towards the middle of April, with Hood's departure looming, Picton faced the prospect of being virtually powerless once the affidavit man returned. Hence the *cabildo*'s address to the Crown on the 13th, hence too the proclamation signed by both junior commissioners on the 27th. It was Picton's way of safeguarding his authority and of maintaining the ascendancy of 'the most respectable proprietors' over the 'despicable set of insolvent Liverpool and Manchester shopkeepers'.

His subsequent actions were consistent with the proclamation. He sent St Hilaire de Begorrat and a posse of men across the island to seek the planters' support of his authority. Not only did they willingly sign the paper placed in front of them, they also purchased in Britain, at their own expense, a sword of honour, which was subsequently presented to Picton by the Duke of York. Picton accepted this 'public testimony', which was 'much enhanced by the time and handsome manner of its declaration'.

The ex-governor then issued a warning to the townspeople that, on the firing of three guns, martial law was to be in force. This was designed to discourage any display of support for Fullarton on his return. Finally, Picton instructed the inhabitants in various parts of the island to resist any attempt at landing that Fullarton might make, and he put the sentinels at the port on red alert.

When the *Start* sailed into the harbour on 6 June the vessel cautiously stood offshore. Picton sent out Brigade Major Pitman with a copy of the Proclamation of 27 April and a letter informing the first commissioner his landing would be forcefully resisted. This was seen by Fullarton as an attempt to contrive 'a scene of civil warfare' which might later be attributed to his own 'violence and insanity'.[64] It was designed, he said, to cast Picton as the island's saviour, offering him the added prospect of a violent confusion in which to 'massacre every individual capable of exposing his delinquencies'. Fullarton chose to avoid this 'bloody trap'. He preferred, as always, to respond by letter, and he sent Picton a proclamation of his own.

It was time once more for Mrs Fullarton to visit her husband on board the *Start*. A handful of supporters similarly dared to incur Picton's displeasure by rowing out to the sloop. Fullarton then moved off with Captain Columbine to inspect the nearby island of Gaspar Grande and the waters of Chaguaramas, dutifully adding the final touches to his survey. It was stalemate, but, with a copy of Hobart's letter in his pocket, the first commissioner was clearly less nervous.

On 14 June, the brig *Nelly* arrived from Barbados with Frederick Maitland on board. He had a letter for Picton from Grinfield:

> I have long seen with the most serious concern the unfortunate disagreements among the gentlemen composing the commission of Trinidad, but I was in hopes that the matters could have been adjusted without a reference to me; but as you and the Council holding the government of that island during the absence of the Commissioners, have addressed yourselves to me, and desiring my interference, I think it my duty to do that which I think will fulfil the intentions of His Majesty; I have therefore directed Brigadier-General Maitland to relieve you in the military command in the island of Trinidad.[65]

That same evening Picton said farewell to Rose and the children, and sailed from Port of Spain, never to return. On his way to England, he would engage briefly in action under Grinfield at St Lucia and at Tobago, where, for a short while, he was commandant. The commander-in-chief would write to London about him as an 'excellent man', whose 'fame will rise the higher for the unmerited persecution under which he now labours', a persecution that was solely attributable to what Grinfield called 'the extraordinary conduct of Colonel Fullarton'.

As for Fullarton, he was not so bold as to accept Maitland's invitation to disembark on the day immediately following his enemy's departure. He suspected Maitland of being a Pictonite and wished 'to guard against new acts of illegality and aggression on the part of the Military Power'. It was three days before the first commissioner could be persuaded, via an exchange of letters, to place a buckled shoe on Government Square.[66]

TWO

LONDON

Libellous Animadversions

I

The London Picton returned to in October 1803 was the world's largest city, teeming with nearly a million specimens of humanity. The virtual doubling of its population in the last century was not solely attributable to the irresistible pull that its commerce exercised on the rest of the country, but also to advances in food production and medicine that had increased life expectancy. Infant mortality still stood at horrific levels; gin-soaking and violent crime had scarcely abated; the poor continued to live in filthy warrens and, for all its splendrous buildings, the capital was a squalid, pestiferous place to the vast bulk of people who made their home in it. Yet beneath the pall of smoke more of them were managing to survive, and London's birth rate had finally overtaken its death rate.

Increased population meant increased size. Horace Walpole remarked in 1791 on the obsolescence of the sedan: 'The town is so extended the breed of chairs is almost lost, for Hercules and Atlas could not carry anyone from one end of this enormous capital to the other.'[1] Growth had gathered pace in the nineties, not just in the poor east and riverside areas, but north of Oxford Street towards Marylebone, where Portman Square and Manchester Square were laid out and town houses were built for the gentry. Only horsepower could compass the new dimensions, and London's streets had become a chaos of equine traffic: the lumbering market-bound wagon, the hired hackney coach, the elegant postchaise and dashing gig with high-stepping steed, milady's phaeton and the West End chariot, whose equipage projected the status of its grand owner.

There was congestion in human traffic too. Horsepower bred a new type of professional: the crossing-sweeper. Much in

demand after a heavy fall of rain, this urchin raked his patch for
a ha'penny tip if a well-shod gent wished to hazard a passage
from gutter to gutter. His first cousin was the chimney sweep, a
fixture of city life since the early eighteenth century when coal
took the place of wood in Britain's hearths and brought
narrower, dirtier chimneys with it. Even lower in rank were the
sewer rats who delved into the city's bowels to retrieve articles
that had been lost or swept away. They were on a par with the
bone-grubbers and ragpickers, scarcely a notch above outright
beggars or scavengers and the myriad types of thief.

Home to the destitute, dissipated and delinquent, the London
street was above all a theatre of varieties, with clumps of
upturned hats to catch tossed coins. Peddlers hawked their
wares and the perennial hordes of prostitutes sought to catch
the eye. There were jugglers, tumblers and sword-swallowers,
musicians, organ-grinders and parrot-sellers, evangelists,
palmists and mountebanks, the latter offering instant cures for
every known malady, especially chilblains and the gout. For
tuppence ha'penny you could buy a newspaper, for a shilling a
broadsheet – very likely illustrated with lurid cartoons. In the
chill winter of 1803 the best-selling line in coloured prints
featured a half-naked mulatto girl being piqueted at the
behest of the infamous governor of Trinidad: Picture of the
girl, pulley, spike and grillos, barked ragamuffin vendors at
passers-by.

Picton complained of the 'indecent caricatures exhibited
everywhere in the streets and windows, and the malignant, scan-
dalous libels which have inundated the metropolis'.[2] He could
buy a souvenir of his time in Trinidad on any street corner when
he stepped from his hotel on Panton Square and headed for the
Haymarket, or strode the few paces to Leicester Square.
Suddenly, he was himself part of the city's scurrilous entertainment, a freak attraction, the latest illuminated spectacle. He felt
like an actor at the Theatre Royal, Drury Lane, entangled, like
Kemble, in some outrageous plot, but one in which victim and
villain were instantly recognized by everyone in the vast audience who alternately hissed him and cheered Luisa Calderón,
the 'most virtuous, interesting young lady whose sufferings have
been painted in such glowing colours to the public'. Hers was
the body displayed in exquisite torment from coffee house to
gin-shop, from gaiety garden to gaming centre and every
debtors' prison in the ogling capital. Alongside this shamefully
abused *mulata*, this emblem of injured womanhood, was Thomas
Picton, the wanton sadist, the Tyrant of Trinidad. His was the
name on every Londoner's horrified lips.

If he picked up a newspaper he was likely to see himself
vilified, in the words of Lord Walsingham, as 'one of those men
whose unprecedented cruelties had deluged our colonies with
human blood'. Nor was his faith in the British press and the
impartiality of the legal system much fortified by reading that
'the blood-stained Governor of Trinidad was in England, and the
friends of humanity were preparing to bring him before the bar
of offended justice, there to expiate his crimes'.[3]

Picton had cut short his service to Grinfield in the Windward
Islands and sped home on hearing that Fullarton had quit
Trinidad on 20 July, less than a month after his own departure.
It was small comfort to know the first commissioner had found
his precious liberal ideas too difficult to put into practice after
all. What troubled Picton was the warning his friends gave of the
damage the affidavit man might do to his reputation at home.
Forsaking his role as commandant of Tobago, he heeded the
advice that his honour would be best served in London.

His first step on arriving back was the bold one of writing to
the prime minister, who faced the threat of a French invasion,
with a plan for the defence of England. In his letter to
Addington, dated 20 October 1803, he wrote of 'the absolute
necessity of placing this country in a permanent situation, so as
to be at all times in readiness to resist sudden enterprises'.[4]
Picton argued that any force Napoleon ferried across from
Boulogne would 'come deficient in two of the most important
departments of an army, cannon and cavalry'. In the event,
therefore, it would be folly to stake the fate of the nation on a
single battle, for an enemy victory would allow them all too
quickly to supply 'their want of those essential arms'. More
politic, Picton argued in his 'rough hints', would be the adop-
tion of harassing tactics that would maximize Britain's advantage
in numbers and the mobility provided by cavalry. In his seven-
teen-point analysis, Picton emphasized the need for an
organized system of recruitment for regulars and, more impor-
tantly, reserves, whereby all males within appropriate age-bands
would be drafted to permanent military centres – at Exeter,
Bristol, Worcester, Salisbury and York – there to receive
specialist training in the artillery or cavalry.

These sensible proposals reflect both Picton's patriotism and
his military acumen. His plan may also be seen, less kindly, as an
attempt to curry favour at the highest level of government at a
time when his reputation was injured and his career prospects
in tatters. He was by no means alone in offering advice to the
government at this time, but few would have tendered as
detailed a military strategy. He doubtless expected something

more in reply than the curt acknowledgement of his letter from Addington's secretary.

It was more gratifying to be able to read in *The Times* of 29 October a report of Brigadier General Maitland's departure from Trinidad in late July. Pointedly omitting all mention of the recently departed first commissioner, the self-styled 'proprietors' of the island took the opportunity to praise ex-governor Picton:

> You came amongst us, Sir, at a most critical period: We were deprived of Brigadier-General Picton, the Pilot who had weathered the storm, who had brought this Government from a state not far removed from revolutionary insurrection, to an unexampled pitch of prosperity; its agriculture promoted, its commerce extended, its population respectably increased, and Port d'Espagne, from a village, risen into a considerable town. The loss of this valuable Representative of his Sovereign would have overwhelmed us with grief and despair, had we not placed the most perfect reliance upon the abilities of an Officer of your high rank and distinguished character.

Maitland responded in kind:

> Gentlemen, I am most grateful for this public testimony of your approbation of my conduct. It rises in my esteem for this reason, that as I replaced a most distinguished and meritorious Officer, so it was more difficult to gain applause. I will not throw away this opportunity of expressing, in unison with you, that I greatly honour and esteem Brigadier-General Picton. In a period of public danger, when the state of this Colony was beset by Traitors, and shaken by the unruly behaviour of a disorderly soldiery, his undisturbed mind awed the factions, subdued the danger, and saved the Colony.

But Maitland could only do his long-distance best for Picton, while fresh deposits of muck were dumped daily on his doorstep. It was the first commissioner, Picton knew, who was behind the malicious rumours and salacious prints. On his return, Fullarton had made his damaging report to Hobart at the War Office. Any interview that Picton might have had subsequently with Hobart must have been wholly unsatisfactory. The die was cast. Public opinion had been raised to such a pitch against 'the bloodstained tyrant' that the clamour pronouncing his guilt was deafening. Fullarton had prepared the ground meticulously, even to the extent of bringing a host of witnesses with him from Trinidad. These included Luisa Calderón, whose now full-grown limbs still bore the marks of M. Vallot's *grillos*.

Picton was summoned to answer charges before a special committee of the privy council on Thursday 8 December 1803. No doubt the case he put to them was essentially that which he later described in an open letter to his former colleague, Hood, namely, that he had been placed in a situation of 'great discretionary power' and that he had done his duty 'zealously and honestly', to the best of his ability:

> You well know, Sir, that I was placed, without any solicitation, as a matter of professional duty, in a most extraordinary situation, at the head of a new conquest, without any legal advisor to guide me in the administration of an intricate system of foreign laws, written in a foreign language; without any magistrate legally constituted, or acquainted with the jurisprudence of the country, to execute them; without any law-books, except such as I could casually pick up on the spot; and without any detailed instructions to supply the deficiency. Thus circumstanced, what more could reasonably be expected of me, than that I should act honestly, to the extent of my abilities, with the best advice I could procure in the place? I am not capable of impossibilities. I trust that the English people are too reasonable to require of me more than they would of any other person of moderate abilities under similar circumstances. Let any one of them suppose himself posted where I was: would he be satisfied to be placed in the midst of darkness, and then punished for not seeing clearly? [5]

This humble plea can have met only with blank looks and deaf ears. On Friday *The Times* briefly reported: 'Yesterday a Privy Council sat for a considerable time at the Cockpit, when General Picton was examined, and Colonel Fullarton attended to substantiate the charges alleged against him. He was afterwards remanded into the custody of Sparrow, the Messenger, for another examination.'

Picton, under arrest, must have felt as much the object of public scorn as the common criminal Robert Redhead, who had been sentenced that same day to 'stand on the pillory, in front of the Royal Exchange, and afterwards be imprisoned in the Gaol at Newgate for the term of two years'. However, there was one significant difference: such crimes as Redhead's did not whet the capital's jaded appetite as did the matter of the governor and mulatto girl. Of the thirty-six charges Fullarton enumerated against Picton in the council chamber at Port of Spain, each of which was conveyed to Hobart, only that relating to Luisa Calderón was pursued in the courts. Public opinion was reflected in the Crown's setting Picton's bail at £40,000, double the amount of the first prize in the monthly state lottery. If not exactly presuming guilt in the accused, the amount showed unequivocally how indignant the Crown was in bringing this charge against one of its supposed servants. Fortunately for Picton, Joseph Marryat, his former agent in London, raised the bond.

A true bill was found by the grand jury and, on 4 May 1804, in the Court of King's Bench, Westminster Hall, Picton was indicted before Lord Ellenborough, the Chief Justice. The indictment was framed in the most inflammatory terms. It was charged, on 23 December 1801, that Picton:

> a person employed in the service of his Majesty, in a civil and military station, in the island of Trinidad, with force and arms, unlawfully, cruelly, and inhumanly, and without any reasonable or probable cause, and under colour of his said station, did cause and procure the said Luisa (being a young woman under the age of fourteen years, in the peace of God and of our said Lord the King then there being), to be unlawfully, cruelly and inhumanly tortured, by the means of fastening and affixing to the wrists of the said Luisa a certain rope, passing through a certain pulley, then and there annexed to the ceiling of a certain room, in a certain prison in the said island of Trinidad, and by such rope raising and pulling up the said Luisa towards the ceiling aforesaid, and lowering her again on a certain sharp spike of wood, so that the feet of the said Luisa fell upon the said sharp spike, and keeping the said Luisa so suspended, and with the weight of her body resting on her said feet on the said spike, for a great length of time, to wit, for the space of half an hour, and alternately raising the said Luisa in the manner aforesaid, and lowering her again on the said spike, for certain other long spaces of time, to wit, for the space of twenty minutes at each of such times, by means of which cruel and inhuman torture, the hands, wrists, arms, and feet of the said Luisa were cruelly and severely strained, bruised, and wounded, and the said Luisa was thereby rendered sick, weak, and distempered, and her life greatly endangered, and hath been ever since rendered weak, and sick, and distempered, to the great injury and oppression of the said Luisa, in contempt of the King and his laws, in manifest violation of the liberties of our said Lord the King, to the great perversion of public justice.[6]

This was in fact the first of seven counts on which Picton was charged in connection with Calderón. The other six were variations on the same theme and recounted in identical fashion the torture by piquet to which Calderón was again subjected on the following day, 24 December, and her subsequent imprisonment in Port of Spain's jail where she was 'put and kept in irons for the space of eight months'.

Picton's defence would centre on testimony that Srta

Calderón, far from being a virtuous minor, was in fact the mistress of a certain trader, Don Pedro Ruiz, with whom she cohabited, and that, furthermore, Srta Calderón had entered into a carnal relationship with a second man, Don Carlos González, whom she aided and abetted in the manner of an accomplice, enabling him to enter the house of Ruiz and rob him of $2,000. Under the law of Spain, which he had been instructed to uphold in Trinidad, Picton had every right as governor to order the application of torture to a person suspected of being an accomplice to a felony. His counsel pointed out to Lord Ellenborough in the form of an affidavit that 'the whole of the proceedings against the said Luisa Calderón were in writing and are a matter of record in the said island', but, having no copies of the records himself, the defendant was under the necessity of requesting a mandamus to examine material witnesses, so that he might proceed to trial with their testimony.

Lord Ellenborough, anxious 'that due and speedy justice should be done', granted the mandamus. In Port of Spain, Thomas Hislop, the new governor, was instructed to examine witnesses at Government House. In London, Picton waited impatiently, determined to clear a name sullied by the evidence of one whom he described as 'a common Mulatto prostitute, of the vilest class and most corrupt morals'.[7]

At Ewenny Priory, near Bridgend, on 23 April 1804, Richard Turberville Picton, Thomas's eldest brother and high sheriff of Glamorgan, saw fit to change his name to Richard Turberville Turberville.

II

On receiving the mandamus in Port of Spain Governor Hislop ordered notices to be posted in Spanish, French and English announcing that court sessions would be held in the council chamber at Government House from 6 December 1804. Dozens of witnesses were called and depositions taken, filling 'sixty sheets of parchment and paper',[8] which, on 7 September 1805, were finally sent to London. The principal focus was on the case against Carlos González, convicted of robbing the tobacco dealer Pedro Ruiz, and on the age of Luisa Calderón, Carlos's alleged accomplice, at the time she was tortured. Picton's defence would prosper if the mandamus showed that González, with Calderón's help, was in fact guilty of robbing Ruiz of $2,000 on 7 December 1801, and especially if it showed that Calderón was not a minor but over fourteen years old when tortured. Unfortunately, neither issue was straightforward.

The evidence that had led to González's arrest was at best circumstantial. What told against him was Calderón's statement in which she confessed to having seen him commit the robbery, which was only said after she had been put on the piquet by *alcalde* Begorrat, who obtained the necessary permission 'to apply the question' ('aplícase la cuestión') from Governor Picton.

Witnesses interrogated by Begorrat in December 1801 were now summoned before Hislop to confirm their statements under oath as evidence for the court in London. It was a matter of record that Ruiz had gone to see Picton at Government House between 6.00 p.m. and 7.00 p.m. on 7 December 1801, forcibly taking Calderón with him. Ruiz complained that he had just been robbed of $2,000, 'the lock of one of his trunks having been broke open, which trunk was deposited in the middle room of three apartments held by him near the marine and government parade'.[9] He said that a plank at the side of the house towards the sea had been forced away. Governor Picton had at once ordered the arrest of Calderón and her mother, María Calderón, a manumitted slave, 'domestics of the said Ruiz', together with González and his partner, Don Pedro José Pérez.

Ruiz's visit to Government House was also described by Sra Calderón:

> The night Pedro Ruiz carried Luisa before Señor Picton, I was standing down below the window of Governor Picton's house, hearing the words that Luisa said, the Governor being below, in consequence of his just having arrived from his walk. He appeared angry and threatened Luisa. When my daughter was telling him she was innocent, he threatened her, and told her that he would send her to the Battery, and that he would draw the money from her.

Picton had promptly ordered both María and Luisa Calderón to be escorted to jail. Soon after he ordered Begorrat to interview all persons who knew anything about the robbery. Typical of the accounts gathered were the following:

Srta Teresa Allen, a 25-year-old *mulata* and next-door neighbour of Don Pedro Ruiz, saw Don Carlos pass by at about 6.30 p.m. on 7 December when he bade her good evening, entered Don Pedro's house and, after speaking to Srta Calderón, went away, by the back, towards the beach. Don José Rodriguez said Srta Calderón came into his chandler's shop after the firing of the gun at sunset and invited his wife to take a stroll as far as the bridge beyond the church, an invite that his wife declined. Soon afterwards Don Carlos appeared and spoke to them about the newly purchased schooner that he was fitting out, whereupon Srta Calderón went off, followed by Don Carlos, without Rodríguez noting which way he went. Other witnesses included the slave Topen and his girlfriend, Nely, who saw Don Carlos making water at the side of the *casa*. When Nely spoke to him about this, it being a place where kitchen articles were usually put, Don Carlos went further up the passage and stood on some planks, seeming to make water there.

The *peón* Joseph Arnaud also saw Don Carlos go towards the passage beside the house of Don Pedro, where he stopped for a time before coming out. Arnaud added that when he saw Don Carlos leave, he did not notice 'whether his hands were engaged, nor whether his jacket was buttoned', a remark that bears on Ruiz's claim to have been robbed in specie, 'doubloons, Portugal pieces, hard dollars, pisteens, rials and half rials'. Finally, M. Honoré Birot, a 48-year-old man, bedridden with the palsy, said that at the time of evening mass he heard the passage door of Don Pedro's house being opened, and a quarter of an hour afterwards he heard blows, as of the breaking open of a trunk, and a short time after that he heard the iron bolt drawn.

These accounts appear to confirm that González visited Ruiz's house and strongly suggest that he followed Calderón there. What is not clear is the purpose of his visit. Interrogated by Begorrat, González claimed he 'talked with Luisa about cohabitation together: she bid him go to the door of the passage, and he stood there, pretending to make water to loiter. He heard the noise of the door, when he approached nearer and met Luisa, who told him to go away immediately, for Pedro Ruiz was coming.'

The *alcalde* concluded: 'The declarations of all the witnesses proved the greatest connexion between Luisa and Carlos.' Srta Calderón, he said, 'confessed to have introduced Carlos into the chamber of Pedro Ruiz, when she yielded to all his wishes, and then retired from the chamber'. González later confessed to having had 'connexion' with Calderón in the passage, this being originally denied by the 37-year-old 'for shame, because he was a married man'. Torture had been applied, said Begorrat, because both the accused had committed perjury and because the testimonies were so strong, particularly that of 'the paralytick, lying in the bed distant from the chamber of Pedro Ruiz about eight or ten paces'.

Did González go to Ruiz's house to rob or to fornicate? González admitted to fornication. The 'paralytick' bore auditory witness to robbery. Begorrat concluded that he did both. Calderón claimed to have granted González her favours and then seen him commit robbery, watching 'from behind the bulk-head or palissade, when Carlos was in the passage breaking open the trunk, and when he took away the money in the sundry bags and purses'. Later, taken by Begorrat from prison to Ruiz's house, Calderón pointed out where she 'concealed herself while she saw Carlos committing the robbery, and a plank whose nails had been drawn of the room, close to where the trunk had stood'.

Was Calderón's change of role, from accomplice to witness, an accommodation arrived at with Begorrat, her statement in exchange for not being charged with a felony? Or did Ruiz – perhaps in cahoots with Picton – make the whole thing up? Was the robbery done to spite a man for stealing his mistress? Witnesses said that it was not the first time that Ruiz claimed to have been robbed. The traders Salazar, Macely and Bartolomé García remembered that, in 1797, Ruiz had said that the huckster's shop he then managed for Vicente Sanda had been broken into one night and robbed of eight joes, which he, Ruiz, blamed on Sanguilot, Sanda's slave. When a trunk was found a few days later 'broke open on the beach' Sanda had forthwith discharged Ruiz.

Ruiz found it difficult to explain that he had borrowed money from González three or four months prior to the alleged robbery. First, he denied all knowledge of such a loan, but pressed by González's attorney, Don Diego de Alcalá, he admitted borrowing from González for a couple of days, 'but the amount he cannot remember, whether it was two or three hundred dollars' nor 'whether it was three or four months previous to the robbery in question'.

Summing up for his client in the original process Don Diego pointed out that 'no one of the witnesses has declared having seen the commission of the act'; that Srta Calderón's confession was made while under torture and therefore 'ought to be considered as null'. Not only was he fully persuaded that the crime had not been committed by his client, but he suggested 'the accusation is false, and the robbery fictitious'. Ruiz had acted out of jealousy and malice: 'It is very probable', Don Diego concluded, 'he may have deceitfully machinated this story to execute his revenge.'[10]

Nonetheless, on 3 August 1802, Picton had found González guilty as charged. 'Inclining to equity and mercy', the governor imposed the penalty of 'perpetual banishment' and ordered González to indemnify Ruiz. As to his alleged accomplice: 'the mulatta Luisa Calderón shall be set at liberty, and considered to have expiated her offence by the long imprisonment she has suffered'.[11] Five days later, González paid his dues and was taken by the high constable to the quay, whence he embarked for Margarita.

The extent of Picton's interest is hard to determine. It is known he had 'several accounts for mules and cattle' with Ruiz, also that when González was in prison the cost of maintaining his new schooner fell on the government, which billed his wife, Juana Talavera. Doña Juana was no fool. She complained at the $900 disbursements, for she had been told 'slight repairs only would be done, as would render the vessel fit to navigate in this gulf, and not such considerable repairs as would render her fit to undertake a voyage to Europe'. Nine hundred dollars was what the schooner originally cost and, item by item, she queried the 'highly remarkable' bill. Item: How was it that caulking on such a small vessel proved so dear, when it had not been caulked below the water line? Most odd was that when the vessel was auctioned, valued at $1,320, nobody came forward to bid and she had to accept the one offer of $1,200 from Miguel Pietry, who was the same government receiver who had billed her for the disbursements![12]

That money was eaten up by boat and court costs, not to mention Ruiz's indemnity. The wages of sin for González must have made him wish he had never clapped eyes on Luisa Calderón. Ruiz had his money by November, but Doña Juana, the wife of González, was in Trinidad long after that, sorting out her husband's affairs.

Did Picton need to worry about Carlos González? Bad as it may have appeared in Trinidad, who in London was going to challenge the conviction? The issue was Luisa Calderón's age when she was tortured. The witnesses were Begorrat, the *escribano* Castro, Vallot and his drunken pair of *alguaciles*, Rafael Chando and Porto Rico, who did most of the hoisting.

Francisco de Castro, keeper of the archives, was the first official summoned by Hislop in the mandamus proceedings that got started in January 1805. Castro described how, after due warning from *alcalde* Begorrat, Srta Calderón was piqueted on 23 and 24 December 1801, and how greatly she had suffered – 'I saw her cry' – though he qualified this: 'It may be there was some affectation in her fainting.'[13] The *escribano* said he had no qualifications in law, having bought his position from the Spanish Crown in the usual way. He admitted that irregularities had occurred in Srta Calderón's examination: 'The appointment of a *defensor* to a minor, and the five days which ought to have elapsed, from the day of giving the sentence to the day of inflicting the torment, were omitted.'[14] There was also the requirement that torture not be applied twice within twenty-four hours, whereas Srta Calderón had been piqueted on successive days at 7.00 p.m. and 11.00 a.m.

This was a matter of acute embarrassment to Begorrat, who had pushed things through in December 1801 before his term of office expired with the year. His shortcomings were defended by two who succeeded him as *alcalde*, Nicholas St Pé and Philip Langston, both of whom swore that Begorrat had challenged the *escribano* about 'omissions and negligencies', quoting Castro as having replied that he had had no time for niceties on 'the eve of the Christmas holidays', when he was up to his eyes taking declarations from Thomas Higham and other members of the 'English Party' over the Walton tavern business. Castro blamed his clerk for mislaying declarations taken down in rough and for slipping up over the Calderón girl too: 'I am sure he has forgot to put the age; it is certain she was questioned as to her age, and that she declared she was more than fourteen.'

The examination of Castro should have continued next day, but he was indisposed. When he appeared again a week later he presented an affidavit prepared by Augustus Hayes, the prosecution attorney, stating that he wished all his previous evidence to be expunged, for it had been 'given under such fears and apprehensions' he had not been able to speak the truth. Even now he felt Governor Hislop would not be able to shield him from 'the subtilty of some men whom it might be equally dangerous for him to point out'. He was 'nevertheless ready to appear before the honourable court in Europe', whenever the trial should take place.

Hislop was not having that. When Castro refused to answer questions he committed him to jail with an alacrity that recalled Picton's days as governor. Nor did he allow Castro's second plea, to be permitted to answer questions in writing from his home. He would respond in court or be charged with contempt. The *escribano* slunk back, his one remaining gesture of defiance being to refuse to take the oath in front of Begorrat. Only when the latter agreed to withdraw did he answer questions put by the counsel for the defence, Archibald Gloster:

'Do you believe the defendant acted in the whole of the prosecution respecting the robbery of Pedro Ruiz, with impartiality?'
'Yes, I believe so.'
'As you often saw Luisa Calderón at the time of her imprisonment, what did her age appear to you to be?'
'I always thought her fifteen, either a little more or less.'

'Was she a woman grown at that time and did her bosom exhibit signs of puberty?'
'I took her for a woman.'
'At the time of her being piqueted, did she protest or object against such punishment on account of her want of age?'
'No.'
'Did Luisa Calderón, or her *defensor*, ever plead her want of age, as an excuse or exemption from torture or punishment?'
'No.'[15]

Castro might have added that her *defensor*, Don Juan Bermúdez, would have found it difficult to plead anything for he was not in fact appointed until after Srta Calderón had been tortured, when four others had declined the position and Don Juan himself was out of town. Castro was already juggling too many balls. Scared of offending Pictonites like Begorrat, he also wanted desperately to prove himself to the first commissioner and book passage to London. He had been packed ready to embark with Fullarton's party on the morning of Wednesday 20 July 1803, but was stopped at the last minute by the wiles of *alcaldes* Black and St Pé, who objected to his deputy Alvarez taking over as official *escribano* on the pretext that he might be of mixed blood. Castro had watched Fullarton's ship sail, with the Srta Calderón and the *borrachones* Porto Rico and Rafael Chando on board, while he, who had enough on Picton to damn him twice over, was left to face his enemies on the quay.

In court his instinct for survival got the better of his urge to travel. He was not helped by the incompetence of Hayes, the prosecuting attorney, whom Fullarton had originally employed to gather evidence against Picton. Hayes's examination of Sra Calderón was particularly inept:

'Are you the mother of Luisa Calderón?'
'Yes, I was delivered of her in this island, and bred her up.'
'State the day and year of the birth of Luisa Calderón.'
'I do not rightly remember when she was born; what I can say is she was born in the month of August, on St Lewis' day, and she was ten years old when she was in prison.'
'Was Luisa more than ten years old when she was in prison?'
'No: rather less than more.'
Archibald Gloster stood up quickly for the defence and ridiculed María's notion of her daughter's age:
'Before Luisa was sent to jail, was she not living with Pedro Ruiz as his mistress?'
'Yes, on a promise of marriage.'
'How long had Luisa and Ruiz cohabited together before Luisa was charged with the robbery?'
'Two years and five months.'

'Had they cohabited together as man and wife?'
'Yes, during the whole time.'[16]

Simple arithmetic showed that, by her own mother's reckoning, Luisa must have begun her life of concubinage at seven, a precocity that, said Gloster, even in Port of Spain, beggared all belief. Hayes tried again, but by the time he got Sra Calderón to say that she believed her daughter was under fourteen when tortured, the woman was no longer a credible witness. Few were now inclined to believe her story that a guard had tried to ravish her daughter in prison. Nor was it likely that Luisa, when she was accompanied by Begorrat to the scene of the crime, had limped all the way, since the *alcalde* himself said that she had freely walked the fifteen hundred paces, 'smoking a segar all the while'.[17] Sra Calderón's naïvety and innumeracy contributed to her lack of credibility, as did her need for an interpreter, but equally culpable was Augustus Charles Hayes, a dim-witted barrister-at-law, whose many court absences suggest a bad case of tropical ennui.

Others were anxious to swear that Srta Calderón had been under the age of fourteen. Don Juan Santiago, her godfather, said she was baptized ten years before being imprisoned, 'a little more or less'. Doña Juana Talavera, still on the island, and keen to do Picton down, said that she had known Srta Calderón since she was two and she was ten when she went to live with Ruiz, adding, with conviction: 'She was not a woman, had no breasts'.[18]

Most were of the opposite persuasion, however, including Cayetano Guevara who had seen Luisa on his arrival in Trinidad in 1786, when she was 'a tiny little thing'. Don Abraham Pinto agreed: Luisa was the same age as his son who had gone to school with her. For Begorrat it was a simple sum: the law fixed the age of puberty at twelve, and Luisa had been living with Ruiz for three years. Farfan said she looked a good sixteen or seventeen at the time, while Vallot topped them all, noting she took tobacco every day: 'From her appearance, she had seventeen or eighteen years at least.'[19]

The man who should have known, Pedro Ruiz, found the question insulting:

'Was Luisa Calderón at that time living with you as your mistress?'
'Yes, in my house.'
'How long had she been living with you previous to the robbery?'
'Between two years and a half and three years.'

'When she first came to live with you was she a woman grown?'
'Surely when a woman goes to live with a man she must be full grown.'[20]

The matter should have been easy to resolve at source: the church's baptismal register. When asked about legal documents, María Calderón had said: 'The curate can answer.' But even here confusion clouded the issue.

Summoned to court, Padre José María Angeles explained, speaking through an interpreter, that the register in question carried a memorandum for September 1788, folio 59b, on which were written the words 'Luisa Vease folio 89', ('For Luisa see folio 89').[21] Turning to this folio, he read out details pertaining to the baptism of one 'Luisa, an infant, natural daughter of María del Rosario Calderón, from Cariaco in Cumaná, on the Costa Firma, born the 25th of August, 1788. To which I give faith; José María Angeles.'

At this point Hayes succeeded in muddying the water:

'Is the memorandum in folio 59b in your hand-writing?'
'Yes.'
'Was that memorandum made at the time of Luisa Calderón's baptism?'
'No: I believe two or three months afterwards.'
'Was the second entry in folio 89 made after the month of December 1789, or before that period?'
'It was made after December 1789.'
'It appears by the registry, that Luisa Calderón was baptised in September 1788: How much time elapsed between her baptism and the making of the entry?'
'I believe one year or more. The sacristan brought me a good number of entries to make: a year and three or four months.'

Even Hayes could see his witness was treading water in a fast-moving river. He threw him a lifeline of sorts:

'By whom was Luisa Calderón baptised?'
'By the sacristan, Don Esteban de Arrago.'
'Do you mean to swear that these entries not being inserted in their right place, is attributable to the sacristan's not having delivered his memoranda of baptisms in due time?'
'Yes, I swear so.'
'Where is the sacristan, Don Esteban?'
'He was at Angustura.'

Hayes sat down, hoping the issue would go away with the sacristan, but Gloster picked up the thread and requested that entries in the baptismal register be examined by a separate member of the clergy. He then cross-examined Padre José María:

'Is any particular age required by the Spanish forms for baptism?'
'The baptisms, according to Roman Ritual, ought to be as soon as possible after birth.'
'That may be the rule; but what is the usual practice?'
'Sometimes a month, sometimes seven years or more.'
'Do you ever require a certificate of birth before you baptise?'
'No: no certificate at all.'

Later, Gloster summoned the Vicar-General of Trinidad, Don Pedro Reyes, who had been requested by the court to examine the register. When asked what observations he had to make, Don Pedro launched into a scathing attack upon the curate's method of recording baptisms. The blank pages found at the end of year-books were dubious enough, he said, but most disturbing was the memorandum for folio 59, *Luisa Vease al folio 89*, which was written in a different ink and 'quite fresh'.[22]

Reyes concluded: 'I consider the entry of baptism of Luisa Calderón as of no authority whatever, and very suspicious.' Later, he petitioned Hislop about 'the great scandal which the curate's conduct had brought upon the ecclesiastical character'.[23] Padre José María was removed from his office, prosecuted for forgery and perjury and committed to Vallot's jail.

In place of the *padre*'s forged entry Reyes found a separate book, *The Register of Ancient Inhabitants*, with an entry for 'Luisa Antonia, infant, daughter of María Nunes, a free coloured woman, with godparents Juan Santiago and Luisa Antonia'. This dated the baptism, by Padre José Antonio Alvarado, as 6 September 1786, one year prior to Padre José Mará's commencement of duties. It also showed, definitively, that the person in question was at least fifteen years and three months old in December 1801.

For the benefit of the court in London Don Pedro wrote: 'I do hereby declare that the baptism of Luisa Calderón, entered in Folio 89 of the register by Father José María Angeles, Curate of the Port of Spain, is false, and of no value, and that that found in the register of the ancient inhabitants is, and ought to be regarded as the true one.'[24]

The person who had put Angeles up to the forgery, however, was already in London and would escape prosecution. Indeed, Don Pedro Vargas, the expert lawyer whom Fullarton had appointed assessor, was to play an important role in the subsequent trial of Thomas Picton.

III

Picton's trial did not come before Lord Ellenborough in the
Court of King's Bench until 24 February 1806. Proceedings in
Port of Spain had been slow and the mandamus depositions,
which required careful study by both counsels, although
dispatched on 7 September, had only arrived in London in
November 1805. Picton, who now lived at 21 Edward Street, near
Portman Square, had to exercise all his patience in the many
months that followed his indictment on 4 May 1804.

Not that Picton was unoccupied in this period, which was
largely taken up with acrimonious exchanges between the ex-
governor and the former first commissioner. It began with
Fullarton's pamphlet of 1804, *Statement, Letters, and Documents
Respecting the Affairs of Trinidad*, which amounted to an outright
attack on Picton for his 'delinquencies' in Trinidad. The document also contained comments on Hood, who that year had
married Mary, the eldest daughter of Lord Seaforth, Governor of
Barbados. Hood, who would soon be nominated a Knight of the
Bath, responded via a letter to Earl Camden, dated Barbados, 1
September 1804, in which he declared Fullarton's account 'false
almost in every page'.[25] This was published with Picton's own
reply of late 1804, *Letter Addressed to the Right Honourable Lord
Hobart*, a collection of testimonies from such officers as Grinfield,
Maitland, Draper and Hood providing 'irrefragable refutation'
of Fullarton's 'libellous animadversions'. In August 1805, Pierre
McCallum published his 350-page *Travels in Trinidad*, which, far
from being an 'unvarnished tale' and 'naked exposition of facts',
as its author claimed,[26] was a rambling diatribe and crude character assassination of Picton. For a response in kind, Picton looked
to Colonel Edward Draper, who was then preparing an account
that, amongst other things, would charge Fullarton with misappropriation of military funds. But this last publication did not
appear until after Picton's trial when it resulted in Draper himself
being brought to court on a charge of libel.

Preoccupied as he was with his pending trial, Picton would
have been no less absorbed by the momentous events taking
place on the world stage. On 2 December 1805, Napoleon had
achieved his greatest triumph when he defeated the armies of
the Austrian Emperor Francis I and the Russian Tsar Alexander
I at Austerlitz. This battle followed Nelson's date with destiny off
Cabo Trafalgar on 21 October, in which he prevailed, despite
Admiral Villeneuve's numerical superiority, and, in the process,
he completely destroyed the Spanish fleet. These famous victo-
ries left the perennial rivals, France and Britain, with absolute

and unchallenged dominion, the one over the land, the other over the sea. Trafalgar effectively ended fears of a French invasion of Britain, while it also gave rise to euphoric confidence at home in the innate superiority of Britain's naval forces. Not only was Britain safe for the foreseeable future, all maritime trade was now subject to her mercy.

Thus the state funeral of Admiral Viscount Horatio Nelson on 9 January 1806 was a solemn act of thanksgiving as well as a grand exercise in patriotism: three days of lying in state at the great Painted Hall of Greenwich Naval Hospital, from Sunday 5 January, when crowds in excess of 20,000 queued outside; the aquatic procession on Wednesday morning when four barges draped in black were rowed up the Thames to Whitehall; the transference, between a double line of troops, of the coffin to the Admiralty; and, finally, the Thursday morning procession, attended by more than 160 carriages and mourning coaches, as well as by most regiments of cavalry and infantry quartered within 100 miles of London, the whole of which moved in stately fashion along the Strand, through Temple Bar, to St Paul's, for the service, which was conducted by the Archbishop of Canterbury.

For weeks London's newspapers had been filled with stories about Nelson. The nation relived those last moments in which he made Hardy swear he would take his body home, not bury him at sea; it repeated his selfless command, 'Tighten that rope!', given when he noticed a slack tiller; and it rejoiced in the words uttered as he lay dying, 'Thank God, I have done my duty'. Column after column detailed the military preparations for the funeral and the order of precedence, beginning with HRH the Prince of Wales. For days ahead of the funeral *The Times* ran advertisements offering rooms with a good view of the procession: from the Turk's Head and the Dundee Arms overlooking the river in Wapping, where five-shilling tickets were on sale at the bar, to upper floors in Fleet Street with commodious bow and double-sash windows, where 'Good fires' and 'Terms easy' were promised.

Within a fortnight, when Pitt died on 23 January, London was contemplating another public funeral. This turned out to be a smaller event. For two days there was a lying-in-state in the Painted Chamber adjoining the House of Lords and, on the morning of Saturday 24 February, the coffin was borne to Westminster Abbey along a route lined with foot-guards. The crowd was sparse and little use was made of the seating on the scaffolds that had been erected. Perhaps the metropolis had had its fill of funerals. Or it may have been a case of a warrior hero having a greater claim on a nation's affection than a politician whose enemies lived at home rather than abroad. William Pitt, the Younger, had filled his country's highest political office nearly as long as Walpole, who held the record with twenty-one years. But his Tory administration had financed the war with new taxes and many thought him too sympathetic towards Catholics and, at least in the early days, not decisive enough about Revolutionary France. On 3 February, in a measure that carried without opposition, the House of Commons voted £40,000 for the payment of Pitt's personal debts. But when it was proposed that a monument be erected at Guildhall to perpetuate his memory, the motion was carried by a majority of only six votes. The inscription on the Guildhall memorial more accurately reflects the mood of the time rather than the full extent of his achievements: 'In an age when the contagion of ideas threatened to dissolve the forms of civil society, he rallied the loyal, the sober-minded and the good around the venerable structure of the English monarchy.'

The death of Pitt left a vacuum. It meant the dissolution of the administration he led, since few of his colleagues were of any consequence. When Lord Hawkesbury declined an invitation to form a new government, deeming it impossible to build on the wreck of the old, the King called on Lord Grenville, who accepted, so long as a place could be found in the cabinet for the Whig Charles James Fox, who had once described the fall of the Bastille, on 14 July 1789, as 'much the greatest event that ever happened in the history of the world'. To everyone's astonishment, George III had agreed and Grenville formed his 'Ministry of All the Talents', which included Lord Ellenborough. The acceptance of a cabinet position by the Lord Chief Justice was controversial. Many felt that there should be a separation between politics and the law. Others doubted that a man as cumbersome as Ellenborough could move with appropriate speed between the Commons, Downing Street, Guildhall and the Court of King's Bench, where he normally sat his bulk down.

Thus, when Picton's trial began on the Monday after Pitt's funeral, the public eye was focused on the Lord Chief Justice, who, from Pitt's death in office until Grenville's appointment, had technically been prime minister. Ellenborough, formally Edward Law, had been elevated to the peerage on being made Lord Chief Justice in 1802, taking his title from the Cumberland village that was his ancestral home. A strong judge, with a reputation for browbeating counsel and jury, he had pursued a career that moved unerringly in one direction:

to the political and juridical right, the French Revolution having cured him of early Whiggish sympathies. The son of an Anglican bishop, he supported the suspension of habeas corpus in Ireland and firmly opposed Catholic Emancipation at home, in which, as in all matters, he sided with the King. In law, he first made his mark as counsel for Warren Hastings, who was impeached in 1788 for misdealings in India. His opening speech lasted three days and, subsequently, his arguments did much to secure an acquittal, in 1795. A decade later, Ellenborough was the judge who helped find Dundas guilty on six counts for misappropriation of navy funds. By then he was famed more for his violent prejudices than his intellect, feared more for his sarcasm than his oratory. He had come to believe the law could not be too severe and had lent his name to ten new capital felonies. With his penchant for pompous phrases, which his Cumbrian accent made even weightier, he seemed to invite mockery, while his shaggy eyebrows, huge frame and ponderous gait made him, like many another feared man, a favourite subject of cartoonists.

The Court of King's Bench was situated in the south-east corner of Westminster Hall, in the Palace of Westminster, which also housed the courts of Common Pleas, Exchequer and Chancery. Once London's principal royal residence as well as the seat of government, the palace had long been a noisy thoroughfare, and the hall was filled not only with judges, barristers and witnesses of all kinds, but also shoppers and stall-holders who sold anything from books to clothing. The Court of King's Bench, so called because the King in person formerly sat there, was England's supreme court and in the Hall itself had taken place such historic public trials as those of Sir Thomas More, Guy Fawkes and King Charles I. Not until the middle of the eighteenth century were the various courts partitioned off so that business might be more audibly conducted. This left the courts small and crowded, and those who wished to obtain a seat at Picton's trial arrived before 9.00 a.m. on the Monday, the hour at which Lord Ellenborough entered in full-bottomed wig and ermine-trimmed robe.

Picton himself, as defendant, was deemed an incompetent witness who could not be summoned for questioning. Wearing a black suit, he spent the day walking the halls of the Four Courts, where, from time to time, he was visited by Joseph Marryat who apprized him of the progress of his cause. Picton placed his faith in counsel Robert Dallas, a polished speaker who had served under Ellenborough in the Hastings trial and who had recently been elected MP for Kirkcaldy. For the Crown there was the formidable William Garrow, a prosecutor whose fertile brain, aggressive courtroom presence and bruising style of cross-examination had, in the last decade, virtually changed the art of advocacy, earning him a reputation as 'the best bar-bully of them all'.

Garrow's plain language, together with a complete indifference to the witness's station in life, was considered by many an assault on the dignity of the courts. Once Garrow defended a farmer against a suit brought by Baron Hompesch, a Swiss nobleman and officer in the British Army, who had charged the farmer with using a hunting dog to poach from his estate in Kent. Garrow brought the dog into court to show it was merely a sheepdog and, stroking the animal tenderly, he stated that the cause was supported by two witnesses, the baron and the dog, 'of which the last was certainly an honest witness'.[27] Worse than this insult was the barrister's blunt refusal to fight the duel that would enable Hompesch to restore his honour. For William Garrow, MP for Gratton, future Attorney-General and Baron of the Exchequer, the only field of dispute was the courtroom, where any ploy was permissible in the interest of securing the desired verdict.

IV

Once Lord Ellenborough had filled his high seat and the grisly indictment against Picton had been read out, Garrow put the case for the prosecution:

> Gentlemen of the jury; the task of stating the particulars of this most extraordinary and horrid transaction, was originally confided to much greater abilities than those upon which it has now unfortunately devolved. I feel, however, some consolation in reflecting that the present is a case which, addressed to a British jury in a British Court of Justice, requires no embellishment of eloquence, nor any factitious aid, to impress it upon the minds of those who are to hear and to decide upon it.[28]
>
> Unless the facts, clearly and fully substantiated by proof, force from you a reluctant verdict of guilty, I have no hesitation in declaring that the defendant ought not to be convicted: I say a *reluctant* verdict of guilty, because there is no individual present, not excepting myself, whose duty it is to conduct the prosecution, who would not rejoice if you could justify yourselves to your consciences and your God, in doubting the truth of this accusation.
>
> The indictment alleges that a representative of our Sovereign,

and Governor of one of our colonial dependencies, who was therefore bound to protect his fellow subjects, has abused the station to which he was raised, and has disgraced the country to which he belongs, by inflicting torture upon one of His Majesty's subjects, without the least pretence of law, without the least moral justification, but solely to gratify his tyrannical disposition, by the oppression of the unfortunate and defenceless victim of his cruelty.

Garrow recounted how Trinidad had been conquered by the illustrious Abercromby, who instructed Picton as governor to continue to administer the island's law, which was so much less severe than that of old Spain and so well suited to that remote area. He then turned to the matter in hand and to the person of Luisa Calderón, who, he said, at ten or eleven years of age had become the mistress of Pedro Ruiz, explaining 'in that hot climate the puberty of females is much accelerated'. He told how Luisa had become engaged in an intrigue with Carlos González, who, in turn, availed himself of the connection to gain access to Pedro Ruiz's house and rob him of a quantity of dollars. Such suspicion attached to Luisa Calderón, said Garrow, she was taken into custody along with Carlos González and examined by a magistrate, to whom she denied all knowledge of the business:

> She persisted in her denial, and whether her object in so doing was to protect herself or her friend is not at all material to inquire. The magistrate felt that he had no authority to adopt any coercive means in order to procure any confession; and therefore he resorted to the defendant, who was invested with the supreme authority of the island, to supply the deficiency; and, gentlemen, I shall produce in the handwriting of General Picton himself, and subscribed with his signature this bloody sentence: Aplícase la cuestión a Luisa Calderón, 'Inflict the torture upon Luisa Calderón'.

Garrow told how the magistrate warned Luisa about her forthcoming torment; she alone would be responsible for her well-being if she did not confess. He then resorted to pure hocus-pocus: 'The punishment was applied which has been improperly called *picketing*. I say improperly, because picketing is a known military punishment.' Garrow explained the distinction: the military torture permitted some relief since it involved an additional rope around the body, which could be rested upon to lessen the pressure on the foot, while the torture suffered by Luisa Calderón afforded no such relief. He concluded: 'Not only for the sake of correctness, but for the sake of humanity, I hope this practice will not receive the appellation of *picketing*, but that of *Pictoning*, that it may be described by the most horrid name by which it can be known, and be shunned as a disgrace to human nature.'

The devastating pun was followed by a detailed account of the torment itself, fully supported by illustration:

> This unhappy creature continued for fifty-three or fifty-four minutes in that dreadful state. The time was ascertained by a watch which the magistrate had before him, not from any fear that she might suffer too much, but because there was some notion of a supposed law, that the torture could not be inflicted for more than an hour; and had it not been for the watch, the pleasure of inflicting the punishment might have induced the magistrates and the spectators to have continued it for a longer period than the time supposed to be allowed.

Here Garrow produced a coloured drawing for the benefit of the jury: 'This gentlemen, is a faithful representation of it, and may give you some notion of the suffering which a human being in such a situation must have undergone.' Remarkably, there was no objection to this shameless incitement of the jury by means of a lurid print and Garrow concluded that Picton had no justification in inflicting torture on a British subject, for 'trial by rack is utterly unknown in England' and even the ancient instrument kept in the Tower, derisively called 'the Duke of Exeter's Daughter', was only rarely used in days gone by and then strictly as 'an engine of state, not of law'. If the harsher laws of Spain allowed torture, there was no practice of it in Trinidad, where Picton had 'all the merit of the invention'.

Luisa Calderón was summoned as the first prosecution witness and sworn in. She was now nineteen and though she wore a plain white dress and muslin turban of the same colour, all eyes in the court were upon her. Despite the fact that she had been living with the Fullartons for nearly three years in London and Ayrshire, she still required an interpreter. Her answers in whispered Spanish seemed to accentuate her vulnerability as Mr Adam, Garrow's junior counsel, took her through her unfortunate life, the enforced concubinage, the robbery, the arrest and the torture, every detail of which was painfully relived. When Adam came to the nuance of whether it was her right or her left foot that had first rested on the piquet, Garrow interjected, showing the witness a coloured drawing:

> 'Is that a faithful representation of it?'
> 'Yes, very good indeed', answered Luisa.

Garrow turned towards Lord Ellenborough:

'I wish your lordship could have seen the involuntary expression of the sensations of the witness upon looking at the drawing.'

The Chief Justice was indignant at the liberty Garrow had taken:

'I do not approve of exhibiting drawings of this nature before a jury, and I shall not permit it till the counsel for the defendant has seen it. I have no objection to your showing a description to the jury, but the colouring may produce an improper effect.'

The print was brought by an usher to Ellenborough, who studied it with a keen eye for the female form, his own wife, Anne, being reputedly a great beauty of the day. It was then passed on to Robert Dallas, who, for his part, was well aware that this and similar drawings were selling by the gross only a few paces beyond the walls of the court. Heavy with resignation, Dallas responded:

'I have no objection whatever on the part of my client that the jury should see it, but it certainly is not the usual course of proceeding in a case of this sort.'

Garrow: 'I have one to which there can be no objection. It is a mere pen and ink sketch.'

He handed the new drawing to the witness:

'Is that a correct representation?'

'Yes, this is correct', said Luisa, innocently passing the drawing to the jury.

Ellenborough was moved to caution again:

'Gentlemen, you will consider that as a description of the position, which we can easily understand from the words of the witness. Nobody wishes that any improper impression should be made by that drawing, it is only to show the nature of the process. You see the suspension by one arm, and the resting upon the opposite foot.'

Luisa was soon illustrating the drawing.

'By which arm were you tied up on the second day?'

'By both arms.'

'One at a time?'

'Yes, first one, and then they changed it to the other.'

'Were you drawn up by the rope the second day so as to remove your foot from resting on the spike of wood?'

'I could just touch it with the end of my toe.'

'Were your shoes taken off both days?'

'Yes.'

'Your feet were naked?'

'Yes, I had no shoes on.'

'What effect did this produce on you; did it make you sick?'

'I fainted away.'

Lord Ellenborough: 'Did you faint away on both days or only on one of those days?'

'No more than one day.'

Mr Adam: 'Do you know whether you were taken down upon fainting away?'

'I do not recollect whether I was or not.'

'Was that owing to your insensibility, or have you forgot it?'

'I do not recollect anything of the kind.'

'How long were you in prison?'

'Eight months.'

'Were you at any time taken from the prison to the house of Pedro Ruiz?'

'Yes.'

'Do you recollect how long that was after the torture?'

'I cannot recollect the time.'

'Were you able to walk there without assistance?'

'I was so very bad that I went all the way quite lame.'

'To what was that lameness attributable?'

'The *grillos* that I was put into.'

Luisa explained that a *grillo* consisted of an iron bar fastened to the ground with pairs of rings attached to secure the limbs. She was shown another drawing and confirmed its likeness to the *grillos*. Eight months in them had left their mark, especially on her wrists, she said, baring them to the jury.

The next witness was Rafael Chando, the *alguacil*, who confirmed the details of Luisa's torture and the likeness to the piquet and the *grillos* found in the drawings shown him by Garrow. Chando described how Luisa fainted into his arms on being brought down from the piquet and how Begorrat revived her by putting a glass of wine to her lips and vinegar to her nose. He swore that no 'defender' was appointed to her, no surgeon was present during her torture, and that the piquet was the first instrument of torture he had seen in Trinidad. Governor Picton instructed him to make a piquet in yard of the soldiers' barracks, and then, about the middle of 1801, another was set up at the jail.

Garrow called Juan Montes, an engineer who had lived in Trinidad since 1793. Montes confirmed Chando's statements and swore that the order, 'Aplícase la cuestión a Luisa Calderón', was written in the hand of the man who had signed it, Thomas Picton. Garrow said he had more witnesses to produce, if necessary, but having regard for the court's time, he was prepared to close the case for the Crown. In doing so he left what seemed an utterly desolate floor to the defence.

Robert Dallas's contribution thus far had been to elicit from Luisa that she had come to England with Colonel Fullarton, and from Lord Ellenborough and a grudging Garrow, that the fateful statement 'Aplícase la cuestión a Luisa Calderón' could only have been written in response to a request. It was time now for matters of substance.

Dallas spoke with *de rigueur* modesty: he was in court only because he had failed to convince his client of his feeble abilities as an advocate, though he did feel duty-bound to defend a gentleman threatened with something worse than ruin, namely, his dishonour. He drew attention to the special problems of a case that was so much in the public eye:

> It is impossible for me, gentlemen, not to feel myself surrounded and pressed upon by difficulties which, for the sake of impartial justice, I would fain remove. I cannot but have felt that a case of this nature, supported as it has been by the exhibition of prints and drawings, exposed to the view of every person in court, and assisted by a species of acting which I at least have for the first time witnessed in a criminal prosecution – I say I cannot but have felt that such a case, founded upon a charge of torture, must in its progress have created powerful sensations, even in men determined to keep their minds as indifferent and impartial as possible – sensations very unfavourable to the party for whom I appear.

Lord Ellenborough interrupted testily: 'I would not permit the drawings to be shown to the jury, until I had your consent.'

'My lord, I acknowledge it; and perhaps I am not correct in now adverting to any advantage that may have been taken of such a concession.'

Dallas continued undeterred: the members of the jury faced another difficulty, that of living in a country where the law was mild, humane and 'most perfectly administered', and having to imagine the practice of a different legal system in a distant clime and in different circumstances. They needed to attend to the facts, in which area the prosecution had been brief. A more correct examination was required, and he invited the jury to consider the two protagonists: General Picton, governor of Trinidad, the supreme military and civil authority of that island; and Luisa Calderón, a domestic who lived in a state of prostitution with Pedro Ruiz, who indulged herself in criminal intercourse with Carlos González, aiding him to rob the man with whom she lived as a mistress. Under the merciful law of England, said Dallas, such a robbery was a capital felony. Both Luisa and Carlos González would have been hanged if found guilty here.

As for Governor Picton, all he had done on hearing of the offence was to refer the investigation to the colony's competent tribunal, ordering all parties accused, not only this young woman, but her mother, Carlos González and González's business partner, to be taken into custody and examined by Mr

Begorrat. Only when every other means had been exhausted by Begorrat was the application for torture made. Governor Picton merely acquiesced to his suggestion, *the first step not having been taken by himself*, and allowed the law to take its course. To impute malice to the defendant was quite extraordinary.

Luisa Calderón had sustained no permanent injury, Dallas observed. In another colony, say St Vincent, the lesser offence of resisting arrest could result in the amputation of a hand, and the magistrate ordering such a punishment would have acted within the colonial law of England and could not himself be charged or held guilty of any crime. It was, said Dallas, important to consider the place where events happened. The defence based itself on three points.

First, by the law of Spain, the infliction of torture in this instance was lawful. Second, should it be argued to the contrary that the order to apply torture was unlawful, it was still not maliciously issued, and the jury must therefore acquit the defendant.

Lord Ellenborough interjected: 'Everything against law is presumed to be malicious.'

Dallas nodded deferentially and continued with his third point: should the jury decide that torture was inconsistent with the law of Spain, it would be shown that General Picton had been misinformed on this, for he had been led to believe it was strictly legal, and the case was then one of a mere error of judgement for which no criminal responsibility attached to the governor.

The defence produced evidence for the legality of torture under Spanish law. Dallas referred to ancient Spanish texts, the *Curria Philippica, Elizondo* and *Leyes de Partida*, citing various instances when torture was permitted. These included crimes of theft, when there was a presumption of guilt in an accomplice, and was especially applicable when a person had been entrusted with the care of property, which was relevant, said Dallas, to the case of Luisa Calderón.

Here, Lord Ellenborough ruled that the case had resolved itself into a point of law, which turned on whether General Picton, as supreme judge, had the authority to inflict torture and was, in so doing, clothed in judicial authority and protected by the law. It was very proper, he said, that the case be turned into a special verdict, leaving any question of law to be decided by the court, and he directed both counsels to put their arguments accordingly.

Dallas cited Abercromby's instructions to Picton and Chief Justice Nihell, broadly to keep the Spanish forms of law in use on the island. He summoned Michel de Gourville, who had lived in Trinidad since 1774 and been an *alcalde* under the Spanish governor Chacón. De Gourville explained how the system had worked formerly and how it had continued under Picton, but Garrow's questions to the witness elicited an admission that the *alcalde* had seen no torture, other than thumb-tying, under Chacón.

Dallas called Archibald Gloster, Trinidad's attorney-general since 1803, who listed the Spanish texts he had been able to consult in Port of Spain. These were reassuringly those Dallas had named earlier when citing references to torture. Soon Gloster's affable equanimity was tested by Garrow's sarcasm:

'I take it you are familiarly acquainted with Spanish?'

'No, not familiarly; I can translate it with the assistance of a dictionary when I wish to look into one of the Spanish law books.'

'Do you know there is another expressly applicable to the colonies which you have not named? What think you of the *Royal Schedula?*'

'What? The *Schedula* published by the Spanish court?'

'Yes', Garrow interrupted with some irony, 'which contains the Regulations for the Population, and the Commerce for the Island of Trinidad? I dare say I have translated that pretty near, though I am not a Spaniard. Have I made a tolerable hit for the first time as a dipper? This is a code which has not fallen under your experience?'

'Yes, I was perfectly aware of it, it is the *Royal Schedula.*'

'There is another book which is called *Recopilación de las Leyes.*'

'Yes, I know that book perfectly.'

'It may have occurred to you to consult these two books?'

'I do not know that I have particularly.'

'Is there one single syllable from the beginning to the end, that justifies inflicting torture in any one of the Spanish islands?'

'I do not know that there is.'

'Upon your oath, do you not know there is not?'

'Upon the oath I have taken, I do not know that there is not.'

Lord Ellenborough: 'Is there in that book any law of Trinidad to regulate the treatment of contumacious witnesses, or of witnesses guilty of prevarication?'

'I do not know that there is, or that there is not.'

Ellenborough: 'You do not found yourself on that book, Mr Dallas?'

'No, my lord; we found ourselves upon the books we put in as containing the general law of the island.'

Dallas explained that the recent declaration of war between England and Spain had prevented the defence obtaining pertinent legal texts. He proposed instead to consider evidence from the mandamus taken in Trinidad. But Garrow intervened to say he would save the court's time, for if it was the intention of the defence merely to show that Luisa Calderón was strongly suspected of involvement in the robbery, he had no objection to Mr Dallas taking the mandamus evidence as read. Dallas was obliged to accept, leaving Garrow to call his last witness, Pedro Vargas, the Spanish colonial lawyer who had been appointed assessor by former first commissioner Fullarton.

Vargas stated that he had been in Trinidad since 1803, having been born on the Main and having spent his whole life there and in various parts of the Spanish West Indies. He was brought up to the law and had practised it in four different places.

> 'Are you able to say that you are acquainted with the laws of the Spanish West Indies?'
> 'I think I am.'
> 'You have studied them in fact as your profession?'
> 'Yes, I have.'
> 'Take that book, and state to his lordship and the jury, whether that is the book you consider as containing the law for the government of the Spanish West Indies?'
> 'I conceive this book contains principally the laws of the colonies of South America.'
> Lord Ellenborough: 'What is it called?'
> '*La Recopilación de las leyes de las Indias de la América del Sur,* ordered to be printed by His Most Catholic Majesty King Charles II.'
> 'Are you acquainted with the contents of that book?'
> 'Yes; that is to say, more or less.'
> 'Is there anything that justifies or alludes to tortures?'
> A sudden hush seized the court before Vargas responded:
> 'No, sir; according to my knowledge of it, there is not anything.'

Garrow let the words hang in the air before he resumed his questioning. At his prompting Vargas swore he had not heard of torture nor seen instruments of torture in any of the countries and islands in which he had resided. The court now resounded to a series of ringing negatives: *Not in New Granada. Not in Caracas. Not in Cuba. Not in Puerto Rico.*

'I never heard that it was practised', said Vargas, adding airily that he had heard of an ancient law of 1260 or 1266, or thereabouts, which authorized torture in Old Spain, but that was held in abhorrence in Spanish America.

Vargas then faced cross-examination by a defence counsel anxious to discredit him. Dallas drew the jury's attention to the fact that the witness had once attempted to pass by the name of Smith while living in England, which was not denied. He also made much of the fact that the witness had only been practising as an advocate for two years, on which point Vargas replied forcefully:

'Those who study the law are obliged by the laws of Spain to study for the space of five years; after that they must practise two or three years; and after that they are examined in full audience; and after that, if approved of, they have a licence to practise. After I was approved of, I practised two years.'

Dallas switched the point of his attack: Could Vargas illustrate his knowledge of the *Recopilación*, which he claimed was the principal legal text for the Spanish colonies?

'Turn to any part that directs what is to be done in the case of a robbery?'

'I think I can produce some; but there are three volumes; it will be difficult. You intend I should produce only one instance?'

'I want to know, whether those books contain any directions to the criminal judge, how to proceed in matters of robbery, or of criminal accusation?'

'I am not prepared for that; but let me see if I can find it.'

The witness began to rummage through the first, then the second of the three volumes. At length his efforts were interrupted by Dallas:

'Will you swear, that there is from the beginning to the end of those three volumes, a single passage that *forbids* the application of torture in the Spanish colonies in any case whatever?'

'In the Spanish colonies I believe there is nothing: not any law.'

Dallas switched again: 'Have you been at any time employed by Colonel Fullarton in taking examinations against General Picton?'

'I believe not, I was not employed officially.'

'I repeat the question to you. Upon your oath, have you not been employed by Colonel Fullarton, to take the examination of different persons against General Picton?'

'I have been employed as an interpreter by Colonel Fullarton.'

'Have you been employed by Colonel Fullarton to take the examinations of different people against General Picton?'

'I was employed.'

Dallas had done much to undermine Vargas's credibility, but he could not make him unswear there was no reference to torture in the *Recopilación*, a book the defence were unable to consult. In his summary, soon after, Dallas argued that the supposed lack of reference to torture in the *Recopilación* simply corroborated his point that torture, permitted by the laws of Old Spain, had not been discontinued in the colonies. The defence, he said, had provided the court with written evidence as to the legality of torture under Spanish law, citing various sources. The prosecution, by contrast, claimed those books were trash and had produced one of their own from which they offered no evidence at all. Indeed, the jurisconsult Vargas, when requested, had been unable to find a single relevant passage in the book, said Dallas:

> He went from place to place; he turned the volumes over in confusion page by page; and he concluded his evidence without referring us to any text upon the subject! Gentlemen, I scorn to detain you by any personal observations about him. I ask, whether, upon the production of a book, out of which not a single passage has been read, you can conscientiously believe that the Spanish law did not sanction the application of torture in the case of Luisa Calderón?

In reply Garrow promised to be brief, noting the time of night, and contented himself with contrasting the two key witnesses now that the case was confined to a point of law: on the one hand, Mr Gloster, whose knowledge of Spanish was so weak he could not even read the title pages of books; on the other, Pedro Vargas, a native of South America, bred to the law, whose contention it was that the Spanish West Indies were not governed by the laws of Old Spain but by a separate code, the *Recopilación*, issued by His Most Catholic Majesty Carlos II in 1680, in which he could find no authority for the application of torture to any person, under any circumstances whatever. All Gloster could say to this, Garrow noted scornfully, is that he once saw those books lying in the *escribano*'s office in Port of Spain, at a time, admittedly, long after Governor Picton's atrocities had been committed, when, as his defence attorney at the mandamus proceedings, he was beating about for any authority at all that allowed torture. Garrow's voice rose to a cruel falsetto:

> I beg his pardon, he goes further and says, 'I do think that once, at the council of which I have the honour to be a member, somebody did produce one, and quote something out of it, and treat it as an authority. Not being able to read Spanish, I am myself totally ignorant whether it is an authority or not, but I am ready to pour in upon you a wheelbarrowful of such authorities, in order to make out a justification of the infliction of torture.'

Garrow's eyes fell on each member of the jury in turn as he asked triumphantly: 'Is this, gentlemen, the way a defendant is to be justified in an English court of justice?'

He concluded with a flourish, reminding them that all witnesses, even those summoned by the defence, were unanimous in saying there had been no practice of torture in Trinidad prior to Picton. There was no such practice and no such law, he said, thrusting his right hand repeatedly at the jury as if it had a cutting edge: 'It is a mere pretence raked up now that the day of retribution has arrived.'

Lord Ellenborough, in the high bench, summed up: The jury were to divest themselves of anything that could possibly inflame their minds and consider a plain question: what was the law of Trinidad at the time of its cessation to Abercromby? Did it or did it not invest the governor with the power to apply torture? The law of old Spain allowed torture, but it appeared neither the *Royal Schedula* nor the *Recopilación* contained anything relating to torture. Witnesses whose memories went back as far as 1774 had sworn there was no practice of torture on the island. Could it be said that the law of Spain was so fully introduced into the island that torture formed a part of its law? The law in the books, he concluded, was to be weighed against the disuse of such a practice in Trinidad.

> If you should be of opinion that it was the existing law at the time of the capitulation, that fact will be inserted in the special verdict. If you are of opinion that, as far as we have any knowledge of the subject, the practice of torture was not in use, and that no such law did exist, I shall have further observations to communicate to you.
>
> At present you will consider whether torture could be applied at the discretion of the judge, and, if so, whether the application of torture to witnesses formed a part of the law of Trinidad at the time of the cessation of that island.

The foreman of the jury consulted briefly with his fellow jurors then promptly addressed his lordship: 'We are of opinion that there was no such law as this existing at the time of the cessation.'

Ellenborough ruled: 'Then Governor Picton cannot derive any protection from that law. If no law obtained in that island at the time which authorised the severities that were practised upon this young woman, your verdict must be that the defendant is guilty.'

The jury's verdict of guilty was then pronounced and recorded:

> Mr Dallas: 'Upon the other points I shall trouble your lordship hereafter upon a motion for a new trial.'
>
> Lord Ellenborough: 'The other points will be open to you upon that motion.'

It was after 7.00 p.m. when Lord Ellenborough raised his huge frame from the King's Bench. Robert Dallas went out into the hall of the Four Courts to confer briefly with an ashen-faced Picton, who looked all his fifty years. Nearby, Fullarton's large party celebrated their victory. By the time they had made their way through Westminster Hall and out into London's night air, Juan Montes, Porto Rico and Pedro Vargas found themselves in need of a strong drink. Luisa Calderón, dressed all in white and protectively chaperoned, looked hard at Picton as she went by, 'smoking a cegar all the while'w.

V

It was Vargas and the *Recopilación* that had sunk Picton. By the end of April the defence had procured its own copy of this elusive text from the London Institute, which had bought it at the sale of the late Marquess of Lansdowne's collection. Dallas at once moved for a new trial on grounds that it was 'other and different from' the way it had been described in court. Vargas had 'grossly misrepresented' the text saying it contained no allusion to torture. The *Recopilación* expressly stated that the law of Spain was to be applied in Trinidad.

Another boon for Picton came in the form of a packet by the Leeward Island mail on Friday 20 June. This contained a report of a meeting Hislop had convened at Government House soon after news of the verdict against Picton reached Port of Spain. The purpose of the meeting had been to ascertain what in fact was the law that applied in Trinidad. To this end Hislop had summoned ex-*alcaldes* Nihell, Black, Begorrat, Rigby and Smith, who resolved, after due deliberation and in sworn statements, that the criminal law of Spain prevailed on the island and that the *Recopilación* did not vary this with regard to torture.

On 7 May Picton wrote to Hislop's secretary, Captain Holmes, to thank him and the governor for the 'handsome and zealous manner' in which they had taken up his affairs: 'I am fully convinced without such attention on your part, my enemies might have succeeded in more effectually and seriously misrepresenting my conduct, though, God knows, notwithstanding, it has been carried to an inconceivable length.'[29] In the following months Hislop obtained evidence to show that the law of Spain had operated under Chacón. The deposition of a now unhesitating Castro was especially important: torture was not only permitted under Chacón, he said, but had been applied in the case of a black man called Francisco in 1790, the whole of which proceedings were dispatched to London.

Another person in Trinidad who tried hard to advance Picton's cause was Edward Draper, formerly a member of the governor's staff. Early in April 1806, Draper published his *Address to the British People*, a lengthy pamphlet that accused Fullarton of having made bogus entries in military returns years before. Draper also quoted Dr John Lynch, an Irish immigrant, to the effect that, when interviewed in London in 1802 by the colonial under-secretary, John Sullivan, he had been told that the man to talk to in Port of Spain was no longer Picton but William Fullarton, for the latter was being sent out to investigate Picton, who would not last six months. No sooner had Draper's pamphlet appeared than an application was made to its publisher, Mr Budd, to stop sales. Draper promptly relieved Budd of several hundred copies, which he continued to distribute for more than a week, an act of loyalty that would cost him a £100 fine and three months' imprisonment in the Marshalsea when Sullivan won his suit against him.[30]

In the middle of 1806 Picton was grateful for Draper's efforts. At least they provided a diversion and even the illusion of turning defence into attack. Picton believed that the result of Draper's trial would have 'considerable effect upon subsequent decisions', and he worked hard on getting Lynch over from Trinidad as a defence witness against Sullivan. He also sent a confidant to Scotland to seek evidence about horses Fullarton may or may not have supplied to the army: 'If we should be able to procure proof', he wrote to Lewis Flanagan, a trainee London solicitor and close friend, 'it would completely despoil his action and turn him disgracefully out of court.'[31]

In his letter of Tuesday 23 September Picton said he had just come back to town from Sydenham after spending the weekend with Marryat. He had worked 'two whole days' on his 'Letter Addressed to Sir Samuel Hood', which would serve as a preface to his new pamphlet, *Evidence taken at Port of Spain* soon also to go on sale at Budd the bookseller's, at 100 Pall Mall. Picton was delighted with his weekend's work: 'It will make a most admirable pamphlet of about ninety pages. Marryat says it is equal in power of spirit and strength of reasoning to anything he has ever read.'[32] Its real strength, however, as Picton well knew, lay in associating him with the rising star of Sir Samuel Hood, which, more than all the eloquent reasoning in the world, promised to increase Picton's stature in the eyes of the public. By contrast, Fullarton's attempt to denigrate Hood a month or so later was in large part responsible for turning opinion against the affidavit man.

Hood's esteem had soared towards Nelson's rarefied heights

when, on 25 September, he had a daring encounter with the French off Rochefort in which his right arm was so badly smashed by musket-shot that it had to be amputated. He returned home a hero to find that Parliament's dissolution and Fox's death in early October had brought on elections. He decided to offer himself to the free electors of Westminster, where two seats were vacant, including Fox's own, and he stood alongside the renowned dramatist and Whig orator, Richard Brinsley Sheridan, their adversary being James Paull, a Scot who had made his fortune in India. The hustings at Covent Garden were a boisterous affair in which, from 3 to 19 November, every day except Sunday, candidates took on a mob whose questions were usually more personal than political in tenor. The banter could be good-humoured, as when Mr Whitbread, a Sheridan supporter, was roared at by one of the crowd:

'If your porter was as strong as your assurance, Whitbread, it would do astonishingly well!'

'But', replied Mr Whitbread, 'if it were as strong as your impudence, I could not live by it!'[33]

The mood soon turned ugly, however, if there was mention of placemen or a hint of bribery. This was frequently the case, since Paull was supported by William Cobbett, the most brilliant radical journalist of the day and founder of the *Political Register,* which often accused Sheridan of venality.

Hood's popularity was expected to see him through. But Sheridan, a less than prudent Naval Secretary in 'the Ministry of All the Talents', was a liability. His great plays had been written thirty years before and he was both physically and financially debilitated. James Paull, in contrast, had money to sweeten the mob's tongue. A dapper little man scarred by smallpox, he surrounded himself with bruisers and showed no respect for status. As ambitious as he was belligerent, he had for some time been formulating charges of financial impropriety against Lord Wellesley, the former governor-general of India and eldest brother of Colonel Sir Arthur Wellesley, the future Duke of Wellington. His refusal to drop them lost him favour with the Prince of Wales and with it one of the pocket boroughs in the Prince's gift. Obliged to stand in open elections, he was not likely to have scruples about the campaign he fought.

On the second day of the hustings, Tuesday 4 November, it was whispered that Colonel Fullarton intended speaking after the close of the poll with a view to attacking Hood over his conduct in Trinidad. Sure enough, after apologies had been made for the ailing Sheridan's absence, Fullarton came forward to address the public. He was astonished to be greeted by a loud hail of rebuke:

'No elector! You have no right to speak!'
'No Fullarton! No treachery! No private malice!'
'Out with him! Out with him! Off! off! off!'
'Hood for ever! Are you not ashamed of yourself? Off! off! off!'

The cries were so persistent that for more than half an hour Fullarton was unable to make himself heard. Fears of a riot grew as voices ran higher and exchanges became more heated. A section of the crowd called on Paull to admit he had put Fullarton up to it. Paull protested, upon his honour, that until he came to the hustings that day he had no more knowledge of Fullarton's intentions than they.

Facing the mob, Fullarton's slight frame looked pitifully isolated, but he was resolute enough to deliver his speech. In the uproar, only those near him could have heard him charge Hood with complicity in Picton's system of terror in Trinidad. He would not go so far as to say Hood practised such cruelties himself, but he had sat in the councils of the governor who caused such practices, and, by not having discountenanced them, he must surely be presumed to have sanctioned them. Fullarton concluded by asking the free electors of Westminster whether they were disposed to choose a man who could sanction such barbarities in a British dependency.

When he retired the abusive clamour subsided and Sir Samuel Hood stepped forward to loud cheers. In uniform, with his right sleeve conspicuously pinned, this gallant officer spoke briefly to the crowd. He would not answer the unfounded charges of his accuser. This was neither the time nor place, though ample refutation would be given before a proper tribunal. He begged leave only to express his sincere thanks to the electors for the signal proofs they had given him of their support, whereupon he withdrew amid bursts of general applause.

On the following days Hood's supporters mercilessly exploited Fullarton's humiliating intervention at the hustings, which had backfired disastrously on Paull. The latter repeatedly disclaimed all connection with his fellow Scot as the jibes rained in: What had become of his 'aide-de-camp'? What news of the man whose calumnies had provoked the voice of popular indignation? Had he vanished in shame from the face of the earth? So favourably did the tide turn for Hood he appeared on the Friday to strains of 'Rule Britannia' and 'Hearts of Oak', while bands of sailors paraded through the Strand beating drums and singing full voice in triumphant pageant. Even Sheridan was well enough to appear on the hustings, and by the end of the second week he too had overtaken Paull to win a seat, the final count being: Hood, 5,478; Sheridan, 4,758; Paull, 4,481. Paull would stand again six months later only to lose to different opponents, a defeat that virtually bankrupted him. Poisoned as much by his own ambition as by the gangrenous leg wound he had sustained in a duel, Paull was reduced to staking his future on the turn of a card. In April 1807 he lost 1,600 guineas in a single night at a Pall Mall gaming house and next day took his own life.

Fullarton had not descended to that level of despair, though there were signs that his mind was disturbed. His response to the débâcle of the hustings was a letter to *The Times*, written at Worton House, Isleworth, on 10 November, in which he announced that his hustings speech was to be published under the title *Address to the Electors of Westminster*. In fraught language he explained that he had had no alternative, if he were not to stand degraded in his own estimation, but to say what he had said and write what he had written about Sir Samuel Hood, for while the latter's naval service gave him 'great claims on the gratitude of his country', his actions at Trinidad could not go without remark when he was seeking the honour of representing the metropolis, at least not without exposing Fullarton to censure. To elect Hood, it appeared, was to insult the worthy William Fullarton.

The former first commissioner ended his letter on a high note of injured honour: 'Those who know me best, will admit that I have, upon all occasions, disregarded personal consequences, when personal honour and character were concerned.' He had challenged Hood once before, in Trinidad, about the need for proper explanations and he quoted the intrepid words directed at the commodore: 'I mean such an explanation as may prove satisfactory to an Officer and a Gentleman.' The precise purpose of this reminiscence in *The Times* was not entirely clear. Was it a mere flourish of his dress sword, or did Fullarton seriously mean to challenge Hood again and seek proper reparation this time? Given the admiral's handicap, the prospect of a duel seemed less unlikely than ridiculous. Yet stranger things happened in these prickly times as two Parisians illustrated when, disputing the affection of an opera-girl, they fought with blunderbusses from hot-air balloons at a height of 1,000 feet, the loser being dashed to pieces on a housetop.

Fullarton's hustings speech, appearing in three folio pages, was a crude attempt to redirect at Hood the charges already levelled at Picton. These were still being considered by the Privy Council and it is doubtful whether the inflammatory remarks about Hood served to further legal action against the ex-governor. What surely discouraged such action was a scurrilous poem published during the election entitled 'The Picton Veil or

The Hood of Westminster'. The object of this anonymous doggerel was to vilify and class as Pictonites all those who were deliberating the charges in the Privy Council, among them Grenville, Eldon, Sidmouth and Castlereagh. It concluded in lavish praise of its presumed sponsor:

> Oh! Fullarton, the brave and good,
> With noble firmness you withstood
> Torture and waste of human blood

while its refrain, repeated ten times, ran:

> It bodes our country little good,
> When murder's cover'd by a Hood.[34]

The punning accusation that there was a cover-up is a measure of the strength of feeling in the Fullarton camp. But there was never the remotest possibility that public opinion would turn against one of the nation's most gallant defenders, and, in practice, the more closely Hood's name was associated with Picton's the safer the latter was from one man's now obsessive persecution. Provoked by the poem and Fullarton's Westminster address, the Privy Council, in January 1807, issued a statement saying there was no foundation for further proceedings on any of the remaining charges brought against General Picton. It was now a question of the rule for a new trial being made absolute.

VI

During this period of enforced leisure, Picton would doubtless have paid close attention to current events if only to understand the changing mood of his times and assess the prospect of acquittal at his second trial. Much of what he saw and read must have puzzled if not astonished him.

On the legal front, Potter Jackson, an ex-slave, came up before Lord Ellenborough in July 1806, having been wrongly suspected of theft and savagely whipped at sea by a certain Captain Livesley. He was awarded £500 damages for the weals on his back, the first such award to be made by a British court to a black man. In March 1807 a landmark in Wilberforce's anti-slavery campaign was achieved when the bill to end the exportation of slaves from Africa reached the statute book. Yet it could not be said that such humane consideration typified the age. It was hardly conspicuous on London's streets: Charing Cross pillory was sure to incite the mob, and executions at Newgate drew vast crowds. Before 9.00 a.m. on Monday 23 February 1807, more than 40,000 people assembled outside the Old Bailey to see two men and a woman launched into eternity. So great was the crush that thirty citizens were trampled to death before the noose tightened on the unfortunate trio.

On the international scene, Picton could not have missed one enterprise of stunning eccentricity, that of Sir Home Popham, who sailed from Cape Town to the Río de la Plata in June 1806 and, with no official orders from Britain, took Buenos Aires with an absurdly small band of soldiers. His initial success, attributable to the element of surprise, was soon reversed once the Spanish troops regrouped, and within a year Popham faced trial in London for his recklessness. What made the venture more incongruous was that at precisely the same time General Francisco de Miranda, or 'el Precursor', as he came to be known, decided to turn his dream of an independent Latin American empire into reality by invading his native Venezuela. Having heard the usual encouraging noises in both England and the United States, but with no greater authority to make war than Popham, Miranda set sail from New York in March 1806 in an eighteen-gun frigate with two accompanying schooners. Picking up fellow revolutionaries in Santo Domingo and Port of Spain, his fleet had grown to fifteen assorted vessels by August when he landed at Vela de Coro on the Main. Unfortunately, the *peones* failed to rally to his side and within weeks he re-embarked for Trinidad, there to dream some more.

What would have distressed Picton about both these adventures was the lack of coordination, which reflected Britain's dilettante approach to Latin America. By contrast, Napoleon's military machine was grinding successive European states into submission and the next phase in his apparently irreversible plan was the subjugation of Britain by means of a Continental blockade. The reaction to this was again piecemeal and cavalier. In August 1806 a small fleet under Earl St Vincent was sent into the Tagus to protect Lisbon, the last port in Europe to which British ships had access. The enterprise ended a year later when a French force of 28,000 men under General Androche Junot was welcomed into Spain in October 1807 and within a month had occupied all Portugal, forcing the royal family of that country to seek sanctuary in their vast realm of Brazil. In October 1806 an unsuccessful attempt was made to sink the flotilla at Boulogne, while the following September Copenhagen was raided and the poorly defended Danish ships were either sunk or taken to England for safe keeping. This attack on an erstwhile ally, only recently brought to Napoleon's heel, was condemned by many members of the House of Commons who felt, like Samuel Whitbread, that the act was 'base and treacherous'. Clearly, Britain's foreign policy was in disarray.

On 13 February 1808, a week after the rule for Picton's new trial was made absolute, William Fullarton died of pneumonia at Gordon's Hotel. This did not end litigation, because Picton was being prosecuted by the Crown, but it did mean much of the prosecution's venom was now spent. Fullarton's death all but escaped public notice, a sign of his waning prestige and of the dwindling support for his overplayed cause. Picton, by contrast, received the comforting approbation of promotion to major-general on 25 April.

At about this time too he received a surprising offer from the Duke of Queensberry, an eccentric octogenarian whose dedication to pleasure had been impressive even by eighteenth-century standards. 'Old Q' sent word to Picton at the Grosvenor coffee house that he was convinced of his innocence and would be pleased to defray his legal costs up to a sum of £10,000. Never having met the Duke, Picton was much moved, but he gratefully declined the offer. His Uncle William had placed his entire fortune at Picton's disposal to meet expenses that would eventually total £7,000. A second offer Picton felt bound to decline was a gift of £4,000 sent by the inhabitants – or, at least, the richer citizens – of Trinidad. News reached London in the first week of July that, on the night of 24 March, a terrible fire had all but destroyed Port of Spain, whereupon Picton nobly returned the money as a donation towards rebuilding homes lost in the blaze.

Picton must have had a sense of what it was to rise, phoenix-like, from the ashes, when, with pride restored, he faced his second trial on 11 June 1808. This was less of a sensation than the first trial, for not only was Fullarton dead but Garrow, uncharacteristically, seemed less than quick. Sparing in his use of the lubricating adjective, the courtroom bully refrained from using the drawings that, he said apologetically, had given offence before.[35] Even Luisa, now a young woman in her twenties, had lost some of her edge as the marks on her wrists faded. She answered in English now, but with an indifference that suggested her future lay in the Caribbean as soon as the trial closed.

It was left to Dallas to make the running. What the jury had to consider, he said, was not the moral fitness or expediency of torture but simply whether or not its application in the case before them constituted a violation of Trinidad's laws. *The Recopilación* was cleared up: it did authorize torture. The ruling of Hislop's court was presented: the law of Spain that prevailed in Trinidad included the use of torture. Other matters were irrelevant, said Dallas: the jail was Vallot's business and the process against Carlos González and Luisa Calderón was Begorrat's. What formalities might have been neglected in that process were his affair. All Picton did was give his assent once the application for torture had been made, which, in effect, he was bound to do in the circumstances. What is more, Picton had the protection of his judicial status: 'Whether he was right or whether he was wrong', said Dallas, 'he unquestionably meant to apply what he considered he was authorised by law to apply.'

Garrow, in reply, warmed a little to his task. Had it perhaps been forgotten that Picton introduced the piquet in Trinidad? Had he been labouring under some delusion in thinking the defence counsel did not even contest the point? Why, if in this country we spoke of 'the Maiden Torture' and 'the Duke of Exeter's Daughter', it must be presumed that 'the new instrument of torture introduced by Picton would henceforth be denominated 'the maiden torture of the island of Trinidad, General Picton's daughter'.

He turned to a point of law: In Chacón's day an appeal was allowed to the superior tribunal at Caracas: a person like Luisa Calderón, facing torture, would have had a *defensor* whose first thought would doubtless have been to appeal to the *audiencia real*. In the case before them, not only did Picton fill Chacón's boots as governor, but, in denying any referral to a higher authority, namely the British Crown – which, God forbid, could not be conceived to sanction torture – he also took upon himself the role of the appellate court. In effect, Picton was both Chacón and Caracas, a judge who sat in judgement on his own judging. 'Was ever anything so preposterous?', asked Garrow, who concluded that the conflation of two judicial offices showed the nature of 'Picton's law' and its 'cruel haste', for, while under Chacón five days was the minimum time set between the application for torture and the infliction of it, under Picton torture was administered on the selfsame day as the order was issued. 'Garrulous Garrow', as Edward Draper called him, had again saved his best point until last.

Summing up, Lord Ellenborough noted that the case had taken on a different aspect from the first trial. It was not a question now of whether torture was authorized in Trinidad under Spanish law, but rather, whether a British Governor could apply the laws of a foreign nation when they were inconsistent with those of his own country: 'Upon this point I will not intimate to you my opinion; but I must state it to be a matter of great doubt.'

Ellenborough cited a case in Minorca, where a British governor was satisfied he had no jurisdiction to inflict torture. He developed Garrow's point about where the appellate jurisdiction lay after Trinidad's 'cessation' to Britain. It seemed unlikely that this was transferred from the *audiencia real* in Caracas to governor Picton: 'Upon this subject, I think the greatest doubt must be entertained. If I were to give my opinion, I should perhaps say that I think he had not such judicial powers; that power remains in his majesty.'

Ellenborough explained his view by quoting the instructions Picton received from Hobart. These indicated his powers were to be equal but not superior to those of the Spanish governor: 'such judicial powers as previous to the surrender of the said island to us were exercised by the Spanish Governor, shall be exercised by you, our governor, in like manner as the same were exercised previous to the surrender of the said island.'

It followed that the additional powers, which formerly belonged to Caracas, did not devolve upon the British governor. Ellenborough concluded: 'Being of the opinion that he was not clothed with the judicial authority of the Audience of Caracas, I think the act done by him is not justifiable.'

On this forceful point Lord Ellenborough instructed the jury to retire to consider their verdict. After a lengthy absence they returned and the foreman gave their view: 'That, by the law of Spain, torture existed in the island of Trinidad at the time of the cessation of that island to Great Britain; and that no malice existed in the mind of the defendant against Luisa Calderón independent of the illegality of the act.'[36]

This, as a verdict, was a halfway house with many doors. It went a long way towards exonerating Picton while at the same time it found him guilty of an illegal act. In effect, it said he had the right to sanction torture under the Spanish law that applied in Trinidad, but not in his capacity as the island's *British* governor. There was no malice on his part towards the person tortured, but he had committed an illegal act and, as Ellenborough said, every act against law is deemed malicious.

There was much here for the judges to discuss when framing their special verdict and arguing upon it. But that would no longer worry Picton. The first part of the verdict would do for him. As for the *illegality* of his act, he knew that the law had a way of exhausting itself like a dog chasing its own tail. Indeed,

later that year an exasperated Lord Ellenborough would explain
to Mrs Marianne Fullarton, when she persisted in bringing the
libel charge against Colonel Draper on behalf of her late
husband, that the matter could go on *ad infinitum*, and though
he was prepared to sit at the bench until his strength was gone,
he felt the honourable lady should know that he believed the
time had come when 'the purposes of justice will be best
answered by suffering the case to remain where it is'.[37]

Picton's case was not finally left where it was until 1812 when,
after intermittent argument, it was thought by the Bar that while
a further judgement would probably go against him, the punishment would be so slight and so little commensurate with the
magnitude of the questions embraced by the case as to reflect
little credit upon the prosecution.

By that time there would be hardly a trace of the ashes from
which Picton had risen.

THREE

WALCHEREN

Between Madness and Folly

I

At the close of his second trial, in July 1808, Picton's finances were in a poor state. His Trinidad properties had become a drain rather than a source of income when the island's economy went into a steep decline after the catastrophic fire in Port of Spain on 24 March of that same year. Five years as an unemployed general had been hard going, especially when the best part of £5,000 had to be raised every October to meet his mortgage payments on the Delaforest plantation. Fortunately, he had his uncle William's support, while his mother Cecil, who died soon after the first trial in March 1806, settled her estate on him when her eldest son Richard opted for the Turberville name and Ewenny inheritance. But Thomas's ready funds were limited and his prospects as a soldier the wrong side of fifty with little active service behind him were not bright. The one thing in his favour was the ominous situation on the Continent.

News of the amazing turn of events in Spain had reached London at the time of the second trial. Eyebrows were raised by reports of a mob storming Godoy's house at Aranjuez in March, when the Prince of Peace narrowly escaped with his life by hiding under a pile of rugs in the attic. This episode was the stuff of comic opera, but the disturbance of 17–19 March known as 'el Motín de Aranjuez' showed how Spaniards felt about the deal Godoy had struck with Napoleon: on the promise of a kingdom in the south of Portugal the upstart prince had allowed the French free passage for 28,000 soldiers to march through Spain on Lisbon. General Junot's army, originally sent to enforce the Continental blockade, was soon massively reinforced and, by the spring of 1808, more than 100,000 foreign troops were on Spanish soil. Under Napoleon's brother-in-law, Joachim Murat, the designated 'Lieutenant of the Emperor in Spain', they occupied the whole country from Madrid north. It was too much for the Spanish patriots who rose defiantly in their capital on 2 May only to be savaged by French bayonets and suffer mass executions the following day, which Goya was moved to record in two of his most famous paintings.

Napoleon had used Portuguese recalcitrance as a pretext to occupy Spain. When the ensuing unrest in Castile prompted Carlos IV's son Fernando, Prince of Asturias, to depose him and declare himself king, the Corsican tyrant saw a new opportunity to profit from chaos. He invited father and son, together with Queen María Luisa and the sycophantic Godoy, to meet with him at Bayonne in early May. María Luisa left her indelibly ugly mark on proceedings: Fernando was her son, she boldly announced, but not the King's, and he therefore had no legitimate claim to a throne on which the Emperor alone should arbitrate. Bastardizing her heir in the presence of husband, family and grandee ministers, made an unedifying spectacle, but it was one that the Queen had doubtless preconcerted with the Emperor, who roundly informed the sorry lot, Godoy included, that they were to be exiled in France and that Spain's new king would be his eldest brother, Joseph Bonaparte.

The patriotic uprising of 2 May – Spain's revered *dos de mayo* – and its bloody suppression the following day, inspired rebellions throughout the country. By June, army units had joined local militia to engage the French in an insidious war waged by *guerrilleros*. There were surprising successes: notably General Castaños's demolition of a French army of 18,000 men at Bailén in July. This débâcle and the rapid formation of *juntas* so worried Joseph he evacuated Madrid and withdrew to the north. Only when his younger brother Napoleon put himself at the head of 300,000 imperial troops did the French re-enter the capital in December 1808.

By then the restive Portuguese had appealed for help to Britain, which, conveniently, had a force of 9,000 soldiers under Lieutenant-General Sir Arthur Wellesley assembled in Cork ready to embark for the West Indies and Venezuela. This force was immediately redirected to Portugal, where, on 30 July, Wellesley made a hazardous landing amidst the Atlantic rollers at Mondego Bay before marching south to Lisbon and achieving a brilliant victory over Junot at Vimeiro on 21 August. The controversial Convention of Cintra, described by Wordsworth as an 'ignoble and shameful transaction', was signed a few days later. It saw the French captives shipped magnanimously home, still laden with specie, while Britain contented itself with having secured a base for operations in Portugal. Wellesley, who neither negotiated nor read the final document until it was published in London on 16 September, was made a scapegoat for the Cintra fiasco. Sir John Moore, who had fought under Abercromby at St Lucia in 1796 and at Alexandria in 1801, assumed command and promptly invaded Spain, intent on supporting rebel operations in the north of the country. By the time he reached Salamanca in late November, however, the Spanish had been routed and, seeing that Napoleon's huge army had entered the Peninsula, Moore decided his only realistic option was to withdraw. Hounded by Marshal Soult's superior forces and with his soldiers suffering terrible privations, Moore effected a perilous retreat to La Coruña over rugged ground in the dead of winter. He won the race to La Coruña, where he turned and fought a pitched battle on 16 January 1809 to protect the embarkation of his army. Moore himself died a heroic death, but the majority of his exhausted troops escaped to fight another day.

The problem was *where* to fight Napoleon. Unmistakably, the mood in Britain had changed since the Spanish army at Bailén, and then Wellesley at Vimeiro, had exploded the myth of French invincibility. John Bull was on the rise and he wanted to meet 'Boney' head on, or at least do the honourable thing by Spain. When, in December 1808, a Spanish fund-raising delegation came to London led by Admiral Apodoca – the same Admiral who, in 1797, had burned the Spanish fleet in Port of Spain rather than fight the British – London's bankers were so willing to subscribe that he sailed home with more than $2 million in cash, no doubt to declare that he had saved Santiago de Compostela a second time. But the government itself could not be so generous. Napoleon's blockade hurt the British economy and there were neither funds nor, after La Coruña, enough fit men to provide assistance commensurate with the challenge posed. Some soldiers had been left in Portugal, where Beresford was training the home troops, and Wellesley would be back to develop the defensive fortifications. But as for a major land offensive, it was a question of finding a chink in Napoleon's formidable armour.

Fortunately, the Austrians had recovered a little in the four years since Austerlitz and by April 1809 were bold enough to sign a treaty with Britain. Archduke Charles, heartened by events in the Peninsula, ventured a surprise attack against the French in southern Germany. He requested help from Britain, suggesting this might take a diversionary form. One possibility was to expand operations in Portugal. Another was a demonstration of strength in Italy, where, in June, Sir John Stuart would seize islands in the Bay of Naples as a preliminary to a mainland assault, which in the event never came. But both these points were remote from Austria. A third, more likely option involved the shores of Northern Europe, where Napoleon's forces had recently been dangerously stripped for the Austrian campaign. The obvious target was the Scheldt estuary in the Netherlands, a kingdom now ruled by Louis Bonaparte, another of Napoleon's brothers.

In the sheltered waters between Flushing and Antwerp, twenty-four hours sailing from the Thames, Napoleon had been steadily rebuilding his fleet. This large naval complex, fed by a river system that brought supplies from deep inside Germany, was, in the Emperor's own words, 'a cocked pistol pointed at the head of Britain'.[1] The British government had long pondered the feasibility of a pre-emptive attack on the Scheldt to deal with this menace. Intelligence in early 1809 indicated that twelve ships of the line were under construction at Antwerp, while ten others had recently been sailed down river for cannon mounting at Flushing. Only the poor state of the troops after La

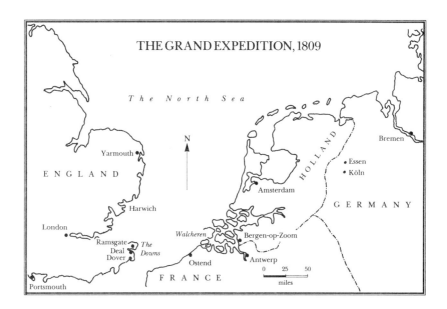

THE GRAND EXPEDITION, 1809

Coruña deterred the early attack urged by Lord Castlereagh, Secretary of State for War. The troops were fit again by June when news reached London of the Austrians' sterling effort at Aspern-Essling, which finally tipped the balance in favour of hazarding the Scheldt expedition. More than 600 ships and 45,000 men were assembled for embarkation at Deal, Dover, Chatham, Harwich, Ramsgate and Portsmouth when news came of Napoleon's riposte, which was to launch the Grand Army upon Vienna.

Picton was in Portsmouth, ready to embark on the seventy-four gun *Aboukir* when he wrote in good spirits to Flanagan, his trainee solicitor friend, on 7 July:

> The Lieut.-Generals having taken their departure for London, I am here in the temporary command of the Forces for the Expedition without any disposition to make anyone feel unnecessarily the weight of my short-lived authority. I am, however, fairly occupied, having no less than five Regiments to Inspect to-morrow morning, and I have just given orders for the Embarkation of all the Artillery. What miserable weather we have had. I fear much, if we don't soon embark, that it may have an ill effect on the health of the Troops. I have begun by feeding my field officers – in which I am singular; but I know a great dinner and a Bottle of Wine dispose people to draw much together, and the cost is not worth attending to. I remove to the Gosport side to-morrow that I may be near my Division. Our Chief, Sir E. Coot, is a gentlemanly obliging man, and my Genl. of Division is esteemed by everyone who knows him.[2]

Picton was clearly glad to be on active duty again, glad too that it was in Europe. He had already 'declined being employed upon Foreign Service', as he wrote in an elliptical letter to Marryat the previous July.[3] Presumably, that was the venture planned for Venezuela, which Wellesley in the end diverted to Portugal, and, presumably, Picton had felt disinclined to return to the West Indies so soon after his trial: 'I shall not be over zealous in coming forward in future', he confided to Marryat, suggesting some hidden offence. A year later and it was HRM the Duke of York who invited him to take part in what would be known as 'the Grand Expedition', a massive amphibious assault on mainland Europe not far removed from the borders of France itself, as the newspapers optimistically pointed out. For Picton it was a privilege to be in command, if only temporarily, at Portsmouth, where nearly half the forces were concentrated prior to embarkation.

However, he had his doubts. There was a compelling logic about the expedition's twin objectives: to provide diversionary assistance for the Austrians and to eliminate the French naval arsenal closest to Britain while this stood relatively unprotected. But there were other considerations that tended to be overlooked, including such simple matters as the midsummer weather in southern Holland, the suitability of the Dutch terrain for invasion and the degree of coordination that could be expected between landlubbers and tars whose mutual disrespect was inveterate. Moreover, while Picton's immediate superiors, generals Sir Eyre Coote and Fraser, were fine soldiers, the expedition's commander-in-chief was the Earl of Chatham, the elder brother of William Pitt, who had not seen active service in years and whose notorious dilatoriness had earned him the sobriquet of 'the late Lord Chatham'. With Moore dead and Wellesley back in the Peninsula, Chatham had got the appointment by default, it was said, mainly because he was the King's friend and because he sorely needed the money. Few believed a lethargic general would get the best out of his soldiers, nor was his distant manner likely to impress Admiral Sir Richard ('Mad Dick') Strachan, who had the naval command.

The expeditionary fleet had assembled in the last week of July, precisely when news came of Napoleon's crushing defeat of the Austrians at Wagram. By then preparations had gained a momentum of their own and, if the diversionary objective was moot, the idea of destroying French warships by a *coup de main* still appealed. Castlereagh and a clutch of cabinet ministers went down from London to view the sails that lay off the Kent coast. Overnight the small bathing towns had come alive with the bustle of embarkation, filled to bursting with sailors and unlikely looking soldiers – *tailors* – who paid double the London rates for last minute items of pleasure. Hapless recruits who feared that English pound notes would be worthless on the other side of the water counted themselves lucky if they got fifteen bob cash for their paper money in the improvised markets. Cheering crowds of well-wishers and tearful wives and children gathered on the quays while local boatmen offered to ferry men to their transports for a small charge. Some sailed out to cheer the troops on their way or ply them with their last saleable commodities. Boney was going to get something to remember them by: a thump on the chin while his guard was down, always assuming John Bull's target for the mammoth expedition really was the best kept secret in the world. At dawn on Friday 28 July, Chatham sailed out in his flagship, *The Venerable*, at the head of the largest combined military and naval force Britain had ever assembled.

That evening the greater part of the fleet anchored in the

Stone Deep ten miles off the island of Walcheren. The next day
being wet and windy, Strachan ordered a number of ships to
enter the Roompot for shelter, from where the uninviting low
line of Walcheren's bleak coast was just visible like a colourless
thread separating the sea from the overhanging sky. Certain
factors then combined to decide Chatham on a change of plan:
the unfavourable weather and winds, together with the presence
of a French fleet off Flushing, suggested it would be unwise to
sail into the West Scheldt, as originally planned, for there the
British ships would come under fire from Breskens on the
Cadsand side as well as from Flushing. Instead, they would
disembark on Walcheren's windswept northern shore and from
there march the sixteen miles across the island to Flushing.
Under the circumstances, this was a safer plan, since the less
navigable East Scheldt could not be approached in numbers.
But the delay would allow King Louis Bonaparte to organize the
defence of Antwerp.

II

Before noon on 30 July some 300 ships of all sizes stood anchored
off the barren wastes of Bree Sand, where, in the course of the
day, 14,000 troops would disembark, including Picton's brigade
of 2,500 men, who landed shortly after 7.00 p.m. Private Wheeler
of the 51st Regiment witnessed the operation as Fraser's First
Division came ashore in flat-bottomed boats:

> The Gunboats had taken up their position along the shore, the
> flats full of soldiers and towed by the ship's boats, formed in rear
> of the Gunboats. On a signal the flats advanced. All now was
> solemn silence, saving the Gunboats who were thundering
> showers of iron on the enemy. Their well directed fire soon drove
> them to shelter, behind the sandbank. The flats had now gained
> the Gunboats, shot through the intervals and gained the shallow
> water, when the troops leaped out and waded ashore, drove the
> enemy from behind the hills where they had taken shelter from
> the destructive fire of the Gunboats.[4]

This show of force was 'most triflingly opposed', Picton wrote
to Flanagan a week later.[5] Indeed, General Monnet, the French
commander, barely had 4,500 men to defend the entire island
and his only recourse was to fall back on Flushing, his men
defending key fortresses as they went. On 31 July Coote's
Walcheren army left Bree Sand in two columns, with Picton's

brigade under Fraser taking the eastern route through the island. Their first task was to take the Der Haak fort and invest the town of Veer, 'which was completely effected by 5 the following morning', according to Picton's account:

> This place, by our Information, was extremely weak and incapable of opposing any resistance, but we found it, in fact, most strongly fortified and surrounded with a formidable Rampart and an unsufferable wet Ditch of more than 60 feet Broad. The Gov. might have given us a good deal of trouble had he persisted to defend the place, for we had neither Battery, Cannon, nor Mortars: but after 10 or 12 hours constant cannonade from the Gun and Mortar vessels (during which four of the former were sunk), he signified a readiness to capitulate, which was most readily taken advantage of, and he surrendered on the following morning.

The bombardment was described in more detail by an officer of the 81st Regiment, whose remarkable *Letters From Flushing* published anonymously later that year levelled many criticisms at the expedition and its leaders:

> Whilst the attack was proceeding on the land-side, the bombs and gun-vessels arrived before it in the Veer-Gat; and Sir Home Popham directed an immediate bombardment. The garrison received it bravely; and though the works were falling about their ears, they returned fire for fire. The effects of the bombardment, however, were tremendous. The report of the cannon was followed by the crash of houses; and bricks, mortar, and timber, struck by the ball, were hurled over our heads into a distant part of the island; whole fragments of chimneys were in this manner driven over the town into the adjacent country. I never saw a cannonade so effectual.
>
> In this manner, tempered only by the rain and darkness, the operations continued during a good part of the night. In the morning the town presented a most melancholy spectacle of ruins. Imagine a heavy circular mass of houses and walls battered by a cannonade of nearly fifty pieces of cannon, and this within three hundred yards of them, and you may form some idea of the horrible spectacle. The town really resembles nothing but a smoking pile of bricks.[6]

Following the bombardment the troops marched through the island's capital, Middelburg, which surrendered without a fight on the same day, 1 August. That evening, Fraser's division took up positions on a dyke one mile from Rammekins fort, which, though small, was strategically important since it controlled the junction of the Slough and West Scheldt. A day was spent

constructing batteries and as soon as these were completed
Rammekins sensibly surrendered before a shot was fired. By the
evening of 3 August on Walcheren only Flushing remained to be
captured.

In a letter of 6 August, Picton describes the conditions that
he and his men faced as they stood east of Flushing waiting 'for
the Mortars and Battery Cannon necessary to commence the
seige':

> The weather has been extremely unfavourable to our operations,
> the rain being almost incessant and the Troops without any cover-
> ing or protection. As the garrison is numerous, and we occupy an
> extensive Line, we have been kept every night until the last in
> continual alarm by sorties and skirmishes, which, though of little
> consequence in themselves, are more harassing to the Troops by
> keeping them constantly upon the alert. I always sleep in Boots
> and spurs on a bundle of Straw, to which I take more kindly than
> I had any idea of, considering the contrary habits of so many years.
> The heavy guns are daily arriving in great numbers, and it is
> expected that the Batteries will open on the 10th Ins[t.] If every
> advantage is taken in the mode of attack, I think the place will not
> hold out many days, though it may, as we now appear to be going
> on, occupy us for some weeks.[7]

Plainly, Picton was already concerned about the pace of British
preparations for he realized that delay at Flushing must jeopardize
any attack on Antwerp, then being rapidly reinforced by National
Guard units from northern France. Chatham and Strachan met on
6 August to thrash out plans and decide the best route to
Antwerp. Unfortunately, they were unable to reach agreement.
Strachan refused to take his ships through the narrow waters of
the Slough. Instead, he proposed that troops should land on
South Beveland, march to Batz and cross to the eastern bank of
the Scheldt, there to protect a naval advance as far as Sandvliet
and attempt an attack on Antwerp. For his part, Chatham disliked
the idea of so many thousand troops tramping South Beveland's
muddy roads, while he was convinced of the need to take Flushing
before moving on Antwerp. Thanks to the Navy's failure to
impose a blockade, said Chatham acrimoniously, Flushing had
daily received new soldiers from Cadsand, and he needed all the
men he had to take the town. The meeting broke up with neither
commander showing interest in the other's priorities.

Picton's appraisal of the situation, contained in the same
letter of 6 August, was pessimistic but close to the mark:

> You know my sentiments respecting the undertaking. The object
> (which was the capture of a few ships) was in every respect paultry
> and most unworthy of the national exertions made on the occa-

sion: and besides, the risque to the Fleet and army employed was great, and the probability of ultimate success very little. It would have been more possible to have marched to Paris than to have seised Antwerp in the midst of all the Fortified Places in Holland, Brabant, and Flanders: there never certainly [were] wasted more folly and madness.

With the capture of this place our operations will conclude, and I rather think John Bull will not think that he has a good penny-worth for his PENNY. This island cannot be retained: it will be more than madness to attempt it.[8]

Picton was farsighted in three respects: in anticipating that the expedition would not proceed to Antwerp; in arguing that any attempt to hold Walcheren would be unwise; and in fore-casting that the British public would not be pleased at the vast expense incurred for so little return. He was perceptive too in remarking that the unwieldy size of the expedition, as Napoleon later observed, made it unsuitable for a swift attack or *coup de main*.

The remainder of Picton's letter painted a favourable picture of the living standards on Walcheren. Years of maritime trading, notably with the east coast of England, plus generous helpings of smuggling and freebooting, had provided a basis for wealth: 'There is no show of poverty anywhere to be discovered. The Houses are extremely neat, and everything has an air of oppu-lence. The Towers are better built than any we have in England.'

He was much impressed by the capital, Middelburg, 'a magnif-icent City', with flowered gardens, a fine Town House amongst its many public buildings, and connected to Flushing by a broad canal and a delightful ornamental avenue. Finally, he elaborated for Flanagan's amusement on how well his creature comforts were being catered for: 'I carry on the War tolerably well', having plenty of good wine: 'Burgundy, Claret, and Hock', 'the finest Potatoes as well as every other variety of vegetables'.

He had one complaint: 'Everything is beautiful here, except the human species which appears in the same costume that Noah's family stept on shore from the Arck. The women are generally extremely plain. I have not seen one of tolerable appearance since my arrival, and I can assure you that I have preserved my Chastity intact.'

The other inconvenience was Flushing itself, a renowned stronghold whose fortifications were conspicuous on the low island. Walcheren was a billiard table of verdant flatness, its sea-restraining dykes and sandbanks protecting inhabitants and prized buildings much as the ledge of cushions on a billiard table guards the inner baize. Once its sea defences were breached, however, Walcheren was destined to flood and turn into what the anonymous officer of the 81st Regiment imagined as 'a round basin, or a deep soup-plate, floating in the sea'.[9]

For centuries, whenever a storm coincided with an especially high tide, there had been flooding, which tested the resilience of all who lived in the appropriately named Zealand, or 'Sea-Land', a province created out of reclaimed land. These were a people, the same officer noted, who lived in dread of sudden rises in the tide and whose lives were spent like those in the neighbourhood of Etna or Vesuvius, 'in hourly danger of extinction'.[10]

Floods could be engineered by cutting the dykes, a military ploy that was put into operation as soon as the British placed batteries against Flushing. The ground outside the town was below sea level at high water and was gradually inundated from 6 August when Monnet ordered the east dyke cut and the sluices opened in the counterscarp of the moat. Discovering from locals that Flushing stood three feet higher than Middelburg, the British gained respite by opening the floodgates of the capital to drain off water. But the level soon began rising again and a thunderstorm on the night of 10 August held up work as the trenches filled with salty slime. Work was interrupted again when Sir William Stuart took ten frigates into the West Scheldt between the guns of Breskens and Flushing, whereupon Picton, on the east dyke, ordered his battery to fire on the town as a diversionary measure, with the result that little damage was suffered at sea. By 12 August the flooding in front of Fraser's division had reached four feet and poles had to be placed to mark the roads. Fortunately, with the batteries themselves now in danger, Chatham was ready to start a full-scale bombardment of the town next day. It had been a close run thing, as Picton reported to Flanagan on 16 August:

> We have got over the business much easier than we had reason to expect. The Prosecution of the Siege was becoming extremely difficult, and our means of carrying on our operations much narrowed by the rapid rise of the Waters which threatened to over-flow all our principal Batteries in the centre of our approaches; and had actually nearly cut off all communication between the different Corps forming the Investment.
>
> The Fire opened upon the Town at 1.00 p.m. of the 14th, and continued with very little intermission until about 4.00 a.m. of the 15th, during a great part of which time the Town was on Fire in various places, and the rapidity of its increase and violence threatened a general conflagration. At this period the Governor sent in a Flag of Truce, with proposals, which were ultimately acceded to, and we are now in possession of the Gates, and the Garrison lay down their Arms. Prisoners of War, to-morrow morning.[11]

The siege had come down to a race between two elements: fire and water. The town itself suffered a double bombardment from land batteries and enfilading sea fire while it was also ignited by the use of the Congreve rocket, an incendiary device first used at Flushing. Private Wheeler was much impressed by the fire-work display: 'This night I was on picquet, it was beautiful and fine, one half of Flushing was in flames, the Fleet and the whole of the Batterys were at it pel mel. At midnight, when on sentry, I often counted fifteen shells and twelve rockets at one time hovering over and descending in to the devoted town.'[12]

But a different sentiment was expressed by the anonymous officer of the 81st who, though finding the bombardment 'prodigious beyond all imagination', had reservations about Congreve's new device: 'He is a very clever, active man, but his rockets are more in favour with your Ministry than they are in the army. We scarcely consider them as fair; they are more destructive than useful. They will certainly reduce a town to ashes; but humanity will teach us that this is purchasing it at a very dear rate.'[13]

The same officer described the fearful scene when both batteries and ships began to open up on the town on the Sunday afternoon:

> Nothing in nature could be more tremendous. The island shook as if under an earthquake, and every report of the cannon was followed by a most horrible crash. Bricks, timber and splinters of wood flew about in every direction; and when the chimnies or any high point was struck, they were sometimes driven almost whole over the walls. The batteries were all so near, that the guns had their full force; they literally appeared as if they were tearing the city up from the roots.
>
> This horrible work continued the whole of Sunday afternoon and night. About ten o'clock on Monday morning Sir Richard Strachan got under weigh, and passing immediately under the sea-line of defence, poured in a most tremendous cannonade, and continuing in his station, repeated these dreadful broadsides for some hours. The brave garrison, for such they were still, stood to their guns; but the ruins now fell so thickly around them, as to bury even their guns.[14]

Outside the town the pressing factor was water. When Monnet first offered to surrender he proposed a 48-hour cease-fire. This Chatham sensibly declined since the water level was still rising. He instructed the British batteries to open up again until speedier terms were agreed. Monnet, perhaps unaware of the full extent of difficulties on the outside, decided to spare the townspeople what he considered unnecessary further suffering. His surrender after less than two days' bombardment would later astonish Napoleon who believed Flushing to be virtually impregnable. Charged later with cowardice and treason, Monnet wisely chose to stay in England for the remainder of the war, avoiding the wrath of the Emperor. As for Picton, he was surprised too and not a little relieved at the speed of the capitulation:

> We certainly expected a more obstinate resistance, considering that the Defences of the Town were in no measure destroyed or even impaired: and indeed the extreme expedient which the Governor had resorted to (that of cutting open the Digues and letting in the Sea) led us to expect a degree of obstinate pertinacity, which we should have great difficulty in overcoming. We were all much pleased to find that our conclusions, or rather, apprehensions, were erroneous; and I believe none more so than our Commanders, who are not calculated to struggle with much unexpected difficulty.[15]

This letter, written a day after the surrender, gave a shrewd analysis of the situation:

> Now we are in possession of the Island what are we to do with it? The best mode, in my opinion, will be to embarrass the Navigation of the Scheldt by sinking some Stone Ships (or Ships filled with Stones) in the Port and Arsenal of Flushing, and then to abandon the Island, which will be extremely difficult and extensive to Defend, if at all practicable. To secure this Place will require 20,000 men, and a large squadron in continual activity. On such Terms, in my humble opinion, it would be a mixture of madness and folly to attempt keeping possession of it. The Heads probably may think otherwise. The remaining part of this dramatical medley remains yet to be acted: but, without any pretensions to divination, I will take upon myself to predict that it will not succeed. Our Fleet was brought into great risque by this Expedition. The navigation was intricate and dangerous in the extreme. Many of the ships were on shore, and in circumstances of great apprehension: fortunately, they have all escaped, though I fear much that some of them have been so damaged as to be rendered useless in future. If they persist in attempting to get up the Scheldt I fear we shall have reason to lament our Madness.

Picton need not have worried. Only Sir Home Popham, the Navy's best navigator, went above the bifurcation of the East and West Scheldt rivers to reconnoitre and, briefly, exchange fire with the enemy before returning to Flushing. It was a further irony that Picton, given his pessimism about the entire expedition, was now appointed to command the garrison at Flushing.

His elevation, which came a week after the town's surrender, was not universally popular. In the opinion of the anonymous officer of the 81st, it was attributable to Picton being a 'ministerial favourite'. Nor was Picton insensitive to the fact that he was now in a position of power for the first time since he left Trinidad, as he revealed in his letter of 25 August to Marryat:

> You will be surprised to find me commanding the garrison of this place. There was a disposition to throw the civil administration and arrangements upon my shoulders, but I declined interfering with any but purely military duties, and even in the performance of these I have again been compelled to make use of severities which occasion painful recollections, but I am not to be deterred from doing what I consider my duty whatever obloquy it may occasion. The first night of my command very great irregularities and disorders were committed but I made so severe an example of the offenders by a drum head court martial next morning and everything has been orderly and quiet since: but by way of showing them that I am in earnest, a similar court martial assembles every morning at guardmounting in constant readiness to administer salutary Justice.[16]

Evidently, Picton had decided that whatever reputation he may have had following his acquittal would not be enhanced by ingratiating displays of leniency. Unfortunately, Chatham was indecisive. In the ten days following the fall of Flushing he showed no sense of urgency. Occupation of the town was not effected until 18 August, though it had surrendered on the 15th. This leisurely approach was reflected in Chatham's meeting with Strachan at Batz, where precisely nothing was agreed. Had the troops moved expeditiously on Antwerp, there would have been every chance of success. But with each day that passed after 20 August a successful outcome became less likely. A definitive decision not to attack Antwerp was finally taken on the 27th, by which time, as Picton's letter of the day before shows, a devastating sickness amongst the men was reducing British numbers as quickly as Antwerp's were being increased:

> I was always of opinion that this expedition was planned between madness and folly: and there never was such a misapplication of the public force. We have taken an island which we cannot keep with all the disposable Army of England. The climate is to the full as destructive as that of the West Indies and will be the Grave of the Army. The garrison of Flushing cost the French last season 1000 and they had generally two thirds of their force in hospital. We are already beginning to be sickly to an alarming degree though the bad season has not yet commenced. The Regiments in

my Brigade have already above 100 each in hospital and the Artillery 80 out of four companies. If ministers are suffered to persist in their quixotic measure of attempting to retain this Golgotha it will be the most costly and disgraceful enterprise which the country was ever seduced into by Empirical Politicians.

The object of the expedition, which was paultry and unbecoming the nation at all times, was only to be effected by celerity and every moment delay rendered it less practicable. But the fact is we are afraid to proceed and afraid to return without doing something. I have it from Naval officers high in Rank and Experience that the Navy cannot Protect us in the Winter Season and from my own knowledge of the Locality I cannot doubt of their correctness. If these people are allowed to proceed in their paroxisms the people of England must be equally mad. I have enjoyed tolerable good health; but in my Family of servants all of seven were taken ill yesterday.

Various factors of hygiene and diet contributed to the sickness that would soon afflict Picton. Not least was the men's practice of hastily downing their daily ration of grog, for this gave rise to an instant and extreme thirst, which in turn was often quenched on unhealthy tank water. Hygiene was not helped by the living conditions in Flushing, which, after the town's surrender, were less than ideal. Most citizens lived in the upper stories of their devastated homes, the ground floor being under water. Those who had died in the bombardment were often buried in shallow graves or communal pits, which soon produced seeping effluvia. As the officer of the 81st commented: 'The air is infected beyond any thing you can possibly imagine. There is pestilence almost in breathing it. I have been in the city once, and have had enough of it.'[17]

Yet the real nature of the infection that was devastating British troops was malarial, and, unbeknown to medical science at the time, it was transmitted by mosquitoes that bred in midsummer on the marshy lowlands of South Beveland and its environs. Within a week of arriving on that island, rifleman John Harris described how he noticed 'an awful visitation come suddenly':

The first I observed of it was one day as I sat in my billet, when I beheld whole parties of our Riflemen in the street shaking with a sort of ague, to such a degree that they could hardly walk; strong and fine young men who had been but a short time in the service seemed suddenly reduced in strength to infants, unable to stand upright – so great a shaking had seized their whole bodies from head to heel. The company I belonged to was quartered in a barn, and I quickly perceived that hardly a man there had stomach for the bread that was served out to him, or even to taste his grog, although each man had an allowance of half-a-pint of gin per day.

In fact I should say that, about three weeks from the day we landed, I and two others were the only individuals who could stand upon our legs. They lay groaning in rows in the barn, amongst the heaps of lumpy black bread they were unable to eat.[18]

From South Beveland in early August the fever spread to Walcheren where, by 1 September, it had infected more than 5,000 men. The virulence of the disease and the fact that there was neither prevention nor cure, caused panic amongst the men. The anonymous officer of the 81st recorded his own amazement that: 'Instances have frequently occurred where, of those who have attended the burial of a comrade, everyone has been seized with a depression of spirits which has invariably proved fatal.' Picton, having witnessed the psychological as well as physical depredations wreaked by yellow fever in the West Indies, ordered, in the interests of morale, that burials were to be confined to the hours of darkness. Nothing is more terrifying than to be attacked by an invisible enemy, as the anonymous officer understood:

> The root of it cannot be successfully reached. It lies in the air we breathe – every inhalation is a putrid poison. The nerves are relaxed by the cold damp which obtains an entrance into the body, and the blood is corrupted by the putrid atoms. The disease commences with every symptom of an ague, from whence it passes into a fever; and after the fever, the blood is putrified. Livid spots break out on the arms, legs, &c. and the unhappy sufferer dies, when, in the absence of the fever, there appeared some hopes of his recovery.[19]

Chatham's prime objective now was to get the men home, although, until otherwise instructed, he was also expected to hold Walcheren in case the situation in Austria changed. Castlereagh's orders to evacuate came on 14 September, by which time almost half the 16,000 or so troops left on Walcheren had gone down with fever. After the Franco–Austrian Treaty of Schoenbrunn was signed exactly one month later, the few remaining British soldiers concentrated on destroying Flushing's dockyards and naval buildings, sinking stone ships to block the harbour, as Picton had suggested. The last troops left on 23 December, but the majority had been evacuated in chaotic fashion in September, aboard ships in which the sick and healthy were often crammed together indiscriminately. Scarcely 100 men were killed in action on the expedition, but some 2,000 died on service in Walcheren and as many more within a short time of being invalided home. The majority of those infected escaped death, but most were left with a permanent debilitation. The

'Walcheren Fever', as it came to be known, not only manifested itself in recurrent attacks of ague, but also in swollen paunches, ulcerated limbs and, as in Picton's case, weak, streaming eyes.

On his return to England in September Picton went to take the waters at Cheltenham and then Bath. Convalescing, he had time to ponder the folly of an expedition that had severely weakened British forces without properly engaging the enemy. The number of fatalities caused by Walcheren Fever was not as great as that caused by yellow fever in the Caribbean. But, somehow, it was harder to bear the sacrifice of able-bodied men so close to home and at a time when an adverse climate was known to be at its worst. The parliamentary inquiry of March 1810 resolved that no blame could be apportioned to His Majesty's ministers over the planning of the expedition. As for Chatham and Strachan, the popular verse summed up their respective capacities for leadership:

> Great Chatham, with his sabre drawn,
> Stood waiting for Sir Richard Strachan;
> Sir Richard, longing to be at 'em,
> Stood waiting for the Earl of Chatham!

When interviewed about the catastrophe, they simply continued their practice of reciprocal incrimination. The alternative was to revert to British type and blame the weather.

On his return, Picton suffered from low spirits as well as poor health. To the stigma of Trinidad had now been added the scars of Walcheren and the prospects of this ageing soldier had never looked more bleak. Fortunately, before 1809 was out he would be summoned to the Peninsula by Lieutenant-General Sir Arthur Wellesley, newly created Viscount Wellington of Talavera following his tremendous victory over the French on 27 to 28 July.

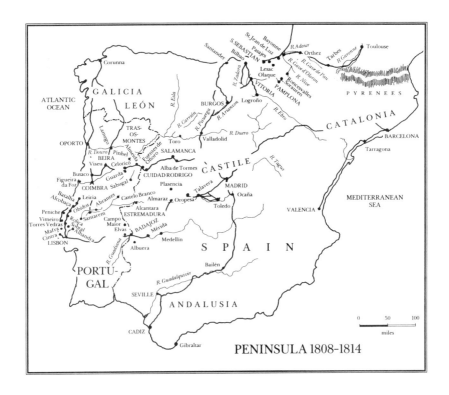

FOUR

PORTUGAL

The Fighting Division

I

Picton was back in Portsmouth on 12 January 1810 waiting for a favourable breeze to sail to Lisbon: 'This is a wretched place to be wind-bound at', he wrote to Lewis Flanagan, having suffered an undignified spill in his rush to get down from London:

> I continued my journey without intermission, fearful of being too late, and the night was so dark that the Post Boy, about three miles on this side of Petersfield, missed the Track, and upset the Chaise into a Deep wet Ditch, where the carriage lay nearly upon its roof, and I was struggling for several minutes with my Servant and Baggage laying upon me. I, at length, however, extracted myself through the upper window, without any material injury, but in consequence of being under the necessity of remaining nearly an hour and a half on the cold wet road (waiting for assistance to replace the Chaise on the Wheels), I have caught a severe cold, which I know how to get rid of as well as any Doctor of them all.[1]

This nocturnal mishap was the last thing Picton needed as he strove to regain full health. As one of Wellington's oldest generals he had no wish to display outward signs of infirmity either to his commander or to the men of the Third Division who awaited his command. But his pessimistic appraisal of Britain's chances of success in Portugal, outlined in the same letter to Flanagan, owed nothing to low spirits or declining health. His pragmatic line was consistent with the view taken at the time by soldiers and politicians alike:

> We shall affect nothing worth talking of in Portugal. We may delay the entire occupation of the country for some months, but certainly not much longer, and that too with a considerable degree of risque: for if we protract our opposition too long we may

experience, I understand, very considerable difficulty in bringing the Army off: for should the Enemy, which we cannot prevent, get possession of the left Bank of the Tagus, opposite Lisbon, our ships of war and Transports must quit the Harbour, and in that case our communication with them will become extremely difficult and precarious.

It was taken for granted that the French could eject British soldiers and recapture Portugal whenever they had a mind to do so. All numerate persons arrived at this conclusion. Wellington had barely 25,000 British, and about the same number of untried Portuguese, troops at his disposal, whereas the French had 300,000 veterans ready and waiting in Spain to march on Lisbon by any of three routes. Actuarially, it was no contest. Other factors would come into play, no doubt, and Wellington's strategy would maximize what Anglo–Portuguese strengths there were. But in January 1810, hard on the heels of the Walcheren fiasco and just one year after Moore's retreat to La Coruña, the only logical prognostication was that the exiguous British force would again have to take to their boats. What troubled Picton was that an enforced embarkation north-west of Lisbon would not be easy:

> Penniche, the other point, is on an extremely dangerous coast, where there is a great surf at all times, and where a re-embarkation must be attempted with very great risque and loss. Under these considerations it will be prudent to press for a timely evacuation, unless some great important object – sufficient to counterveil the exposure, should be attainable, of which I have not the least conception.

It would be some time before Picton had a conception of Wellington's deep-laid plans, for so intent was the latter on preserving an element of surprise he was reluctant to confide even in his divisional commanders. In the meantime, Picton embarked for Lisbon with hopes no higher than when he left for Walcheren. The city itself would have impressed him when he saw it from a frigate's deck in the Tagus: the Torre de Belém at the water's edge where it had saluted generations of intrepid explorers; the Manueline splendour of the Mosteiro dos Jerónimos set back from the river's curve; the port and commercial centre of Lisbon, rebuilt by Pombal after the earthquake of 1755, swaddled in leafy hills and overlooked to the right by the hilltop Castelo de São Jorge. The view had struck Sergeant William Grattan of the Third Division's 88th Connaught Rangers when he arrived the previous October and saw the city before him 'standing like a huge amphitheatre'.[2] But Grattan was sorely disappointed on setting foot ashore: 'The fine gardens all vanish, not into *thin* air, but into the most infernal pestiferous atmosphere that ever unfortunate traveller was compelled to inhale.' Grattan was glad to quit the city of beggars and famished dogs and continue on his way to join his regiment at Badajoz.

By the time Picton arrived in late January, Wellington had withdrawn from Badajoz to the Mondego valley in central Portugal and had set up headquarters at Viseu. After his victory at Talavera in July of the preceding year he had intended holding Badajoz, the gateway to Andalucía and to Lisbon, but he was also determined not to expose his troops in battle with the numerically superior enemy. He was horrified in November when the Spanish army, inspired by Talavera, fought on and was duly routed at Ocaña by Soult, to whom Napoleon had handed over. This allowed the French to invade Andalucia at will. On 1 February 1810 King Joseph Bonaparte entered Sevilla and by the spring only the impregnable Cadiz, a virtual island city, defied them. With Andalucía lost, Wellington saw little point in keeping his troops in cantonments on the exposed plains around Badajoz, where their numbers had been depleted by shortages of food and infections spawned in the Guadiana river. He decided instead to concentrate on the defence of Lisbon, whose environs he had carefully studied the previous October.

Lisbon was no Cadiz. Whereas the latter is a narrow isthmus, Lisbon stands on a twenty-five-mile breadth of land that separates the Tagus from the Atlantic. Nonetheless, Wellington resolved that this peninsula could be fortified, with Portuguese labour, while the bulk of his army would stand further north to meet the advance of an enemy who would surely come that way to avoid crossing the Tagus. Spaniards saw Wellington's withdrawal as a betrayal. To the weak Perceval administration in London, desperate for a victory to cheer, it was ignominious retreat. Yet Wellington believed the French had erred in taking Andalucía: now with even more territory to garrison, they would have correspondingly fewer men to hurl at Portugal. If the Portuguese could be trained, an Allied force of 70,000 might suffice to defend Lisbon and stick fast to the last rock in Europe.

Picton left Lisbon for Viseu on 14 February, having the previous day written to Despard Croasdaile: 'I have received orders to proceed to the Head Quarters, about 200 miles from here, and shall commence my journey early tomorrow morning, and as I travel with the Baggage I shall not be able to exceed 6 Leagues or 24 English miles per day.'[3] In fact, he later reported to Flanagan that it took him nine days of travel 'through the most miserable country'.[4] He noted that the land grew rapidly less hospitable once he had left the banks of the Tagus at Vila Franca: 'There were few, and those very confined spots, capable of producing corn of any kind. The Features of the country were generally bold, rocky, and covered with Heath, arbutus, rosemary, small furse, and some other productions of an unproductive soil.' Whether he knew it or not, this letter from Viseu outlined the difficulties that the French troops would meet should they invade and have to forage in a land of 'worse mountain than ever I saw in any part of Wales'. Picton admired the hardiness of the Portuguese and their ingenuity in working every bit of usable land: 'These people get rich where a highlander would starve.' He cheerfully complained of 'cold rooms, hard beds, bad fare', but was pleased to find 'good civility and respect from all classes' and a 'most inveterate hatred to the French'.

He had begun to feel the excellent spirit of cooperation that prevailed amongst the British soldiers and their comrades-in-arms, the Portuguese, who, as always, were emboldened by a will to outdo their Iberian neighbours: 'Lord W[ellington] is a great favourite with every one, high and low, and they are all persuaded that he would have certainly destroyed the French Army at Talavera had the Spaniards at all co-operated'. A sceptical Picton was impressed by his commander's meticulous preparations, which capitalized on the logistical problems facing the French:

> We are here *in utrumque paratus*, either to advance or retreat, though I rather think we shall make more forward movement, but if we should be under the necessity of falling back, as far as I am judge, every measure of prudence has been adopted to enable us to do so with credit. We are here on the Frontiers near the Enemy, and have nearly consumed what the frontier provisions contain for the support of man and beast, keeping the country in our rear to supply us in case of necessity: and the enemy cannot advance without bringing everything with them to subsist upon.

By 20 February 1810 Picton had reached his Third Division, stationed at Trancoso, some '50 miles in advance of Head Quarters' north-east of Viseu.[5] The practice of grouping together a number of brigades into the larger unit of a division had been introduced by Wellington the previous year. It had the presumed advantage of putting untried and veteran regiments together. Thus in Picton's Third Division were brigades led by Colonel Henry Mackinnon, General Lightburne and Colonel Harvey, and while Harvey's brigade consisted of two regiments of Portuguese infantry, Mackinnon's included the trusted 88th Connaught Rangers led by the resolute Scot, Colonel Alexander Wallace. William Grattan, himself newly enlisted in the 88th, recalled that it was 'with no little anxiety' that his comrades looked forward to meeting their divisional commander for the first time:

It would be impossible to deny that a very strong dislike towards the General was prevalent; his conduct at the island of Trinidad, while Governor of that colony, and the torture inflicted, by his order, on Louise Calderon, a torture which, by the way, had been given up in our army as being worse than flogging, had impressed all ranks with an unfavourable opinion of the man.[6]

A few days after his arrival the whole division was ordered to assemble under arms to receive their commander:

Punctual to the appointed time, General Picton reached the ground accompanied by his staff; every eye was turned towards him, and, as first impressions are generally very strong and very lasting, his demeanour and appearance were closely observed. He looked to be a man between fifty and sixty, and I never saw a more perfect specimen of a splendid looking soldier. In vain did those who had set him down in their own minds as a cruel tyrant, seek to find out such a delineation in his countenance. No such marks were distinguishable; on the contrary there was a manly open frankness in his appearance that gave a flat contradiction to the slander, and in truth Picton was *not* a tyrant, or did ever act as such during the many years that he commanded the third division.

But if his countenance did not depict him as cruel, there was a caustic severity about it, and a certain curl of the lip that marked him as one who rather despised than courted applause. The stern countenance, robust frame, caustic speech, and austere demeanour, told in legible characters that he was one not likely to say a thing and not do as he said. In a word, his appearance denoted him as a man of strong mind and strong frame.[7]

Picton watched the division perform evolutions and, according to Grattan, was visibly impressed by the line marching and echelon movements of the 88th, which earned Colonel Wallace praise of the new commander. Just when the parade was about to be dismissed, two straggling Connaught Rangers arrived with a stolen goat. There and then Picton ordered a drum-head court martial. The two men were promptly found guilty and flogged in the presence of the entire division. Still Picton had not finished. He proceeded to lash the men of the 88th with his tongue, abusing both their religion and their homeland, then bellowing uncontrollably in his fractured voice: 'You are not known in the army by the name of Connaught Rangers, but by the name of Connaught *foot-pads!*'

When the men were finally dismissed, Colonel Wallace let his brigade commander, Colonel Mackinnon, know that he was distressed by Picton's abuse of his regiment. Wallace and Mackinnon were disciplinarians themselves, but neither had heard such language from the mouth of an officer. In time Picton found a way of reassuring Wallace, inviting him to dinner and expressing his entire satisfaction with the much maligned 88th. Wallace was appeased, but his men would always be wary of their vituperative divisional commander.

Picton's behaviour was consistent with his treatment of delinquency in Trinidad and Walcheren. Indeed, it seems to have become a point of principle with him to react harshly whenever he smelt the issue of his supposed tyranny in the air. At Trancoso, meeting his troops for the first time, he may well have had other reasons for behaving as he did. Wellington, he knew, set great store by courteous relations with the natives, a point that he had no doubt impressed on Picton in person when he passed through Viseu. It was one thing for the French to indulge in indiscriminate foraging, not to say downright plundering, but the British were guests in Portugal and had to respect their hosts at all times. Picton may also have felt his elevation to divisional commander owed something to his reputation as one who upheld what he liked to call 'the wholesome severity of the law'.[8] Certainly the patient, defensive strategy that Wellington was preparing to frustrate the French had as much need of disciplinarians as heroes. It was also the case that, fairly or unfairly, the Connaught Rangers had acquired the name of the army's most ardent pillagers, a practice often ascribed to picaresque habits fostered by the poverty of their native land. Was it coincidence, Picton may have wondered, that such notorious characters were placed in the Third Division under his command? He seems, at least, to have been only too ready for them.

There was another side to Picton's nature. He could be sympathetic and even see the humour in a situation that may have offended officers with more aristocratic airs. Lieutenant Grattan reported that one day, when out riding with an aide-de-camp along the Côa river, Picton saw a Connaught Ranger on the opposite bank with a huge goat on his back. Since food rations had been somewhat scanty of late Picton was resolved to capture both the goat and the young soldier. Having no time to consult his map to ascertain the whereabouts of the nearest ford, he was reduced to bawling:

> 'Pray sir, what have you got there?'
> 'A thieving puckawn, sir', the soldier replied.
> 'A *what*?'

'A goat, sir. In Ireland we call a buck-goat a puckawn. I found the poor baste sthraying, and he looks as if he was as hungry as myself'.

'What are you going to do with him, sir?'

'*Do* with him, is it? To bring him with me to be sure! Do you think I'd lave him here to starve?'

'Ah! you villain, you are at your old tricks, are you?' Picton shouted, his face crimson with the effort of making himself audible above the sound of water. 'I know you, though you don't think it!'

'And I know you, sir, and the *boys of Connaught* know you, too, and I'd be sorry to do any thing that would be displaising to your honour; and, sure, iv you'd only let me, I'd send your sarvent a leg iv him to dhress for your dinner, for by my sowl your honour looks could and angry – hungry I mane'.

The young Connaught Ranger then held up the goat by the beard and shook it at Captain Tyler, Picton's aide-de-camp, before moving smartly off through a grove of chestnut trees.

'Well,' said Picton, turning breathlessly to Tyler, who was nearly convulsed with laughter, 'that fellow has some merit. He would make a good out-post soldier, for he knows not only how to forage but to take up a position that is unassailable.'[9]

II

Picton continued at the walled town of Trancoso, twenty miles west of the Côa, with his division spread in 'rather extended cantonments' over neighbouring villages. Trancoso, where, in 1283 Dom Dinis married Isabel of Aragón, was, in Picton's eyes, a 'wretched Town'. Standing nearly 3,000 feet above sea level, it had yet to shake off winter's grip:

'During the last week', Picton wrote in mid March, 'we had one of the heaviest falls of snow I ever remember to have seen, and the rain has been incessant ever since, so that there is no venturing out of Doors.'[10] Had he gone out, like Rifleman George Simmons, he would have seen 'innumerable prints of wolves' in the snow, which gave a chilling edge to the 'rocky, wild, and romantic' landscape.[11]

Picton was in fact housed in the Casa Real, 'destined to receive the Prince whenever he made his visits to this part of the Kingdom'.[12] But while the house was 'capacious enough' it offered few comforts. In depressed mood he reflected on the military situation:

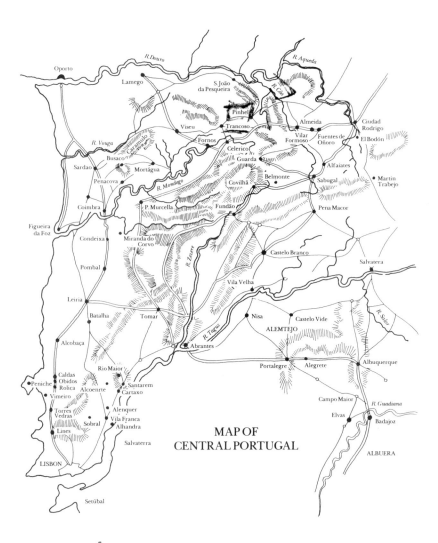

MAP OF
CENTRAL PORTUGAL

We are as ignorant here of what is going on in our neighbourhood as if we were in the mountains of Wales or of Wicklow. The French, I conceive, are collecting their forces to break in upon us from different points at the same time. To say the truth, we are in no force to make anything like a successful resistance, and as soon as they commence their operations, we must fall back and concentrate our forces without loss of time. Our line of communication with Lisbon is of immense extent, and if the enemy make use of their usual activity, we may experience great difficulty in preventing them from slipping in before us. They will probably make the invasion with 150,000 men at different points: from the side of Galicia, that of Ciudad Rodrigo from Plasencia, and into the province of Alemtejo. We cannot bring into the Field above 20,000, and the Portuguese have about 30,000 regulars of all descriptions: with so inconsiderable a Force, and in a country affording no strong military Posts, what probable result can you reasonably look forward to? We cannot remain here long under such circumstances, and the sooner we give up a hopeless cause the better, all this in confidence.

Picton was not the only one to write home 'in confidence'. Understandably, Wellington's penchant for secrecy fostered widespread speculation, which, under the circumstances, could only lead to pessimistic conclusions about British prospects. Nothing angered Wellington more than gloomy reports home, for he knew what their cumulative effect would be when morale was fragile, the government in Westminster precarious and, after Walcheren, every taxpayer keen on his military pennyworth. It was just as well that the Duke did not have sight of Picton's letter of 20 March, which concluded:

Considering everything, I am clearly of opinion that it will be something very nearly allied to madness to attempt seriously the Defence of this country. The Country affords few if any good Positions, where you can, with safety, await the attack of a superior Army. A very few weeks will, I conceive, finally settle the business, and the sooner it is done the better, for England is squandering immense sums of money to no possible good Purpose.[13]

What worried Picton, first, was the exposed nature of their position, for the French might use forced marches to cut them off from Lisbon, and second, the untried temper of the Portuguese soldiery: 'They appear good, able men and perform their military movements with considerable precision, but they are so miserably Officered that we can have but little reliance upon their co-operation. I have 2800 attached to my Division, and *entres nous* I had much rather be without them.'

As he waited for the snow to melt and military action to start in earnest, he was struck down by a recurrence of Walcheren Fever. On 7 May he wrote to Flanagan:

> Your Letter came to hand in due time, but, at the period of its arrival, I was so ill of a Fever, which terminated in a severe inflammation of the Eyes, that I was totally incapable of reading it for nearly three weeks, and it is not without considerable difficulty that I now make use of my Eyes to read and write, which I am directed to do very sparingly, for fear of bringing about relapse in that delicate organ.

In early May, his sight returned with the sudden warmth of spring, when he gratefully resumed active habits:

> My Health and strength are, however, tolerably well re-established. I am on horseback every morning at four o'clock, and ride nearly three Hours before Breakfast. By regularly going on in this way I trust I will be able to guard against another return of the Walcheren Complaints, the last attack of which was considerably more severe than the original one, though I have shaken off the effects of it with less difficulty.[14]

He was now at Pinhel, near the Côa river, about fifteen miles to the east of Trancoso and the same distance from the frontier fortress of Almeida. There he resided in the elegant bishop's palace, whose grounds occupied the only flat area in the steep town. Picton found the incumbent cleric 'a well-informed liberal-minded man', whose conversation was a delight after his recent tribulations. He noted with approval that, despite his status as one 'who may be expected to entertain considerable Prejudices in favour of the old Establishment', the bishop 'acknowledges that nothing could exceed its corruption and imbecility, and he expresses his apprehensions that the [Royal] Family have carried with them to the Brazils civil and political vices enough to contaminate any Country'. This uncompromising episcopal stand clearly influenced Picton's own opinion of King Dom João VI and his fugitive court: 'They escaped by flight from Portugal', he wrote scornfully, 'and the probability is that they will eventually be turned out of the Brazils.'

Picton seems to have been so influenced by the bishop's scarcely concealed Francophile tendencies as to question the entire British purpose in Portugal:

> This country, in every political and civil consideration is, without contestation, one of the most miserable in the world, and the arrival of the French cannot fail to ameliorate the situation of the Inhabitants in general. We are throwing away immense Sums to

no purpose, we cannot succeed, and, if we could, I by no means think it desirable, upon a liberal view of the subject, as it would be perpetuating the misery of this unhappy opprest people.

The suggestion that it would take French rather than British influence to improve the common lot in Portugal is revealing. Certainly living conditions in the rugged upland regions were primitive, as Rifleman Simmons testified:

> Our present quarters are truly miserable; on all sides stupendous mountains; the people wretched in the extreme, clothes hardly sufficient to cover themselves, and positively not a degree above savages – I mean as to their method of living. Of a morning they will turn out of their wretched cabins and are to be seen sitting in rows upon the ground in the sun picking lice off themselves and out of each other's heads.[15]

Picton still had complete confidence in Wellington: 'I go on perfectly well with our Commander of the Forces, who appears to me, from what I have been able to Observe, to possess the Talents, decision, and personal qualities necessary for his Situation.'[16] But in terms of strategy his aspirations were limited to the possibility of effecting a dignified evacuation: 'I trust we shall, at all events, come off with some degree of Eclat so as to satisfy our friend, John Bull.'

His orders at this time were to observe, without directly engaging, the French, who were now moving in large numbers from Salamanca on Ciudad Rodrigo, the imposing Spanish twin of the small fortress at Almeida. Ahead of him were three battalions of light troops under General Robert Craufurd, which functioned as an advanced observation corps. Craufurd, to Picton's alarm, had been making daring sorties into Spain, annoying the French with skirmishes at Barba del Puerco, Villar de Ciervos and various points along the Agueda river. The Third Division, however, like Cole's Fourth Division at Guarda, was to stay out of trouble, though, as Picton himself noted, it had 'Orders to support him [Craufurd] in case of necessity'.[17]

The French siege of Ciudad Rodrigo began in earnest on 22 June when the first parallel was established. There had been continuous skirmishing near the town during the previous weeks when the *guerrillero* and folk hero, Julián Sánchez, 'el Charro', made a number of daring sorties. By mid June, the French had brought 35,000 men and a massive siege train to invest the fourteenth-century fortress whose stone battlements and sturdy cathedral rose steeply above the Agueda to cut a yellow glow in the crisp blue sky. The British expected a quick capitulation, for the town, they said, was only defended by 6,000 Spaniards, an observation that imputed as great a deficiency in national character as numerical force. They had reckoned without the town's governor, however, Lieutenant-General Andrés Pérez de Herrasti, a veteran soldier who inspired his men to such heroic resistance that the prolongation of the siege became an embarrassment to Wellington. Why was it, his own soldiers asked as the siege wore into its third and fourth week, that they must stand aloof and watch their gallant Ally suffer unaided?

'The Spanish are astonished at us remaining idle', wrote George Simmons: 'The young women, with whom we joke and talk, make no scruple in calling us cowards, and say if we fought as well as we eat and drink wine, we should be fine fellows indeed.'[18]

British caution was seen as a mark of treachery: it was all that could be expected of heretics; another betrayal to match the shameful retreat into Portugal after Talavera. But Wellington was not to be drawn from his Lusitanian redoubt. He refused to risk his precious forces in open conflict, especially on a plain where the superiority of the French cavalry would be decisive. He declared: 'There is a great deal of difference (particularly in the blood to be spilt) between fighting in a position which I choose, or in one which the enemy choose.' In the end it was a simple matter of mathematics, as Wellington explained in a letter of 31 July to his devoted elder brother William Wellesley Pole, 3rd Earl of Mornington: 'If I had attacked them I could not have gained any important success before they would have been joined by the 8th corps, which were never farther from them than León. There would then have been 57,000 men against 25,000; and whatever might have been my first success, I must have retired with loss.'[19]

Picton's letter of 4 July, written during the siege, shows both his sensitivity to the situation and a growing understanding of Wellington's strategy:

> We have remained in this situation on the Frontiers of Spain much longer than any of us expected, but we are now certainly upon the eve of a movement: *not forward*. The enemy has collected so great a Force to besiege Ciudad Rodorigo that we could not, without too much risque, venture to its relief, though our advance Posts have constantly been in sight of the Enemy and the Place which has been Invested for more than a month.
>
> The Batteries of the Besiegers opened Eight days ago, and the Fire from Guns and Mortars has been incessant ever since. The garrison (considering the miserable state of the Fortification, which has no casemates or cover for the Troops) has certainly

made a most gallant resistance, and repulsed three attempts to carry it by storm, in which the Enemy sustained very great loss. The Fire still continues, and nearly the whole Town has become a prey to the conflagration, which has continued to rage for four days and nights.

They have exhausted their stock of ammunition and Provisions, and must, therefore, surrender at discretion in a day or two. To be spectators of such a scene, without the ability to take part in it, cannot be very gratifying to our Feelings: but a forward movement to attempt to raise the Siege would have been too dangerous for prudence to have risqued, considering the great disparity of our numbers, as well as the unfavourable circumstances of our Situation.

Picton knew they would have to retreat in haste once Ciudad Rodrigo fell:

As soon as the Town has surrendered we must fall back without delay, for we can no longer remain here, in this distant and exposed situation. The French Army, in our Front, under Marshal Ney is above double our numbers, and the disproportion in Cavalry is still greater, nearly four times more, so that we are but ill prepared to contend with them in an open Champaign Country such as lies between the Rivers Coa and Agueda.[20]

He correctly perceived that the main effort would come deep inside Portugal, though he still saw this primarily as a matter of saving face:

When we get within about 35 miles of Lisbon, and collect all our Forces, which will amount to nearly 50,000 men, we may venture upon a Battle. All we can gain by a successful Fight is Honor, for considering every thing, and the Enemy's great facility of rein- forcing their armies to any amount, it would be more than Quixotic to expect ultimate success in so disproport[ionate] a struggle.

Militarily, he disliked the frontier position not only for its openness, which left it 'rather in the Air', but also because of the reduced state of the Côa 'which is now so nearly dry as to afford scarcely any barrier, and may be easily forced everywhere'. At the same time he knew full well that the French would find it hard to forage in the area once the British did retreat: 'The necessaries of Life are almost wholly eaten up here by the long residence of our Army.'[21]

Picton's appreciation of the situation underlies his highly controversial decision not to assist Craufurd when his Light Division was surprised by Ney at Almeida on 24 July, two weeks after the fall of Ciudad Rodrigo. His refusal to lend support when Craufurd's 4,000-strong corps came under severe attack from 20,000 French infantry and 3,000 cavalry was, at face value, in contravention of Wellington's order to support Craufurd 'in case of necessity'. Bad blood very likely existed between the two generals, for, in Picton's view, Craufurd took unnecessary and unauthorized risks. The younger general had an unrivalled reputation for outpost work; but if harassing the enemy while it engaged in the siege of Ciudad Rodrigo involved a tolerable risk, it was altogether foolhardy in Picton's eyes to camp in front of the neighbouring frontier fortress on the Portuguese side, Almeida, because the only possible retreat was via a single narrow bridge over the Côa gorge two miles west of the town. To persist in that position and then expect support on being surprised by a massive French attack beggared Picton's patience and belief.

Rifleman Simmons recalled that on the evening of 23 July he and his colleagues in the Light Division 'drank success to their defence of the fortress' with Portuguese troops. They then left Almeida and took up positions in the rocky country outside, where they were instantly greeted by a torrential storm of thunder and lightning. Next morning, as the men checked the readiness of their guns and ammunition, they were attacked in vast bodies: 'The whole plain in our front was covered with horse and foot advancing towards us.' With the utmost difficulty, and sustaining heavy loss of life, they retreated down a rough track and clambered over the stone walls of drenched vineyards to the suddenly swollen Côa, 'which river was running furiously in its course'.[22] Simmons himself was shot through the thigh as he, like many others, sought to protect the division's evacuation via the small bridge. Later, it was the turn of the French to suffer heavy losses as they tried several times, in vain, to storm the bridge before evening brought an end to the gory action.

Later that year, in a letter to *The Times* that was published 20 November 1810, Craufurd gave a detailed account of the action at Almeida on 24 July. The ostensible point of his writing was not to criticize Picton but to repudiate Masséna's claim that the French had scored a notable victory and had put British soldiers to ignominious flight over the Côa. Craufurd reported that his men, though outnumbered in the order of six to one, had inflicted at least twice as many losses on the French as they suffered themselves and that they had 'performed in the presence of so superior a force one of the most difficult operations of war, namely, a retreat from a very broken and extensive position, over one narrow defile'. He also insisted that 'the retreat was made in a military, soldier-like manner, and without the slightest precipitation'.

At issue was not the bravery of the Light Division, still less that of its commanding officer. The Côa incident provoked a controversy over Picton's apparent disobeying of an order as against Craufurd's arguably reckless conduct. Both men had a case. In essence, Picton's decision was consistent with Wellington's refusal to aid the beleaguered Herrasti at Ciudad Rodrigo. As for Craufurd, he had doubtless delayed his retreat in order to encourage the Almeida garrison before it in turn came under French fire. Ironically, in this noble objective he had perhaps been spurred to new heights of bravura by the British passivity at Ciudad Rodrigo. But the price – 333 British soldiers killed, wounded and missing – was a heavy one to pay. It would have been considerably higher if Picton had committed his Third Division and a general action had ensued.

Wellington expressed himself with characteristic vigour on the subject in his letter of 31 July from Celorico to his brother, William Wellesley Pole. In this he wrote of 'the foolish affairs in which Craufurd involved his outposts', noting:

> I had positively desired him not to engage in any affair on the other side of the Coa and had expressed my wish that he should withdraw his infantry to the left of the river. After all this he remained above two hours on his ground after the enemy appeared in his front before they attacked him, during which time he might have retired across the Coa twice over.[23]

The philosophy of the Commander of the Forces is revealed in his conclusion: 'You will say, if this be the case, why not accuse Craufurd? I answer, because, if I am to be hanged for it, I cannot accuse a man who I believe has meant well, and whose error is one of judgement and not of intention.' Little wonder that Wellington always had the respect of his generals whom he customarily allowed a good deal of discretion when it came to following orders. Little wonder, too, that Craufurd chose not to press his complaint against Picton.

III

After Craufurd's retreat from Almeida, Picton's position at Pinhel became 'perfectly untenable', as he wrote from Linhares on 1 August: 'I, in consequence, left it at three o'clock on the morning of the 26th, and arrived here on the Evening of the 28th.'

Linhares was a small village on the eastern flank of the Mondego valley, down whose steep sides the Third Division descended like water cascading off the nearby Serra da Estrela: 'We have made a retrograde movement during two days', wrote Picton, 'and have shortened our distance from Lisbon by about 35 miles.'[24]

At Linhares they could draw breath, for the French had not pursued them with urgency after the Côa engagement. 'They might have compelled us to fight upon ground much less advantageous to us than what we now occupy', Picton informed Marryat on 8 August: 'They advance with great caution, and leave as little as possible to Fortune.'[25] In fact, the French had concentrated on much needed foraging and, from 15 August, on the siege of Almeida itself. This tight fortress, under British Governor, General William Cox, fell on 28 August, when a leaked trail of gunpowder leading to the main magazine was ignited by shell fire and the town rent apart in a volcanic eruption that cost nearly 700 lives. Almeida's two weeks of resistance did not compare with the forty days of Spanish heroism at Ciudad Rodrigo; nevertheless, for Masséna it was another of those irksome delays, which, in aggregate, would prevent his army approaching Lisbon until the worst time of year for foraging had arrived.

In August the weather had turned 'excessively hot', Picton reported, 'to the full as much so as in the West Indies'.[26] For the wounded, like George Simmons who had to endure the journey on a jolting bullock cart, the heat and the flies were excruciating:

> Several of our poor fellows died from the rough usage they suffered, and several soldiers who had neglected to cover their wounds now became one frightful mass of maggots. We had no means of keeping off the swarms of insects, and the slow pace that the bullocks went, made us feel the vertical rays of the sun with redoubled force.[27]

Picton was scarcely more comfortable in Linhares: 'We are absolutely devoured by every kind of Vermin. It is almost impossible to Sleep for Buggs and Fleas.'[28] Cured now of his Francophilia, he noted that the locals had such dread of the enemy that they deserted their villages as soon as the British troops moved out: 'They betake themselves to the mountains with everything they possess. It is a lamentable thing to see *Veteres migrare colonios* ["Old peasants on the move"].' Though he had yet to confront the enemy himself, he felt able to reflect piously: 'These modern Franks make war like the Goths, Huns, and Vandals of old, whose devastations they refine upon.' His anguished conclusion was worthy of Goya: 'The world has certainly arrived at an extreme state of wretchedness and misery, from which there is no prospect of approaching relief. *Paciencia y Cojer los Ombros* ["One has to be patient and shrug one's shoulders"].' Indeed, in the stoical vein prescribed by the Spanish proverb, Picton shrugged his flea-bitten shoulders for a full week in Linhares.

As ever, in moments of idleness, his mind turned to financial problems: 'I have not heard a word from Trinidad since I have been in this miserable country', he wrote Marryatt, 'and I am in consequence desirous of knowing how my affairs are going on there, particularly those of the Union.'[29] He also had time to share with his fellow officers the sensational news of 9 July when Lord Ellenborough sentenced William Cobbett, the most brilliant radical journalist of the day, to two years in prison and a £1,000 fine. Cobbett had been prosecuted for an article published the year before in his *Political Register* in which he had protested against the flogging of five Ely militiamen for the crime of refusing to march without pay, the 'marching guinea' to which they were entitled by law. To quash this mutiny four squadrons of Hanoverian cavalry had been sent in from nearby Bury St Edmunds and had flogged the 'free-born Englishmen', moving Cobbett to write:

> Five hundred lashes each! Aye, that is right! Flog them! flog them! flog them! They deserve a flogging at every meal time. Lash them daily! Lash them daily! What! Shall the rascals dare to mutiny? And that, too, when the German Legion is so near at hand? Lash them! Lash them! Lash them! They deserve it, Oh, yes! they merit a double-tailed cat! Base dogs! What! Mutiny for the price of a knapsack? Lash them! Flog them! Base rascals![30]

Not surprisingly, Cobbett's *saeva indignatio* was not appreciated by Picton who held a very different view of military authority. He supported the punitive action taken against the Ely militiamen and rejoiced in both the sentence and the staggering seven years' bond imposed on the radical agitator who had spoken out against 'the odious punishment of flogging':

> Cobbett has made a most miserable display of his oratorial Talents. The Libel itself was a most vulgar, malignant production, much below his general writings, and I am much surprised how, with his apprehension of the Consequences and general Prudence, he could have committed himself in so palpable a manner. You may well say that they have closed his political speculations by the sentence which keeps a Halter about his neck for seven years.[31]

Picton's main thoughts in the Mondego valley centred on his immediate military situation. His knowledge of Wellington's plans was becoming more detailed now, as he revealed in a letter dated Linhares, 1 August, in which he first mentioned Torres Vedras:

> About 25,000 men are collected within 4 or 5 miles of this place, in readiness either to take advantage of an imprudent movement of the Enemy, or to continue our retreat towards the Positions, between the Tagus and Torres Vedras, where we calculate to make a successful stand, at least for some time, so as to carry our reputation unimpaired aboard the Transports, which are in readiness to carry us off.

He reflected too on their recent speedy retreat down the Mondego valley, where the Third Division had been joined by Cole's Fourth descending from Guarda: 'By this movement we have gained two objects', he informed Marryat; 'we have transferred the theatre of operations to a more enclosed country, where numbers will lose many of their advantages, and we have secured the reunion of the different corps of the Army whenever events may render such a measure desirable.'[32] Nevertheless, it was still thought to be only a question of time before the inevitable evacuation: 'there will probably be a good deal of hard fighting before the enemy will be able to reach the neighbourhood of Lisbon: but as their losses will be supplied by continual reinforcements, and we shall be daily diminishing in numbers, without any hopes of succour, it is clear that they must eventually succeed'.

Wellington's tactic after the surrender of Almeida was to fall back on Lisbon, and, as he withdrew, to lay waste the land. This was designed to take maximum advantage of the French reliance on requisitioning. For though Napoleon had conquered Europe by the speed of his advances and the audacity of his attacks, made possible by his army's practice of travelling light, living off the country and sleeping in bivouacs, Wellington knew that French soldiers could not stay in one place for any length of time since they soon cleared it of all sustenance over a radius of twenty miles. They were obliged either to forage further afield, in which case they might fall prey to *guerrilleros*, or else press on to pastures new. Wellington, by virtue of his command of the sea, had a steady line of supply from Oporto and points along the coast. He also had the goodwill of the indigenous population since, unlike the French, he paid promptly for services rendered. In all, he was much better equipped to play a waiting game.

Yet Wellington was also aware that the Perceval administration in London was on a knife edge and under constant attack for its handling of the Peninsular campaign, which, critics claimed, was hopelessly lacking in vigour and needlessly expensive. He knew that a victory over the French would change all that and it would do something for Portuguese morale.

Accordingly, Wellington brought his army to a halt on the barren heights of the Serra do Buçaco and, from 21 September, awaited the French. The imposing eight-mile mountain ridge north-east of the old university town of Coimbra barred the main route south to Lisbon. Its steep, heathery slopes littered with outcrops of rock afforded an excellent defensive strong-hold to the combined British and Portuguese army. It was as good a place as any to 'blood' his ally.

Why Marshal Masséna should have accepted the invitation to attack such a position is altogether less clear, for the option remained of skirting Busaco and attempting to turn the enemy. It is true that Masséna, whom Napoleon had created Prince d'Essling in January following his stunning displays against the Austrians, at Aspern-Essling and Wagram, had yet to confront the British, whom he may have held in as little esteem as the untried Portuguese. To this *enfant gâté de la victoire*, the choice of terrain may have seemed inconsequential when set beside the advantage in numbers enjoyed by his irresistible, battle-hardened hordes. But General Marbot, Masséna's second aide-de-camp, revealed a number of reasons for the marshal's precipitate attack.

In the first place it is clear that, after leaving Almeida on 14 September, Masséna had taken an inferior route by eschewing the Mondego valley and passing via Celorico to the town of Viseu. This choice of a more westerly route was 'déraisonnable' in Marbot's view since the roads it provided, 'les plus affreux du Portugal', were quite unsuited to the French army. There was also little sustenance to be found in the locality: 'Les environs de Viseu ne produisent ni céréales, ni légumes, ni fourrages. Les troupes n'y trouvèrent que des citrons et des raisins, nourriture fort peu substantielle.'[33] French problems were compounded by the fact that their maps were poor and their guides were long-term captives rather than local volunteers with specific knowledge of the area. Masséna would spend six days requisi-tioning at an empty Viseu, 'La cité de Viseu était totalement déserte lorsque nous y entrâmes.' This prompted Marbot to remark on Wellington's scorched earth policy, 'cette terrible mesure de résistance', which proved so much more effective in Portugal than in Spain because, he argued, the Portuguese were 'plus dociles' than their neighbours and hence more readily persuaded to the sacrifice.[34]

Very likely the chronic lack of sustenance, coupled with a real fear about future provisions, gave special urgency to French plans. Yet Marbot had reason to believe his commander was influenced too by purely personal considerations, notably the comfort of his mistress, who accompanied him everywhere dressed in an aide-de-camp's uniform and who tired of the horseback treks she had to make on roads too rough for coaches. 'Sombre et misanthropique', Masséna had come to rely on his companion for solace, tending to prefer her company to that of others.[35] Her presence was required even when he dined with his senior officers, among them generals Reynier, Junot and Montbrun. This fuelled discord and damaged communication at the highest level of command, especially with Marshal Ney.

When, on 26 September, Masséna arrived at the village of Mortágua, twelve miles east of the Busaco ridge, the French commander's first priority was to secure comfortable lodgings where his companion might rest. As a result, Masséna did not join his advance posts until late in the afternoon. There in the Moura foothills he was promptly briefed by generals Reynier and Junot, who had already made up their minds that the British position was not as strong as it appeared: were the command in their hands, they would not hesitate to attack. Masséna, who had sight only in one eye, made but the most perfunctory of surveys before responding, 'Eh bien, je serai demain ici au point du jour, et nous attaquerons', whereupon, to the stupefaction of his assembled generals, he turned his mount and headed back to Mortágua.[36]

Marbot was alarmed that the decision to attack could be taken without proper reconnaissance. If there was no chance of bypassing the Busaco ridge at its southern end where the Mondego river flowed through a gorge, surely it was worth checking the possibilities to the north. Unable to speak directly to Masséna, a privilege reserved for Pelet, his first aide-de-camp, Marbot contrived under cover of night to communicate his concern by loudly debating the situation with fellow officers in the darkness while pretending to be unaware that his commander was within earshot: Was it conceivable that the inhabitants of Mortágua had lived for so many centuries without a link to the main highway between Lisbon and Oporto? What effort, if any, had Reynier, Junot or Ney made to discover such a road when they passed through Mortágua?

Masséna, whose ears functioned rather better than his eyes, instructed generals Marbot and Ligniville to find a local guide as soon as they returned to Mortágua. This was easier said than done, for almost everyone had fled the town. Eventually, they found an old gardener who had stayed behind to tend a sickly monk, and it was the latter who gave them the information they needed: Yes, he had often travelled from Mortágua to the Oporto

road 'par une bonne route', whose fork, barely a league from the
monastery, the soldiers had unaccountably missed. Marbot and
Ligniville soon verified the monk's account and, little more than
an hour later, reported back to Masséna, who was poring over
maps with Pelet when they arrived. Pelet, however, was disinclined to credit the news his subordinates brought. He had
examined the mountain himself by daylight with a telescope and
had seen no passage to the right. If there were one, did they not
suppose Marshal Ney would have found it during his sojourn at
Mortágua? It was midnight and Masséna would need to leave at
four to reach Busaco by daybreak. It was time for bed.

At dawn, Marshal Masséna scanned the vast ridge of Busaco as
far as his good eye could see. Through the patches of mist he
noted that its heights were undulating but smooth, unlike the
rugged escarpments on its sides. The relative flatness of its
upper reaches would give the enemy, hidden behind the skyline,
an ease of communication and allow them to collect their forces
swiftly wherever the French chose to ascend. In his mind's eye
Masséna saw the British and Portuguese waiting on the reverse
slope of the ridge, but he had no accurate idea of their numbers.
By contrast, his own army was there on full display and could be
counted by the enemy to the nearest squadron of men. All he
could make out of the British was a sprinkling of sharpshooters
halfway up the mountain, where they waited for the first foolhardy French to come within range. Directly below them was a
ravine that stood like an immense moat scooped out by nature,
its sculpted rocks providing a formidable battlement and
rendering the crest inaccessible at that point to French artillery.

For a moment Masséna appeared to hesitate as he turned
thoughtfully towards General Marbot and said: 'Il y avait du bon
dans votre proposition d'hier.'[37] Almost at once General
Reynier, Pelet and Marshal Ney rode up and informed him that
everything was ready for the attack and for his 'victoire certaine'.
He would drive the hideous British leopard into the sea, just as
Napoleon had instructed.

It was not yet 6.00 a.m. when Masséna gave the order for the
battle to begin.

IV

The British and Portuguese meanwhile had encamped patiently
on the reverse slope of Busaco ridge, where their numbers had
been steadily reinforced in the last week until they reached

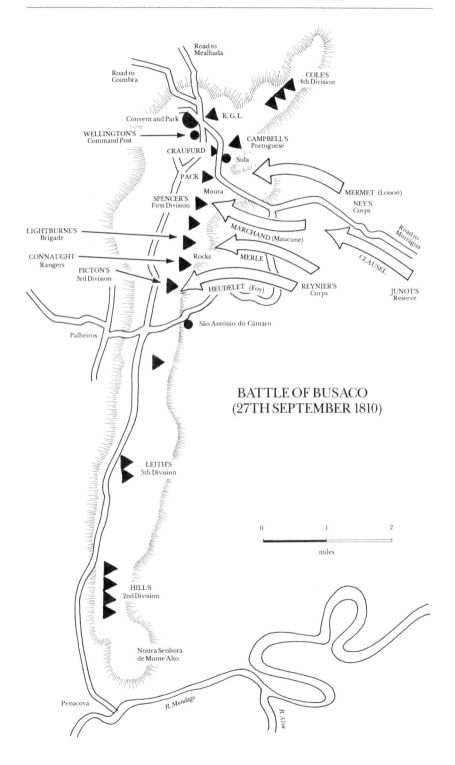

Road to
Mealhada

Road to
Coimbra

COLE'S
4th Division

Convent and Park

K.G.L.

WELLINGTON'S
Command Post

CAMPBELL'S
Portuguese

CRAUFURD

Sula

PACK

Moura

MERMET (Loison)

NEY'S
Corps

SPENCER'S
First Division

Road to
Mortágua

LIGHTBURNE'S
Brigade

MARCHAND (Maucune)

CONNAUGHT
Rangers

Rocks

MERLE

CLAUSEL

PICTON'S
3rd Division

HEUDELET (Foy)

REYNIER'S
Corps

JUNOT'S
Reserve

São António do Cántaro

Palheiros

BATTLE OF BUSACO
(27TH SEPTEMBER 1810)

LEITH'S
5th Division

0   1   2

miles

HILL'S
2nd Division

Nostra Senhora
de Monte Alto

Penacova

R. Mondego

R. Alve

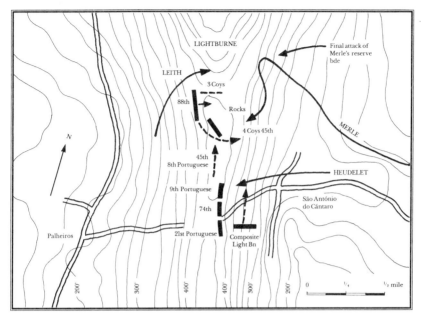

BUSACO (3RD DIVISIONAL SECTOR)

52,000, half of whom were Portuguese. This was considerably more than Masséna estimated, but less than his own army, which was 66,000 strong. Many on the summit, like Picton, doubted whether the Allied force was adequate to defend an eight-mile line.

Wellington had placed Picton and his Third Division roughly at the centre of the ridge, where a track rose from tiny São António do Cántaro and crossed in a shallow pass towards the scarcely larger village of Palheiros on the Coimbra side. The Third Division, numbering 4,700, had been allocated a mile and a half of the ridge to defend. Picton kept the bulk of his men near the Palheiros track, though Lightburne's Brigade, at Wellington's orders, was moved to a higher plateau a mile to the north. After sunset on the eve of the battle Picton prudently detached the 88th Regiment, Colonel Wallace's Connaught Rangers, to fill the large gap between him and Lightburne. During the night the Allied soldiers camped without tents and fires, which left them exceedingly cold on the mountain. One young officer, Moyle Sherer, recounts how the Allied army, including the likes of Picton, spent the night: 'We lay down, rolled in our cloaks, and with the stony surface of the mountain for our bed, and the sky for our canopy, slept or thought the night away.'[38] Schaumann, an officer in the King's German Legion, walked to the top of the ridge to satisfy his curiosity, whence he viewed the darkening plain below with awe:

> I was little prepared for the scene which met my astonished vision. For as far as the eye could see, I could discern three dark columns of a colossal army advancing under cover of clouds and dust, and gleaming with the glint of arms. And so this was the famous French army, the terror of the world, the conqueror of Italy, Spain, Egypt and Germany! It had been victorious at Jena, Austerlitz, Marengo, Ulm, and Vienna, and on the morrow we were probably going to try conclusions with it.[39]

Two hours before daybreak the men were under arms, eager to have sight of the enemy. But, as Connaught Ranger Grattan reported, at one time in the morning 'the haze was so thick that little could be seen at any great distance'. Only gradually did he become aware of the encroaching conflict:

> A rolling fire of musketry and some discharges of cannon in the direction of S. Antonio announced what was taking place there; and the face of the hill immediately in front of the Brigade of Lightburne and to the left of the 88th Regiment was beginning to show that the efforts of the enemy were about to be directed against this portion of the ground held by the 3rd Division.
> The fog cleared away and a bright sun enabled us to see what was passing before us. A vast crowd of tirailleurs was pressing forward with great ardour, and their fire as well as their numbers was so superior to that of our advance that some men of the Brigade of Lightburne, as also a few of the 88th, were killed while standing in line.

It was at this early point that the Connaught Rangers distinguished themselves, for Colonel Wallace quickly recognized the danger, dismounted from his horse and led a charge against those French who had reached a rocky vantage point precisely where the Third's line was weakest: 'All was now confusion and uproar', wrote Grattan, 'smoke, fire, and bullets, officers and soldiers, French drummers and French drums knocked down in every direction. British, French and Portuguese mixed together, while in the midst of all was to be seen Wallace fighting like his ancestor of old at the head of his devoted followers, and calling out to his soldiers to 'press forward'. It so happened that Wellington himself came upon the scene at this moment and witnessed the brilliant success of Wallace, the 88th and 45th Regiments, which moved him to report: 'I never saw a more gallant charge.'[40]

The Third Division thus bore the brunt of the French assault, as Picton anticipated:

> I had no doubt, from a variety of circumstances, that the extended post I occupied in the position would be the first and principal object of their attack. It proved so. The whole of their artillery and several heavy Colums were brought to bear upon the Pass of St. Antonio de Alcantara [Cántaro] at day break, and the attack was continued with great obstinacy on the different points of the Line occupied by my Division, until 12 o'clock, when they desisted, after being driven back on every occasion in great confusion and with great loss.[41]

General Jean Louis Reynier commanded the assault on Picton's own position near the Palheiros track. His First Division, led by Merle, formed columns, which ascended to the north of the track and roughly parallel with it, while his Second Division, under Heudelet, kept to the easier gradient of the winding track itself along which they brought up what artillery they could. Once Merle's Division came under heavy fire from the Connaughts above, they found it impossible to maintain disciplined columns on the steep slopes and degenerated into swarms. Heudelet's advance was more orderly on the track but subject to the devastatingly accurate fire from sharpshooters and from two batteries of Portuguese 6-pounders. The French gained momentary hope when some of their light troops took possession of another cluster of rocks that stood to the north, beyond the Connaughts, from which prominence they were able to offer some cover to the right flank of Merle's dishevelled columns.

Doubtless there is an element of exaggeration in Picton's claim that 'the whole of the real attack was upon the position of the 3 Division, and the Demonstrations upon the other points were merely feints'. Nonetheless, it is clear that the Third, which henceforth would be known as 'the Fighting Division', was busier than any other in Wellington's army that day, while Picton himself, in his first major battle, was sorely pressed coordinating his defensive positions over the extended line. When he realized that Heudelet's progress up the Palheiros track was safely contained, he left Colonel Mackinnon with some 2,000 men to guard the pass and headed north along the ridge instructing the companies of Major Birmingham, Colonel Meade and the 8th Portuguese to follow. Passing the 88th Regiment's position, which was now vulnerable since Wallace, after earlier engaging the French, had pursued them down the slope, Picton headed towards the troublesome gap that separated it from

Lightburne's Brigade. There he was alerted to the French occupation of a second rocky prominence near the summit:

> Having repelled the Principal attack, against which they brought the whole of their Artillery, I was gallopping to the other Extremity, which was at the same time closely engaged, when I found a Colum of the Enemy had penetrated to the centre of my Line, and had actually established themselves on a strong Rocky point, which commanded every thing around. There was nothing at hand but the Light Infantry Companies of the 74th and 88th Regiments, which had been dispersed and were returning in Disorder, in this extremely critical situation, with the assistance of Major Smith of the 45th Regiment, I rallied them with some difficulty, and after a few words led them to a charge, from which I had but faint hopes of success.

The few words with which Picton exhorted his men to hurl themselves at the enemy were no doubt choice and uttered in his voice like thunder. On this occasion his men were also much taken by the fact that when Picton urged them on he raised his top hat to reveal the nightcap with which he had armed himself during the chill night. This impromptu comic display had the effect of rousing the men, who rushed forward spiritedly under Smith to oust the French from their rocky stronghold: 'Major Smith fell like a true Hero on the summit of the Rock, in the moment of Victory, and we completely succeeded in dislodging them, and with the assistance of a Portuguese Regiment, which arrived at the moment, we dispersed them and drove them across the ravine with great slaughter.'[42]

It is perhaps not surprising that the bulk of Merle's divisions were more easily repulsed for his undernourished soldiers must have reached the Busaco summit in a state of exhaustion. Moreover, their ascent in the time-honoured French formation of the column was inappropriate on this terrain since it provided a large, slow-moving target to the long line of Allied sharpshooters who curved around them on the crest. The rounds of destructive fire that rained down as many as a thousand musket balls at any one time were followed, typically, by a charge with fixed bayonets, which completed the gory operation, sending the French who survived scurrying in confusion back down the escarpment.

Having witnessed such an effective repulse of Merle's columns, Reynier might have been excused had he decided to withdraw and regroup. Unused to such setbacks, however, he impetuously sent in his reserve divisions led by General Foy, who climbed the slope under the same terrible fire, 'receiving all and giving nothing'. Foy was in fact the only Frenchman to scale the ridge on horseback, a distinction that served to attract the bullet that gravely wounded him. The same fate awaited General Simon, whose belated attack at the northern end near the convent of Busaco was repulsed by Craufurd's Light Division, whereupon the battle effectively concluded.

Marbot described the second attack ordered by Reynier against Picton's position as 'cette folie',[43] for clearly it contributed to the substantial French losses on the day of at least 1,000 dead – Wellington put it nearer to 2,000 – and about 4,500 wounded. By contrast, the Commander of the Forces was able to write 'our loss was really trifling', and indeed he had won his *bataille politique* by which he hoped to secure reinforcements from London of men and treasure. He was delighted too with the Portuguese effort in the field, for which so much was owed to Beresford's drilling, and he commented with some glee: 'The battle has had the best effects in inspiring confidence in the Portuguese troops both among our croaking officers and the people of the country. It has likewise removed an impression which began to be very general, that we intended to fight no more, but to retire to our ships.'[44] His only gripe was that Busaco was not the decisive battle he had hoped for, claiming that he would have stopped the French there and then 'had it not been for the blunders of the Portuguese General commanding in the north', who failed to hold the road by which the French eventually turned the Allied position and thereby obliged them to retreat. As far as Masséna was concerned, it was a case of better late than never. Marbot, critical to the last, argued that both commanders were at fault, the one for not taking better care in covering the route that the other neglected to take.

Picton's view was that the Portuguese contribution, recognized with a knighthood for Beresford after the battle, was largely attributable to their good fortune in being under the wing of his division, which he now lavishly extolled in letters:

> The 3 Division was the only one seriously engaged. We repulsed three heavy Columns with the Bayonettes after they gained the Summit of the Hill, and a fourth, which was unable to gain an inch of ground though supported by the incessant fire of 14 Pieces of Cannon. We take to ourselves the Credit of making a Kt of the Bath: for it was chiefly my report of the Portuguese Troops attached to the 3rd Division that gave them the Eclat which has called forth this distinguishing mark of Royal Favor.[45]

If Picton was piqued, it is perhaps because the Third – and its commanding officer – had not been similarly recognized: 'We were certainly rather huddled together in the commendations part of the Commander of the Forces letter', he carped, 'and some part of it is awkwardly enough expressed.' As for the Portuguese, things should be kept in perspective:

> You must not, however, run away with the Idea that these Troops are, in any degree, to be compared with the British. They are certainly gaining ground both in discipline and in confidence, and with the example of our Troops will, I doubt not, do well, but I should be sorry to see them out alone or in any considerable Bodies against the French. Their officers are generally speaking most miserably bred, and wholly destitute of the spirit which ought to actuate a soldier, and without which he can never do anything respectable or Praiseworthy.

Much to Picton's embarrassment, one of his more expansive letters home was excerpted in the London *Courier*. Though he could not be certain, the letter was probably one he had sent to the old Duke of Queensberry. 'This indiscretion on the part of one of my friends', he wrote Marryatt, 'has occasioned me much concern, and has placed me in an Awkward Situation, as if I meant to arrogate to myself the whole merit of that action.'[46] He felt obliged to write to Wellington on 10 November in order to offer a more sober account of events as he saw them:

> In consequence of an extraordinary report which has circulated with great assiduity, it becomes necessary that I should make a written detailed report to your Lordship of the circumstances which preceded and attended the action which took place upon the heights of Busaco on the morning of the 27th September, inasmuch as they relate to myself and the troops I had the honour of commanding on that occasion.[47]

He was anxious to correct a misconception under which Wellington had apparently been labouring, namely that he had himself participated in the assault led by Colonel Wallace against a group of French soldiers ensconced in a rocky crest: 'I can claim no credit whatever in the executive part of that brilliant exploit which your Lordship has so highly and so justly extolled.' He explained that he had been actively engaged elsewhere at the time, repelling Heudelet at the Palheiros pass, and that he was not disposed to deprive Wallace and his comrades of any merit to which they were wholly entitled.

It is likely that further tension had arisen between Picton and the Connaught Rangers, who may have felt they were not receiving proper recognition from the divisional commander in his reports. But the confusion might also have resulted quite innocently from the fact that Picton later led a similar assault.

Indeed, this very similarity reminds one of Wellington's remark that 'the history of a battle is not unlike the history of a ball', it being exceedingly difficult to reconstruct a myriad simultaneous and sequential occurrences in any accurate form.

Picton was obliged to write a separate apology to Colonel Williams for having neglected to mention in his reports the latter's heroic deeds in the ravine of São António do Cántaro. Elsewhere he offered the excuse of being 'constantly under fire' at Busaco, arguing that 'in a complicated business of the kind it is not possible that the general who commands can see everything, and we must be satisfied with the relation of what he imperfectly discerns through the smoak and fire'.[48]

No doubt Picton rued the fact that Wellington had witnessed Wallace's charge, not his own.

V

Once the French had found the way to skirt Busaco there was no point in the Allies waiting hopefully on the heights for Masséna to attack again. Consequently, on 28 September, Wellington withdrew.

'We expected that the Enemy would have renewed his attack on the following day', Picton wrote from near Lisbon some weeks later, 'but it appeared that he had already got a surfeit. He decamped on the 28th at night, and attempted to reach Coimbra by a circuitous route, but Lord Wellington, aware of his Movement, cut in by a more direct road, and reached it before him, which we did early on the 30th.'[49]

The Allies scarcely drew breath amid the decorative turrets and spires of Coimbra, 'it affording no advantageous position', as Picton observed. Instead, together with the majority of its inhabitants, they quit the city within a day, having ransacked it and set it ablaze before the French arrived on 1 October. So swift was the British passage across the River Mondego that, in the resulting confusion, much baggage was left behind. This slowed down Masséna's famished soldiers, who, for three whole days, mercilessly looted King Dom Dinis' seat of learning and thereby lost any opportunity of overhauling the Allied army. Marbot thought this a 'déplorable perte de temps'[50] for in his view they could easily have caught and inflicted heavy losses on the British, whose flight was hindered by the presence of women, children, the elderly and the infirm, many of whom struggled pitifully with their possessions, as Sergeant William Lawrence observed:

I never before or since saw such a wholesale move as this was, for
everyone seemed anxious to carry as many of his effects as he
could find room for. The farther we proceeded the more confused
our retreat appeared, for multitudes were obliged to rest weary
and exhausted by the roadside, and often were found dying or
even dead from their hard exertions, and the road was everywhere
strewn with pieces of all kinds of furniture, which the poor fugitives had vainly attempted to get forward.[51]

Passing a convent, Lawrence saw that 'a great many of the
nuns were crowding the balconies to watch', and one of these
unfortunates fell from a height in her eagerness to escape. A
number of grenadiers were immediately ordered to break open
the doors, whereupon 'the poor women came out as thick as a
flock of sheep', wrote Lawrence, 'and a great many of them soon
passed us bound for Lisbon, being fearful of consequences if
they took any other direction'.[52]

The Allied troops were not above pillaging. At Coimbra
Wellington had been induced to pardon looters from the 45th
Regiment, 'in consequence of the gallantry displayed on the 27'
at Busaco, but his patience was spent by the time they reached
Leiria, where, on 4 October, a British soldier and a Portuguese
soldier were hanged. In an order that probably owed something
to the Connaught Rangers, the Third Division was singled out :
'Major-General Picton is requested not to allow the troops of his
division to enter any town unless necessarily obliged to pass
through it, until further orders.'[53]

These blemishes apart, Wellington was able to express his
general satisfaction with the conduct of the operation. From
Leiria on 4 October he wrote: 'Since the 30th I have continued
the retreat of the army without inconvenience, or loss, or hurry.
This day we all halt, and I shall fall back no farther until I shall
see what the enemy's arrangements are.'[54]

The pace of the withdrawal became more leisurely after
Coimbra. Near Lisbon on 3 November, Picton wrote: 'The whole
business of the Retreat, and everything connected with it, has
been conducted with great judgement and regularity, and the
Enemy have been completely foiled in all their attempts and
expectations, and unless great efforts be made to extricate
Massena, he will be completely disgraced and defeated.'[55]

Though Wellington had entertained hopes of stopping the
French in their tracks at Busaco, his deep-laid plans were for a
withdrawal to Lisbon and the area of Torres Vedras some twenty
miles north of the capital, which had been carefully fortified in
readiness for a French assault. It was heartening for the British
to observe the sturdy Lines behind which they now retreated,

while it must also have been comforting to know that the terrain they left to the French was utterly desolate. The Lines of Torres Vedras were in fact a series of redoubts: the first stretched eastward from the Sizandro river and the town of Torres Vedras, turned south towards Sobral, which was the largest redoubt, and reached the Tagus at Alhandra; the second broadly followed the same route but was five miles or so closer to Lisbon, while the third, the least ambitious, fringed the capital itself.

The Lines of Torres Vedras impressed the newly arrived Sergeant Lawrence:

> We took up our position at some fine breastworks which Lord Wellington had for some time previous ordered to be thrown up by the Portuguese peasantry in case of the retreat of our army. Now we found how much we needed them, for on the 10 October the French came in sight of our strong position, where we had drawn up, determined that they should not proceed one step farther towards Lisbon. The cold and rainy weather having now set in, Lord Wellington had provided as well as possible for the best reception of his troops, who were mostly now in cantonments, while those of Masséna's army were subject to hardships of the worst description, owing to the cold, wet, and above all insufficient food and raiment.[56]

No less aware of the contrasting fortunes experienced by the two armies, Picton wrote on 26 October:

> We have retreated above 200 miles with the greatest regularity and good order, and the Army is now in high spirits, health, and excellent order, with every prospect of being able to defeat the Views of the Enemy at least for this Campaign. The Army of Massena is on a most miserable situation. It has not had bread for more than a fortnight, and its other resources of subsistence begin to fail, and the Disertion is, in consequence, very great. Upon the whole our Prospects are rather flattering. The only resource of Massena now is to throw himself into the Alemtejo, where he may find some resources, and open a Communication with Spain. His communications on all other sides are completely cut off, and all his sick and wounded have fallen into our Hands.[57]

In fact, following their three-day romp in Coimbra, the French had quit the city with virtually all their able-bodied men, leaving 3,000 wounded at the convent of Santa Clara under the protection of half a regiment of *matelots*. Consequently, the city was swiftly retaken on 7 October by Portuguese militia under the command of Colonel Nicholas Trant of whom Wellington later said: 'Trant, poor fellow! a very good officer, but as drunken a dog as ever lived.' The Portuguese were little inclined to treat their prisoners well, Masséna having, as Lawrence put it,

'kindled a spirit of revenge'. Marbot claims that more than a
thousand of his compatriots were massacred at the convent,
while the rest were marched to Oporto, stragglers being slaugh-
tered on the road. Marbot laid the blame for these atrocities
squarely with the English commander: 'aussi le nom de Trent
[sic] est-il devenu infâme, même en Angleterre'.[58]

Behind the Lines of Torres Vedras Picton became ever more
conscious of French difficulties. On 3 November he wrote:

> The situation of Massena is certainly most critical: his Army is
> suffering greatly from want of provisions and if a very consider-
> able Army and gigantic supplies of provisions, stores, etc., do not
> arrive within a couple of Months, he will be under the necessity of
> attempting to escape as well as he can, and in the actual state of
> this country, where every thing in the country he must retire
> through is either destroyed or consumed, he will not be able to
> extricate himself without the complete disorganisation of his
> Army. Under these prospective circumstances Lord Wellington
> would not be excusable in trusting to the Event of a doubtful
> action, for our Force is greatly over-rated.[59]

Picton need not have worried. Wellington had no intention of
risking a battle: 'I have determined to persevere in my cautious
system', wrote the Commander of the Forces on 8 December, by
which time he calculated that his own numbers actually
exceeded those of the French in Portugal. 'Including Spaniards
and Portuguese, and supposing that Masséna has lost 20,000
men *hors de combat* since he entered Portugal, I have now 10,000
men more than he has; that is, I have 60,000 men in their shoes,
and he has 50,000.'[60]

But time was more important than numbers, and there was no
earthly reason to attack an enemy who was daily being starved
to death: 'It is wonderful that they have been able to remain in
the country so long', wrote Wellington, 'and it is scarcely possible that they can remain much longer.' Confident of the
inexorable triumph of his strategy, he added:

> If they go, and when they go stay, their losses will be very great,
> and mine nothing. If they stay, they must continue to lose men
> daily, as they do now; and I don't think that the troops engaged
> in the seige of Cadiz, joined to those now here, could enable them
> to beat me in our position between the Tagus and the sea.[61]

The French would not have been oblivious to an irony in the
situation: they, the powerful aggressors, were effectively cut off
from their lines of supply by the vast areas of devastated land
that they had conquered, while the retreating enemy, besieged

in and around the Portuguese capital, had no such problems since it enjoyed perfect communication by sea with its distant headquarters in London.

Yet if young Sergeant Lawrence could say without undue exaggeration that he and his fellows in the regiment 'lay as comfortably as if we had been living in peaceful times',[62] it was not quite such a quilted experience for some of his senior officers. The 53-year-old Picton, for one, was starting to feel in his joints the rigours of the campaign and the onset of winter:

> My bed has been a bundle of Straw ever since I left Pinhel, and I always sleep in my clothes. My Quarter, at times, have been good, but for these last four weeks I inhabit a miserable Hovel with a rotten Floor, in which there are a dozen Holes, yet I enjoy my Health, and indeed never was better. The Season here at present is as cold as with you in England, and we have no fires or indeed means of having any, the Houses being entirely without Chimneys. *Saevas curr per Alpes ut pueris placeas et Declamatio fias* ('On, on, you madman, drive over your savage Alps, to thrill young schoolboys and supply a theme for speech-day recitations').[63]

Picton's citing of Juvenal, Dr Johnson's favourite poet, with its implied reference to Hannibal's privations, suggests that the prospect of military glory meant rather less to him now than his immediate physical well-being. In mournful mood he concluded: 'I begin to find that I am getting too old for this kind of Labor, and the Ambition which supplies the necessary fire is long since extinguished, or but faintly glows unperceived in the Embers.'

No doubt the reference to fire was deeply felt. But if the divisional commander was prepared to test his level of resistance to hypothermia, others were not, as may be seen from Wellington's order on 'the practice of burning doors and windows', which he wrote at his Cartaxo headquarters on 12 December:

> Within these few days the furniture and doors in the Quinta of the Duque de Lafões, in the neighbourhood of Alcoentrinho and Alcoentre, have been carried off and burnt. The Commander of the Forces is ashamed to acknowledge that the British troops have, in many instances, done more mischief to the country in this manner than had been done by the enemy.[64]

Another discomfort was the rain. Lieutenant Grattan of the Connaught Rangers, while appreciating that his 'situation was, in every respect, better than that of the enemy', lamented the shortage of straw which might have provided a thatch against the continual downpours. He describes a typical scene in an Allied hut at night:

At one end might be seen a couple of officers, with their cloaks thrown about them, snoring on a truss of straw, while over their heads hung their blankets, which served as a kind of inner wall, and for a time stopped the flood that deluged the parts of the hut not so defended. In another corner lay someone else, who, for want of a better, substituted a sheet or an old tablecloth as a temporary defence. Others more stout and convivial, sat up smoking cigars and drinking brandy punch, waiting for the signal to proceed to our alarm-post, a duty which the army performed every morning two hours before day.[65]

Picton returned to the subject of his health in a letter from Torres Vedras on 25 November: 'my eyes become daily more cloudy with respect to reading and writing, though I still discover objects at a distance as well and as particularly as ever. I am turned of 50, and I *nolens volens* must make my mind up to what is reasonably expected at that age.'[66] Two weeks later, from the same location, he continued stoically:

In points of health, I am going on as well as I could wish, but I begin to grow tired of our Employment, which requires youth and ardour to follow with any great degree of spirit. Ambition is the *primum mobile*, a disposition which I am perfectly cured of, and I may very truely say that I am now activated by no other motive than a Sense of public Duty.[67]

While Picton reflected on his declining powers the younger men went about their work shoring up the defensive lines. Rifleman George Simmons, back with his regiment after a spell convalescing in Lisbon, wrote: 'The whole British and Portuguese troops had been daily employed in strengthening the position from the Tagus to our extreme left at Torres Vedras, cutting down trees and forming *abatis* wherever the ground was not bold and precipitous. Our days were now spent in making the position as strong as possible, scarping the ground and throwing up field-fortifications.'[68]

It was a miserably wet October in which Marshal Masséna stood before Torres Vedras, hesitant and finally disinclined to commit his army to an assault. No doubt, like General Marbot, he marvelled at the 'arc immense' of fortifications that the Allies had constructed. What appalled Marbot was that French intelligence appeared not to have communicated to Masséna 'la moindre notion sur ces travaux gigantesques!'.[69] It was 'vraiment incroyable' that, with agents everywhere, they had remained ignorant of so massive a military undertaking, over a year in the making, as the defence of Lisbon.

As the autumn rains fell with tropical force, Picton had time to assess the situation: 'War, when not decided by great Battles, always becomes a matter of calculation', he mused, specifying his own with some accuracy:

> If the French can reinforce Massena, before his stock of provisions is exhausted, and can bring along with them a sufficient supply for themselves and his Army, the decision will again be referred to the Bayonette, if not, he must submit or escape as he can. The Difficulties of reinforcing him, and supplying themselves and his Army with Provisions, is incalculable. The state of the Country, execrableness of the Roads, total deficiency of the Means of Transport in the Country they are to pass through, and the extreme distance of the Communication, altogether form obstacles which no government, except the Monocracy of Napoleon, could even think of surmounting.[70]

Convinced that the Peninsular campaign would prove decisive, Picton expanded with irrefragable logic:

> The Fate of Spain, and in a great measure that of all Europe depends upon the result, and we should spare neither pecuniary nor other means to secure a favorable issue. If Buonaparte fails in this Expedition, it will be the greatest and most sensible reverse he has ever suffered, and it will be extremely difficult to renew the Invasion, as the means of supplying so large an Army as will be required for another attempt must be brought all the way from France by land, as Spain will be able to contribute little if any: besides, his want of success here will conjure him plenty of enemies throughout the Peninsula.

On 14 November Masséna ordered his drenched army to withdraw to Santarém, one of the strongest fortresses in Portugal, where they might find better foraging on the Tagus. The Allies immediately gave chase. Rifleman Simmons detailed the horrors they encountered on the way:

> In the morning we marched through a place, Alenquer, which was entirely sacked by the enemy, the windows and doors torn down and burnt, as well as most of the furniture in each house. They had left numbers of miserable objects behind them in the houses, that were so ill as not to be able to march; these were of course put to death by the Portuguese when we happened to miss finding them out... I examined several encampments that the enemy had occupied and found them in a most filthy state, and in several huts I found dead men who had fallen victims to the inclement weather.

Next day, marching along the Tagus from Vila Nova to Azambuja, Simmons reported:

> We took a number of stragglers who had been suffering sadly from

starvation and disease. The road was found strewn with rags and pieces of Frenchmen's appointments and caps, and occasionally a dead horse, mule, or jackass to enliven the scene. [71]

Many British soldiers, believing that the French had set off for the richer foraging grounds of Spain, were sorely disappointed to see them halt at Santarém. In this military stronghold 'la pénurie était immense',[72] as Marbot confirms, but at least it offered a base from which the French could maraud into the Alemtejo. Once Masséna was securely installed at Santarém, both armies settled down quietly for the winter and even the venturesome Craufurd was persuaded to withdraw behind the lines. Ten kilometres from Santarém at Cartaxo, Wellington contented himself by directing small operations on the enemy's flanks and rear, sniping at the French foragers. 'Masséna is an old fox, and is as cautious as I am', he wrote on 8 December: 'he risks nothing. But it is astonishing what a superiority all our light detachments have assumed over the French.' Clearly ready to hibernate, he concluded: 'although I may not win a battle immediately, I shall not lose one; and you may depend upon it that we are safe, for the winter at all events'.[73]

It was left to the men to idle away the hours as best they could. Officers could escape to the Lisbon fleshpots, at least for the forty-eight hours that Wellington famously said was long enough for any man to spend in bed with the same woman. Generals had the occasional entertainment to break the monotony, like the banquet at Mafra to celebrate General William Carr Beresford's knighthood. As for the men, Grattan remarked how appreciative they were that Wellington, so far from imposing unnecessary drills and duties, was 'a most indulgent commander', letting them do virtually as they pleased. So long as they were ready when the time came, 'with sixty rounds of good ammunition each', it mattered little to the Commander of the Forces how they spent their leisure or even how they dressed. As Grattan observed, scarcely any two officers were dressed alike: 'Some with grey braided coats, others with brown, some again liked blue; while many from choice, or perhaps necessity, stuck to the "old red rag".'[74] Even amongst this motley crew Picton would have been conspicuous, for besides the beacon of his black top hat, which he always insisted on wearing, to save his weakened eyes from streaming, he now found it necessary to carry an umbrella whenever he stepped outdoors.

When not distracting themselves by competing for the most *outré* cut of uniform or hair, the British soldiers engaged in the time-honoured sports of the field, shooting, hunting and, preeminently now, since it encompassed both sport and fashion, horse-racing. 'Jockeys, adorned with all colours, were to be seen on the course', wrote Grattan, 'and the harlequin-like appearance of these equestrians was far from unpleasing. Some of the races were admirably contested, and afforded us as much gratification as those of Epsom and Doncaster do to the visitors of those receptacles of rank and fashion.'

A sad corollary of this exportation of home pursuits to foreign parts was the British soldier's imperviousness to the local culture, which, to the vast majority of Wellington's men, who were unable to speak the Portuguese language, remained a complete mystery. John Bull's proverbial stand-offishness, which would have more serious repercussions in Spain, is only fatuously explained by Grattan: 'There were a few who applied themselves to learning the Portuguese language, but these instances were rare, and seldom attended with much success, and for this reason – that we had no native society sufficiently agreeable to compensate for the purgatorial punishment we were obliged to endure when approaching the Portuguese females.'[75]

As the winter wore on Wellington's mind turned to political events at home. Parliamentary friction, exacerbated by disagreements over the powers as Regent of the Whig-minded Prince of Wales during the illness of his father, George III, might easily have caused a change of heart towards the Peninsular campaign: 'I doubt whether this government (I mean the existing administration in England) have the power, or the inclination, or the nerves to do all that might be done to carry the contest on as it might be', Wellington wrote on 11 January 1811.[76] He remained confident of his military strategy: 'I am tolerably certain of the result; and I am equally certain that if Buonaparte cannot root us out of this country, he must alter his system in Europe, and must give us such a peace as we ought to accept.' But he lamented the fact that his powers, in sharp contrast to those of his monocratic foe, were severely circumscribed:

> I am commander of the British army without any of the patronage or power that an officer in that situation has always had. I have not authority to give a shilling, or a stand of arms, or a round of musket ammunition to any body. I don't think that government ought in fairness to make a man what they call commander of the forces, and place him in the perilous situation in which they have got me, without giving him in specific terms either power or confidence, or without being certain of having a majority in Parliament to support him in case of accidents.

In these lean months the only cause for rejoicing was the

stream of French deserters, who provided ample evidence of the privation at Santarém. Picton had little else to report in his letter from Figueiros on 8 February:

> We are quietly in winter quarters, without any kind of movement on either side. As yet the probabilities in favor of my conclusions appear on the increase, and their difficulties in procuring a wretched subsistence for their Troops, by all accounts, are daily augmenting and the three worst months, Feby., March and April, and I may add May, still remain to be laboured through a perfectly exhausted country. The Deserters and Prisoners are all in a wretched miserable plight, to all appearances half-starved, living mainly on what they can casually pick up on the licensed marauding Parties. Their Sick, in consequence, is immense; the last Prisoner I examined said that the Company in which he was began the campaign with 115 men, had not lost a single man in action, and at that time was only 43: at that rate the loss must be incalculable.[77]

On 4 March two more deserters reported that 'the enemy was burning everything that they cannot remove', a clear signal of Masséna's intentions. At 2.00 a.m. on 6 March 1811 the French withdrew and, as Simmons recalled, the Light Division quickly assembled and entered the city at daybreak to find its 'few miserable inhabitants, moving skeletons' and 'many streets quite impassable with filth and rubbish, with an occasional man, mule, or donkey rotting and corrupting and filling the air with pestilential vapours'.[78]

VI

The scenes witnessed in the wake of the French retreat were so chilling as to suggest that those who perpetrated them must have been reduced by deprivation to a subhuman state of frenzy.

George Simmons found Santarém 'dreadfully sacked', and, pursuing the French through 'several towns on fire', likened those he met on his way to the living dead: 'The unfortunate inhabitants have the appearance of people who have been kicked out of their graves and reanimated.'

Private Wheeler entered Leiria, forty miles north, to find it 'completely gutted, doors, windows, shutters, and in many places the floors were ripped to pieces for fuel, furniture broken to pieces and thrown into the streets; the churches did not escape, the graves were opened, and the dead dragged out'. In one church, on the steps of the grand altar, sprawled the body of a priest who had been stabbed to death; nearby lay a woman 'covered with blood, having received from the French soldiers eleven bayonet wounds'.[79]

At Porto de Mós Sergeant Donaldson stumbled into a chapel that was still on fire and beheld a macabre scene:

> As it was quite dark I caught up a burning piece of wood to inspect the place –but what was my horror, when I entered and found the half-consumed skeletons of human beings on every side; some lying, others kneeling, and more of them standing upright against the walls! Of those who had sunk on the floor nothing remained but the bones: while the others, who were in a kneeling or standing posture, were only partially consumed; and the agonized expression of their scorched and blackened features, was awful beyond description.[80]

Wellington divided his forces in three to pursue the French, who, according to Colonel Jenkinson of the Royal Artillery, 'ran the whole way to Pombal'. In the middle group was the Third Division, which marched on the main Coimbra road and, passing through Pombal, also put to the torch, caught up with the French rearguard under Marshal Ney in a strong position near Redinha. Picton reported:

> No time was lost in commencing the pursuit. The Third Division marched on the latter day [6 March], and after five severe marches over rocky almost impracticable mountains, came up with the Enemy's Rear guard, commanded by Marshal Soult [=Ney], near Pombal on the 11th. A general attack was ordered on that Enemy, but some of the Divisions, which were to have cooperated in the enterprise, not coming up in time, owing to the extreme badness of the Roads, it was postponed until the following morning. The Enemy, however, disappointed us, and profited of the obscurity of the night to withdraw to a more commanding situation. We continued our pursuit, and after a march of three Hours came up with him strongly posted, with a show of considerable Force, and a disposition to stand fast.[81]

Jenkinson described how Picton's men moved upon the enemy's left flank and appeared with a suddenness that shook the French: 'their consternation when they discovered the Third Division was very great, and increased by the advance of the whole army in a line, which was formed as if by magic'. Picton's account is even more circumstantial:

> Every point was carried with little resistance, but the ground being favourable to Defensive Operations they withdrew to a commanding woody Hill, where they showed a good countenance, and assembled their forces as if resolved to stand an attack: but the 3rd Division being detached over a rocky mountain to turn their left,

and appearing suddenly in their Rear, they abandoned it with considerable precipitation, and retreated upon the town of Condeixa, where they established themselves behind an extremely deep, rocky river.

Masséna, having originally intended to take his troops to the fertile area south of Oporto, now reluctantly decided to pass by Coimbra and head east, for Trant's Portuguese troops had blown the bridge over the swollen Mondego rendering it impassable. Ceding the burning town of Condeixa to the Allies during the night, Masséna moved off hurriedly towards Mirando do Corvo, which stood eight miles south of Coimbra at the head of a strong pass above the Mondego valley. Again Wellington trusted to the mobility and verve of the Third Division to dislodge the French and he dispatched Picton, as the latter recounted, in a wide outflanking movement that struck like a right hook at the enemy's ribs:

> On the 13th at 5 o'clock in the morning, this Division was again Detached over Goat Paths and Precipices, to make a Demonstration on the Rear of the Enemy's left, and if possible to Pass the River in their Rear. After many hours laborious marching over shelving rocks, and through difficult ravines, where we, with difficulty, crawled on one by one, we at length suddenly appeared considerably in their Rear, which again made them Decamp, and we succeeded passing the River at a Ford and Defile where twenty men might easily have stopped the Whole Division, and we Bivouaced within half a mile of the Enemy's rear Posts. On the 14 the Light and Third Divisions pushed forward at a very early Hour, and we engaged in a continual series of skirmishes until near 5 o'clock in the Evening. This Day afforded a complete military lesson in this kind of warfare.

It was clearly a novel experience to have the French on the run, even if, as chance dictated, the rugged terrain conspired variously with morning fog, evening darkness or plain gun smoke to allow the enemy an unlikely escape from a number of tight corners. Picton, keen to pit his wits against the best of the French generals, thrived on the independence this kind of skirmishing provided. He was strangely mistaken, however, about the identity of his adversary, for Marshal Soult was then at Badajoz, which, on 10 March, he had snatched from Spanish hands, much to the disgust of Wellington, who had ordered General Beresford south to invest Badajoz and keep an eye on Soult. That it was Ney, not Soult, who opposed Picton in these encounters hardly detracts from the latter's achievement, nor would it have diminished the pride he so evidently took in it:

Marshal Soult [=Ney] commanded the Enemy's Rear guard, and displayed great ability in all his Dispositions, and being wholly left to myself on this occasion, during the whole of the Day, I accompanied all his movements, and by successively taking up positions in the Rear of his left, he was obliged to fall back continually before the Light division which closely harrassed him and pressed up his Rear during the whole of the Day.[82]

From 15 to 18 March the French crossed, in turn, the rivers Ceira and Alva, blowing up bridges as they went and deploying strong rearguards to delay the Allies while their main body headed east towards Guarda and the Spanish border. The French retreat, 'une des opérations les plus difficiles de la guerre', was, in Marbot's view, conducted by the French 'd'une manière régulière et concentrée'.[83] Picton gives a close account of his own Division's movements during these three eventful days:

The Enemy again profited of the night, and of a very thick Fogg on the morning of the 15th, to withdraw to a strong position, covered by the river Ceira, leaving a very strong rear guard to cover the Bridge of France de Raine [Foz de Arouce] and the approaches on the main road. We did not march until near Eleven o'Clock owing to the obscurity of the morning, and it was near Two o'Clock before we ascertained the situation of the Enemy's Rear Guard. It was full four before the necessary dispositions could be made for the attack, which was again allotted to the Light and 3rd Divisions. After a severe contest of about two Hours, they were completely dispersed, and had not darkness unfortunately intervened, the whole of them must have been sacrificed. On the 16th, the Enemy having blown up the Bridge, made a great display of their Force on the Commanding Hills behind the River, and the whole day was employed in Reconnoitring and making the necessary dispositions, and at Day break of the morning of the 17th, the 3rd Division was Detached by a forced March to possess itself of a passage over the River, and turn the Enemy's left, whilst the other Divisions of the Army menaced their Front. Suspecting our movements, they Decamped about the same time, and by a forced march passed the River Alba at the Ponte de Murcella, and took up a strong position on its right bank, which could not possibly be forced by an attack in Front. On the 18th the 3rd Division was again Detached to make a lateral movement and Demonstration on the Enemy's rear, which completely succeeded, as the Enemy, on discovering it, immediately abandoned the Position, and fell back with great precipitation, which left open the River to the Divisions which followed the main road.[84]

The Allies not only had to contend with the enemy's impeccable tactics in retreat but were also slowed down by the need to ensure a continued supply of their own provisions. It was the turn of the French to leave nothing in their wake but devastation: impedimenta, including ammunition ditched to lighten their load, had first been made unusable, while pack animals had been hamstrung. This last practice horrified British soldiers. William Grattan described the chaos that confronted him on 15 March, when the road was 'covered with a number of horses, mules, and asses, all maimed; but the most disgusting sight was about fifty of the asses floundering in the mud, some with their throats half cut, while others were barbarously houghed'.[85] Sergeant Donaldson vividly recalled the scene at Miranda do Corvo where the road was littered with French and Portuguese dead:

> One part of it was covered with asses, which the French had hamstrung before they left them. It was pitiable enough to see the poor creatures in this state; yet there was something ludicrous in the position the animals had taken, when thus cruelly lamed; they were sitting in a groupe upon their hinder end, staring in each other's faces, seemingly in deep consultation on some important subject, and looking as grave and dull as many an assembly of their biped brethren at home.[86]

The French found the Mondego valley '[une] des plus fertiles', in Marbot's words, 'et l'armée y vécut dans l'abondance'.[87] For the Allies, the problem of supplies now grew steadily more acute, as Picton explained:

> Our Army depended wholly for its subsistence on what we were able to Transport from Lisbon on the backs of mules, which every day's march, indeed, every mile in advance rendered more difficult. The Enemy, on the contrary, retreating through an untouched country, met with greater facilities in proportion as they fell back: we were, in consequence, under the necessity of halting to wait for our resources, which could not possibly keep pace with the rapidity of our continual movements. Under such circumstances, the Enemy easily gained ground, and increased his distance, so that we did not again get into his neighbourhood until the 20th, when he occupied the Strong Position of Guarda.[88]

Masséna's face-saving plan at this juncture was to link with Soult at Badajoz, re-enter Portugal by the Alemtejo and march on Lisbon. Ney, 'qui brûlait du désir de recouvrer son indépendance',[89] opposed this, arguing that the men, who had not had bread for six months, were in no condition to engage in a new campaign. The disagreement ended with Ney departing for Almeida, whence he eventually proceeded to Paris. For his part,

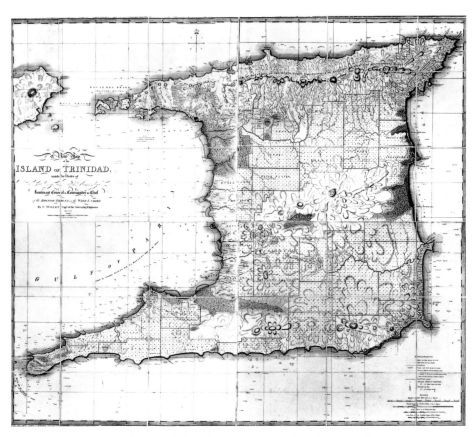

A New Map of the Island of Trinidad, made by Order of His Excellency Sir Ralph Abercromby Lieutenant General & Commander in Chief of the British Forces in the West Indies, by F. Mallet, Captain of the Surveying Engineers, 1797
(W. Fadden, London, 1802).

Governor Picton's Torture upon Louisa Calderon (B. Crosby, London, 1 March 1806).

Edward Law, Lord Ellenborough.

Being Nervous and Cross-Examined by Mr Garrow, T. Rowlandson, 1806 (British Museum cartoon 10841).

View of the Hustings in Covent Garden – Vide. The Westminster Election, Nov.ʳ 1806,
J. Gillray (British Museum cartoon 10996).

Map of the Island of Walcheren with the Foftifications (sic) *&C.* (J. Stratford, London, 10 February 1810).

Het Bombardement Van Vlissingen 1809., I. H. Koekkock. (The Bombardment of Flushing.)

Sir Thomas Picton.

The Duke of Wellington.

Genl. Sir Thomas Picton Storming the Moorish Castle of Badajos, March 31.st 1812.,
aquatint by T. Sutherland (J. Jenkins, London, 1 April 1815).

Death of Sir Thomas Picton., aquatint by M. Dubourg (Edward Orme, London, 1 January 1817).

Masséna was no doubt glad to be rid of so rebellious a general, especially since Ney's reluctance to communicate with him had nearly resulted in his capture by the Allies a few days earlier at Condeixa, where, amazingly, oblivious to the enemy's proximity, the French Commander had chosen to dine out under some trees with his cherished companion.

Guarda, with its fortress-like, granite grey cathedral, is the highest town in Portugal, and very likely its most inhospitable, having a reputation of being 'fria, feia, forte e farta' ('cold, ugly, strong and self-sufficient'). It was 'a most stupendous Post', in Picton's words, 'covered by a Rapid, Rocky River, the access to which, from the nature of its Banks, is every where difficult, and except in a very few places actually impracticable'.[90] Once again the Third Division, with the 6th and Light Divisions, was given the responsibility of taking the town. Early in the morning of 29 March, they made good progress up the steep slopes, as Picton recalled:

> The 3rd Division passed the River Mondego at an unguarded Ford before Day light, and, by a rapid March, fortunately got possession of the Commanding Ridge, on which the City of Guarda is situated, and suddenly appeared within 400 yards of Massena's Head Quarters, before he had any notice of its approach. The Great General lost his head on the occasion, and instead of immediately attacking the Division, which, though strongly posted, he might have overwhelmed with numbers, he immediately withdrew, with precipitation, the Bodies opposed to the other Columns, and commenced his Retreat, filing off about 20,000 within Cannon shot of the Division. If the whole of our Army had been up so as to take advantage of the favorable conjunction which presented itself, I have no doubt but we should have annihilated his whole Corps. They marched off, followed by some squadrons of Cavalry for a few miles, and retreated under cover of the night.

Donaldson recalled that the soldiers were 'much fatigued in ascending' to Guarda and 'entered the town with empty stomachs'.[91] A pleasant surprise awaited them, however: 'the French had left their dinners for us ready cooked, as in their haste they had left them on the fire in the different houses where they had been lodged'. One French soldier had a keen sense of humour: on a table where dinner had evidently been interrupted they found 'a mule's head in the centre, with a label in its mouth on which was written *Pour Mons. Jean Bull*'.

Not all the scenes in Guarda were so amusing. Simmons found that the ancient cathedral, saved from burning by the Third Division, had done duty as a stable, its organ 'hacked about in the most wanton manner'.[92] This no doubt was for firewood, as

Guarda was still very cold in March. In addition, both Simmons and Donaldson testified to horrific scenes of rape and pillage in the neighbourhood, while Picton remarked: 'The atrocities of the French are scarcely conceivable. On various occasions we have found the women who have been ravished by them, shut up in Houses which they had set fire to, and from which they were rescued by our soldiers extinguishing the Flames.'[93]

From Guarda Masséna's army beat a hasty retreat, taking up a position twenty miles south-east at Sabugal on the Côa. 'The Want of Provisions would not allow of our following them until the 2nd of April', Picton recalled. 'On the 3rd we found them strongly posted behind the River Coa and determined to Dispute our further Advance'. Again the Third and Light divisions were asked to carry the attack to the enemy:

> The Light Division was to make its attack on the right, where the country became more level, and the Banks of the River of easier access. The point where the Third Division was to Penetrate was much more difficult, both with respect to the Ford itself, as well as the means of approaching it. The Light Division easily effected its Passage, and engaged the Enemy, while the 3rd was perserveringly struggling with the local difficulties and untoward nature of the Ground. However, after much labor at length succeeded, and came up to the assistance of the Light Division, at a moment when it was nearly overwhelmed by numbers.[94]

Rifleman Simmons found that the Côa was deep – up to his armpits – and that once the Light Division crossed, they were given a torrid time by the French on the steep brushwood slopes opposite. A little later, still under heavy fire, Donaldson crossed with the Third Division and climbed the hill in an attempt to bring relief to the riflemen. When the two forces joined they formed a line at the order of their commander: 'General Picton rode up in front of us, with his stick over his shoulder, exposed to the heavy fire of the enemy, as composedly as if he had been in perfect safety. "Steady, my lads, steady", said he, "don't throw away your fire until I give you the word of command".' The thunderous volley, when it came, caused the French to take to their heels instantly. Moments later, as Donaldson wrote:

> a severe rain storm commenced and darkened the air so much that we lost sight of them completely: when the sky cleared up, they were discovered, about a mile forward, scrambling their way over hedge and ditch without any regularity. The ground which they had occupied, now lay before us, strewed with the dead and wounded: and the Portuguese regiment belonging to our division were busy stripping them naked.[95]

From Sabugal the French escaped as best they could into Spain, as Picton wrote on 11 April:

> they have since retreated so incessantly night and day that we have scarcely got sight of them since. They are completely out of Portugal on the other side of the River Agueda, continuing their flight towards Salamanca, perfectly dispersed and disorganised. If we could have accompanied ourselves with Provisions sufficient to enable us to march everyday, scarcely a man of Massena's army would have reached the Frontiers of Spain.[96]

But the Allies had needed to pause to await supplies, tend their wounded and, on the night after the Sabugal engagement, cope with another wretched downpour. So wet was the night, as Donaldson remembered it, that fires had to be kindled in the hollow trunks of chestnut trees, which burned up high as the branches, creating an eerie spectacle: 'The flickering lurid glare which these fiery columns threw on the naked bodies of the slain, the indistinct objects in the background, and the groupes of soldiers which flitted around them, presented a scene, at once sublime and picturesque: it looked like the midnight orgies of some supernatural beings.'[97]

For three days the Light and Third divisions remained nearby at Quadrazais, Vale de Espinho and Alfaiates, but marching north they crossed the frontier at Vilar Formoso to Fuentes de Oñoro just within Spain by 8 April. Cradled in a shallow ravine, Fuentes struck Donaldson as 'beautiful and romantic', its houses being much superior to those of Portugal, while nearby stood a large wood in which 'the voice of the cuckoo never was mute'. The Allies massed at the border with the twofold purpose of blockading the fortress of Almeida, ten miles to the north, which General Brennier still held for the French, and of surveying Ciudad Rodrigo, fifteen miles into Spain. Wellington calculated that Masséna would need time to recover after his ignominious exit from Portugal, where, by Marbot's estimate, he had lost at least 10,000 men as well as quantities of horse and guns. He consequently decided that his most positive plan for the moment would be to march a detachment south to join Beresford in the siege of Badajoz, leaving General Spencer to command the army remaining at Fuentes, and General Campbell to conduct the siege of Almeida.

Wellington departed, admonishing those he left behind in his usual fashion: they were not to commit any depredations for fear of their lives; those not engaged in the siege of Almeida must take the trouble to exercise themselves daily; certain regiments were to smarten themselves up, notably the 3rd and 15th

Portuguese, who were in such a 'shameful state' they risked
being turned out of the army as 'unfit to do duty with the other
troops'.[98] He left on 15 April and within three days had reached
Nisa, 100 miles south on the other side of the Tagus. However,
receiving news from a worried Spencer that Masséna was
regrouping much sooner than expected, he at once changed his
plans, returning post-haste to Fuentes de Oñoro. 'And it was
lucky that I came when I did', he wrote some weeks later. 'The
French collected every vagabond they had in Castille in order to
raise the blockade of Almeida, and we had two very severe but
partial actions with them on the 3rd and 5th, in which we gave
them a terrible beating.'[99]

The two-day Battle of Fuentes de Oñoro was a triumph for
Wellington and his Allied force of 36,000 men, at least 10,000
fewer than the French. Each of the two actions had its own character: the one on 3 May centred on Fuentes, while 5 May saw a
more open conflict as the armies confronted each other on the
border between Fuentes and Vilar Formoso.

On 3 May the French approached from Ciudad Rodrigo in
three columns led by generals Loison, Junot and Reynier. The
Allies faced them, holding a seven-mile line that extended
southwards from the ruined fortress of Concepção near Almeida
down to Fuentes de Oñoro, west of which Wellington deployed
the bulk of his force, including the Third and Light Divisions.
Donaldson recalled that, on the plain outside Fuentes, the
morning was 'uncommonly beautiful, the sun shone bright and
warm', and that when the French advanced massively in the
afternoon, 'their arms glittering in the sun, bugles blowing,
drums beating', the scene realized all he had ever imagined of
the pomp of war.[100] It happened that there were German hussars
amongst the cavalry on both sides and this occasioned an
exchange of 'insulting language, as well as shot'. Confusion
resulted too from the fact that the French Hanoverians wore red
and were mistakenly fired on by their comrades. The French
advanced on the village of Fuentes in such numbers that, while
parts of the village were taken and retaken several times, the
Allies were finally 'obliged to give way, and were fairly forced to
a rising ground on the other side, where stood a small chapel'.
Marbot confirmed that 'il devint impossible de les déloger de
cette importante position' and night came with the French
having failed to secure a definitive capture of Fuentes.[101]

The next day, 4 May, saw no serious engagements but was dedi-
cated to reconnaissance and to bringing in the dead and
wounded, a practice that often involved the British and French
assisting one another in the most cordial manner. Masséna

deduced from intelligence reports that the Allied line was weakest at its southern tip, which was protected only by Spanish *guerrilleros*. Consequently, he determined to deploy the bulk of his army in that quarter, making the customary feints elsewhere. They would cross the Duas Casas river where its sides were less steep and they would drive the Allies back towards the Côa, punishing them severely when they tried to escape via the sole bridge at Castelho Bom. An alert Wellington had detached the 7th Division under General Houston to the high point of Poço Velho two miles south of Fuentes to guard against just such an eventuality.

The fighting on 5 May proved to be confused and uncoordinated. The enemy cavalry outnumbered its Allied counterpart and could not be held in check everywhere in the open country. For their part, the Allies were superior in artillery, and in the woodland and rugged river sections they repulsed all attacks by the French infantry. As Donaldson reported, the turning point came shortly after midday, when Masséna ordered the Imperial Guard to occupy Fuentes and 'brought down such an overwhelming force, that our troops were fairly beat out of the town'. It was then, as he recalled, that Wellington ordered the Connaught Rangers, who had been surveying the action from a vantage point above the village, to go in: 'the 88th regiment, led on by the heroic Colonel Mackinnon, charged them furiously, and drove them back through the village with great slaughter'.

Grattan, who was with Mackinnon, recalled: 'The battalion advanced with fixed bayonets in column of sections, left in front, in double quick time, their firelocks at the trail. The enemy were not idle spectators of this movement; they witnessed its commencement, and the regularity with which the advance was conducted made them fearful of the result'. The Connaughts quickly gained ascendancy and 'drove the enemy through the different streets at the point of the bayonet, and at length forced them into the river that separated the two armies'.[102]

When they returned from this charge General Picton exclaimed:

'Well done the brave 88th!'

Some of the Connaught Rangers, who had been stung by his earlier reproaches and resented the aspersions cast on their homeland, cried out:

'Are we the greatest blackguards in the army now?'

'No, no', replied Picton, with a broad smile, 'you are brave and gallant soldiers. This day has redeemed your character.'[103]

He could be well satisfied with his Third Division. They had played the key role in hounding the French out of Portugal, or as he himself put it: 'The 3rd Division was principally engaged in every action which took place during the whole course of the Retreat; indeed, with little exception, the whole was devoted between the 3rd and Light Divisions.'[104] Moreover, at the critical moment, when Masséna's counter-attack seemed likely to succeed, the 88th had entered the fray and handed the French Commander an unaccustomed defeat. Soon the great Marshal Masséna would be recalled to France on grounds of ill health, to be succeeded by Auguste Marmont, Duc de Ragusa, at age thirty-six, the youngest of the marshals. The Third Division, in recognition of its exploits, henceforth would be known as 'the Fighting Division'.

A major disappointment was in store for Wellington. Five days after the Battle of Fuentes de Oñoro, which effectively prevented the French from relieving Almeida, General Brennier succeeded against all odds in breaking out of the fortress and guiding his men under cover of darkness through the Allied blockade to Ciudad Rodrigo. Wellington wrote to William Wellesley-Pole:

> I was then quite sure of having Almeida; but I begin to be of the opinion that there is nothing on earth so stupid as a gallant officer. They had about 13,000 men to watch 1400; and in the night of the 10th, to the infinite surprise of the enemy, they allowed the garrison to slip through their fingers and to escape, after blowing up some of the works of the place! They were all sleeping in their spurs even; but the French got off.[105]

Nonetheless, Wellington had accomplished his mission in Portugal. The French had been expelled. It was now time to focus on Spain.

FIVE

SPAIN

With the Cold Iron

I

The keys to Spain were the border towns of Ciudad Rodrigo and Badajoz, two formidable fortresses, to the north and south respectively, both of which would have to be taken before Wellington could entertain thoughts of action in the interior. General Beresford had been prosecuting the siege of Badajoz for some weeks, hampered by a lack of suitably heavy guns, which remained for safekeeping in storage ships on the Tagus, and by a shortage of basic siege materials – picks, shovels, sandbags, gabions, fascines and the like. Toiling in his preparations against the four outpost forts that protected the Extremaduran citadel, Beresford was apprehensive that at any moment Soult might turn his attention from Cadiz, where the patriotic Cortes had been charting the future of free Spain since 24 September. On 14 May 1811 Wellington dispatched his Third and Eighth divisions from Fuentes de Oñoro to bolster the investment of Badajoz.

The Third Division would have been glad to quit Fuentes which, as Donaldson wrote, was now 'sadly altered' by the recent conflict: 'there still remained some bodies lying about swelled and blackened by the heat of the sun, and the streets were dyed with the blood of the combatants'.[1] Vilar Formoso was no better, having become a 'receptacle for the wounded', according to Sergeant Grattan who watched the surgeons, 'stripped to their shirts and bloody', go about their grisly duties with saws and red-hot irons: 'a number of doors, placed on barrels, served as temporary tables, and on these lay the different subjects upon whom the surgeons were operating; to the right and left were arms and legs, flung here and there, without distinction'.[2] The shallow pits that eventually received these useless limbs would, in turn, attract flocks of vultures that hovered unnervingly in the blue sky. Grattan concluded: 'each hour made our position more disagreeable, from the increasing putridity of the dead men and horses with which the plain was covered'.

Picton's men were soon presented with fresh horrors as they headed south in forced marches along the Portuguese side of the border. Having crossed the Côa near Sabugal, where six weeks earlier the French had showered them with bullets, Rifleman Simmons came upon a grisly memento: 'We bivouacked in a wood of chestnut-trees, where several of our brave fellows had been buried, and whose bones had been dug up by wolves and were strewn above their graves.'[3] Simmons searched for the cadaver of an erstwhile friend, the young Adjutant McDiarmid, hoping he might have escaped the abomination: 'I found his skull lying at some distance; the hair was still in patches on it. There was no mistaking it; his hair, when alive, was auburn and very curly. His bones were partly eaten and thrown about. I collected the straggling relics and replaced them and covered them over as the last tribute I could pay him.'

They arrived at Campo Maior, near Elvas, on 23 May, having covered, by Picton's reckoning, '180 miles in nine days'. This was a week too late, however, for 'a most sanguinary action had been fought before our arrival, on the 16th, between Lt. Genl. Beresford and the Corps under Marshals Soult and Mortier'.[4] When he heard that Soult was coming up behind him, Beresford had raised the siege on the 15th and taken up a position, which Wellington had chosen for him, at Albuera, fourteen miles south-east of Badajoz. Picton summed up:

> It was the most bloody affair that, probably, ever took place, and the one in which there was most individual gallantry displayed. More than half the British troops engaged were either killed or wounded. The affair was long undecided and even unfavourable to us, but the invincible spirit of the Troops at length wearied the Enemy out, and they gave way at a time too when we were uncapable of any further exertion. Such of the Portuguese as were engaged performed well, and the Spaniards showed more nerve than on any former occasion.

Beresford's despatch to Wellington from Albuera on 20 May was heavy with remorse for the number of Allied fatalities, which he put at 4,500, the French losses being significantly greater. Clearly shaken, he admitted that his decision to stand and face Soult had been 'very unwise', that 'the battle ought not to have been risked', because, as he wrote, 'I certainly risked all that you had been so long in gaining'.[5] Wellington, who visited the scene of the battle on 21 May, did not chastise Beresford for the tactical errors that many attributed to him, or for his vain attempt to retreat from the field which was only thwarted by his troops' refusal to comply. Instead, the Commander of the Forces was anxious to stress that the battle had been a victory and, in sharp contrast to Picton's analysis, he put the blame for the massive fatalities elsewhere: 'Beresford's was a terrible fight; but he would have succeeded without much loss, if the Spaniards could have moved: nevertheless there they stood like stocks, both parties firing upon them, and it was necessary to apply the British everywhere.'[6] Within a week, on 27 May, in an extraordinary session, the Cortes at Cadiz voted to confer on Beresford the title of Marqués de Albuera. On 17 June, however, following adverse remarks about the conduct of the Spanish troops at Albuera, their official expression of gratitude was reduced to that of awarding Beresford the rank of Captain-General.

In this the bloodiest and least conclusive battle of the war the laurels of victory went to Beresford if only because Soult finally withdrew to Sevilla, thereby allowing the Allies to recommence the siege, their sole object in doing battle. 'We again undertook the Siege of Badajos', wrote Picton on 22 June, 'with very incompetent means of Artillery and amunition, in consequence of which we were under the necessity of converting it into a Blockade, which we were obliged to relinquish on the 17th instant in consequence of the approach of a fresh French Army.'[7] The spareness of Picton's comment on this second phase of the siege is indicative of the small esteem in which he, like most Allied soldiers, held siege warfare as compared to the glories of the well-fought field. No doubt it also reflects his frustration at what was an ignominiously abortive operation.

At Badajoz Wellington's plan was to breach the walls of the Alcazaba, or main castle, and its outpost fort, San Cristóbal, 500 yards across the Guadiana river. The dangers involved in preparatory work – digging trenches and throwing up batteries within range of crack shots on the enemy battlements – were soon clear to Private William Wheeler, newly arrived in Spain with the 51st Foot. As Wheeler noted, though the work was done at night, the cover of darkness was, at best, intermittent:

> As soon as the Enemy hear the pickaxe they give us light by throwing out a quantity of fireballs. This would be very accommodating on their part if they did not open as many guns as they can bring to bear on the place. These balls give a great light around the place where they fall [which] enables them to point their guns with greater precision.

By day the men kept to their trenches, 'almost suffocated for

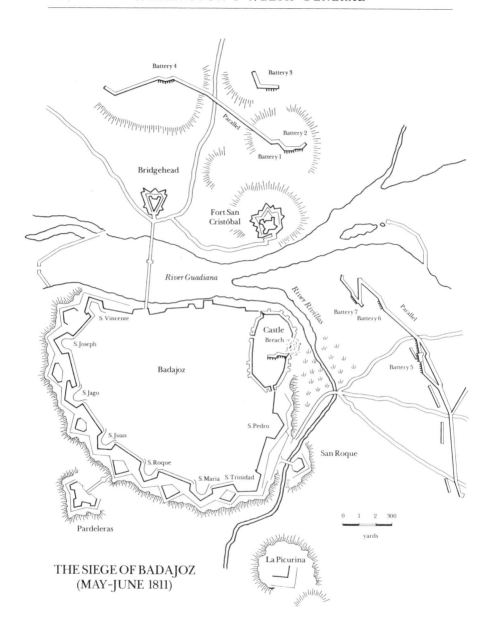

THE SIEGE OF BADAJOZ
(MAY–JUNE 1811)

the want of air and nearly baked by the sun, parching with thirst, with a beautiful river close to us but might as well be an hundred miles off – for if any one only indulged the eye with a peep, bang goes half a dozen muskets at his head.'[8]

Progress was delayed by the French having cleared most of the topsoil around San Cristóbal during the Allies' absence at Albuera, leaving them solid rock in which to dig. Firing finally commenced on the morning of 3 June when it became apparent that the antiquated brass guns that had been obtained at Elvas were unable to provide a sustained pounding: overheating occurred in the bore of smaller pieces, while 24-pounders drooped at the muzzle unless the rate of fire was greatly reduced. By firing steadily at a fixed point, even with this inferior ordnance, it was possible to make an impression, over time, on the city's defences. However, the resulting breach in the masonry revealed a wall of hard clay beneath. In comparison, San Cristóbal was considered an easy target by engineer Lieutenant Forster, and it was decided to launch an assault at midnight on 6 June. This was to be spearheaded by a 'forlorn hope' of twenty-five volunteers, led by Ensign Dyas of the 51st, and supported by two companies bearing twelve-foot ladders. Among this force of 180 men was Private Wheeler:

> We advanced up the glacies close to the walls. Not a head was to be seen above the walls, and we began to think the enemy had retired into the town. We entered the trench and fixed our ladders, when sudden as a flash of lightning the whole place was in a blaze. It will be impossible for me to describe to you what followed. You can better conceive it by figuring to your minds eye a deep trench or ditch filled with men who are endeavouring to mount the wall by means of ladders. The top of this wall crowded with men hurling down shells and hand granades on the heads of them below, and when all these are expended they have each six or seven loaded firelocks which they discharge into the trench as quick as possible. Add to this some half dozen cannon scouring the trench with grape. This will immediately present to your imagination the following frightful picture. Heaps of brave fellows killed and wounded, ladders shot to pieces, and falling together with the men down upon the living and the dead. Then ever and anon would fall upon us the body of some brave Frenchman whose zeal had led him to the edge of the wall in its defence, and had been killed by their own missiles or by the fire of our covering party.[9]

What must have jolted Wheeler was the manner in which this gallant assault culminated:

> In the midst of all these difficulties, great as they were, we should

have taken the Fort but for an unforseen accident that could not
be remedied – it was the ladders were too short. Several men who
had gained the top of the ladders could not reach the top of the
wall with their firelocks. As soon as this was discovered all hopes
of gaining possession was abandoned, and the order was given to
retire.

The ladders were too short. It might be thought that Wheeler is
generous to a fault in describing this oversight an 'accident'.
Volunteers would surely be forgiven for assuming that every care
would be been taken by those who planned the action in calculat-
ing the length of ladder required. The bloody shambles at San
Cristóbal, in which more than 100 men were killed, was the work
of heroes and fools alike, but the latter would have made the
greater impression on the French when they saw the dwarf
ladders that the Allies left standing against the walls.

The fiasco was not complete. Once the dead and wounded
had been brought in on the 7 June, Wellington, still concerned
that Soult might return with reinforcements, ordered the
bombardment of the satellite fort to continue for two more days.
This was done to such good effect that a second assault was
launched on the 9th as soon as it was dark enough for the men
to approach undetected. The undaunted Dyas, who had mirac-
ulously survived the first assault, again led 'the forlorn hope',
now bearing six ladders up the considerably enlarged breach,
while a second party with ten ladders simultaneously attempted
to scale the front face of the fort. Other troops were detailed to
keep shooting at the parapets of the castle to deter sniper fire.
Wheeler continued his account:

> This second attempt was attended with the same ill success as the
> first. It is true we had profited by the discovery of the ladder being
> too short, but the old fox inside was too deep for us. He had
> caused all the rubbish to be cleared out of the trench. This again
> placed us just in the same predicament, our ladders were again
> too short and if possible we received a warmer reception than
> before. The ladder I was on was broken and down we all came
> together, men, firelocks, bayonetts, in one confused mass, and
> with us a portion of the wall.

The injured Wheeler only escaped with his life by resorting
to a subterfuge. He drenched his side in the blood of a
comrade who lay dead nearby, so that the French patrol that
found him thought his hip was shattered and, after relieving
him of his boots, left him for dead in the rubble where he lay.
Later, in the darkness between shots, he inched his way down
the debris until by morning he had reached the plain below

the fort. There he chanced his luck and, barefoot, ran as best he could through a hail of musket fire to the safety of a battery. Another 140 men, two-thirds of the attacking force, fell in this second assault on San Cristóbal. But Wheeler had the same charmed life as Ensign, soon to be Lieutenant, Dyas, who also reached camp unhurt, his sword shot off at the handle and his coat perforated with lead.

Wellington raised the siege on 16 June, on receiving intelligence that the French were approaching in massive numbers from opposite directions, Soult from the south and Marmont, who had replaced Masséna, from the north. Picton put the French at '50,000 Infantry and above 6000 Cavalry: a force so superior to what we could possibly collect that it was judged expedient to give up the blockade and take up a position on the right of the Guadiana, in the rear of Elvas and Campo Mayor'.[10] Wellington is said to have commented testily that he would be his own engineer next time he laid siege to a fortress. Picton's assessment was more pointed: 'Lord Wellington sued Badajoz *in forma pauperis*.'[11]

In effect, the Commander of the Forces had asked too much of his men. Badajoz could not be taken in a hurry, at least not with museum-piece guns.

II

The débâcle of Badajoz kept Picton in low spirits for some time. From Campo Maior, on 22 June, he wrote: 'We now wait on the movements of the Enemy who extend between Badajos and Merida. It is not yet ascertained whether they intend to carry on offensive operations or will content themselves with the brilliant exploit of relieving Badajos, which would certainly have fallen within a few days.' He was finding it more difficult now to bear the hardships of a campaign that involved continual movement:

> Until these last two days I have never had my clothes off since July last year. I have begun to find that this kind of Life is too trying for a constitution of 54, which has experienced so many Changes of Climate and so many other circumstances which overstrain the Nerves, and I certainly shall take an early opportunity of withdrawing from public exhibition lest I should fall into the situation of Gill Blass's Master, the old Arch Bishop of Granada.[12]

Very likely Picton was alluding to the notion of vanity, or the belief that one is indispensable, as is illustrated in the unbounded conceit of Lesage's apoplectic cleric whom he had no doubt come across in Smollett's translation of 1750. As a soldier, moreover, he could identify with the *pícaro* and his precarious life. In any event, Picton offered an appropriately hard-nosed view of the military situation in his letter to Marryat of 2 July: 'You appear everywhere to entertain sanguine expectations of our ulterior successes. I am concerned that I cannot say anything to keep up so pleasant a delusion.' He felt bound to point out that the number of regular British soldiers was small, below 20,000, 'a paper force', which would soon *undeceive* British opinion at home. He also observed that what success the Spanish freebooters enjoyed in harassing the French was offset by their tendency to alienate the locals 'who dread them to the full as much as they do the enemy', and he concluded, for the benefit of the MP in London: 'We are playing, in my opinion, a very losing game in carrying on the war with our own money, *at an immense expense.*'[13]

Fortunately for the Allies, the French at this time had no concerted plan. Soult continued to view Andalucía as his priority and, to Marmont's fury, took the better part of his army there in late June. Marmont headed back north to revictual Ciudad Rodrigo, having heard that Wellington was at last bringing his siege train from the Tagus to bear upon that fortress. For his part Picton was unconvinced: 'The insuperable difficulty (from distance and the nature of the roads) to the transporting forward the heavy ordnance and stores for a siege, will effectively prevent our attacking Ciudad Rodrigo, but we shall push on towards Salamanca.' He would soon be undeceived himself by the Allies' pertinacity in transporting huge battering guns up the Douro and then across 100 miles of the Peninsula's most rugged country to Ciudad Rodrigo. For the moment, however, Picton confined himself to serenading Marryat with a by-now familiar refrain: 'As long as we have money in abundance, supplies of all kinds find us out; but as soon as the means fail us, we are obliged to go the Lord knows where in search of them. Dollars here are the only sinews of war.'

He was still carping on August 26, *en route* to the blockade of Ciudad Rodrigo:

> We have been in constant movement ever since the 5th March, and upon the whole we have marched nearly 1200 miles, always through miserable exhausted country affording no articles of human existence. We are now within two days March of Guarda, only five leagues from our old quarters of Pinhel. I am growing tired of this vagrant Life, and I find it too late, at my age, to pass my days in continual marching & my nights sometimes in the

Open Air, almost generally in miserable Hovels, and always upon a Bundle of straw where I can procure it.

His disenchantment was fostered by a sense of having missed out on pecuniary and other rewards, all of which gave rise to a desire to return home:

By way of economy we are made to Perform the Duties of Leut. Generals with all the expense of an increased Staff, upon Major Genl's Emoluments, and the rising Sun concentrates all his raies upon those who have never Done an hours service except about St. James's. I shall very shortly request permission to return from the staff, and let those who have all the Loaves and fishes do the business.[14]

Wellington had sensibly taken his men from the environs of the Guadiana, which was a notorious breeding ground of malaria in the summer months, and had again positioned them in the healthier, if less comfortable, mountains of Portugal. Picton, along with a good many others, was already suffering a recurrence of Walcheren Fever, as he explained to Flanagan on 3 October: 'At the time your two last Letters arrived I was so seriously indisposed with a fever, and its consequences, a violent inflammation of the Eyes, that I was totally unable to decipher them.' Indeed he had been quite unwell in the last week of September, which saw notable action when a large body of Marmont's soldiers was detached from Ciudad Rodrigo in a bold counter thrust:

I was scarcely able to Mount my Horse when the Division was ordered to move forward and take up a Position in the immediate vicinity of the Enemy, who had advanced in great Force to Relieve Ciudad Rodrigo. They passed the Agueda on the night of the 24, and early on the morning of the 26th attacked the left of the position occupied by the 3rd Division (where there were only three weak regiments, amounting to about 1100) with two Divisions of Infantry and 28 Squadrons of Cavalry with a large proportion of Artillery. These three weak Batns. and five squadrons of Lt Cavalry engaged the Enemy for several Hours, and repeatedly drove them back, and finally effected their retreat in a most masterly manner, though the Enemy's Cavalry had surrounded them on all sides.[15]

The French surprised the Allies, who had mistakenly believed that Marmont's reinforcements under General Dorsenne would simply enter Ciudad Rodrigo to revictual the town. But Dorsenne, with 25,000 fresh recruits, had other ideas and was eager for spoils. Learning that the Allies were ill-prepared for action in their scattered encampments south of Ciudad Rodrigo, he saw an opportunity for his cavalry. Picton was eight miles

south at El Bodón, with part of his division under Wallace at
Pastores to the east and another part at Fuenteguinaldo near
Portugal. These unsupported infantry looked like easy pickings
for the French cavalry, but in practice the fire of the French
horse artillery was less effective than it might have been and
steadiness on the part of the British infantry held the day.
Lieutenant William Grattan recalled the orderliness of the
British retreat to Fuenteguinaldo when Picton rode alongside
the Connaught Rangers:

> Montbrun, at the head of fifteen squadrons of light horse,
> pressed closely on our right flank, and made every demonstra-
> tion of attacking us. But General Picton saw the critical situation
> in which he was placed, and that nothing but the most rapid, and
> at the same time most regular movement upon Guinaldo could
> save his division from being cut off to a man. For six miles across
> a perfect flat, without the slightest protection from any incident
> of ground, without artillery, and I might say without cavalry, (for
> what were four or five squadrons to twenty or thirty?) did the
> third division continue its march, during the whole of which the
> enemy's cavalry never quitted them; a park of six guns advanced
> with the cavalry, and taking the third division in flank and rear,
> poured in a frightful fire of roundshot, grape, and canister; many
> men fell in this way, and those whose wounds rendered them
> unable to march were obliged to be abandoned to the enemy.
> General Picton conducted himself with his accustomed coolness;
> he remained on the left flank of the column and repeatedly
> cautioned the different battalions to mind the quarter distance
> and the *tellings off.*
>   'Your safety', added he, 'my credit, and the honour of the army,
> is at stake: all rests with you at this moment.' [16]

Donaldson recalled how Picton inspired his officers, helping
them to focus on their duties rather than the enemy's threatening manoeuvres:

> General Picton showed that coolness and intrepidity for which he
> was so much distinguished; for some time he rode at the head of
> our square, while a strong body of French hung on our right,
> waiting a favourable opportunity to charge. The captain who
> commanded us (both field-officers being sick) was throwing many
> a fearful glance at them, and was rather in a state of perturbation.

'Never mind the French', said Picton, 'mind your regiment; if
the fellows come here, we will give them a warm reception.' [17]
    At about this time Montbrun came 'within half pistol-shot of
us', Grattan continued:

Picton took off his hat, and holding it over his eyes, as a shade from the sun, looked sternly, but anxiously at the French; the clatter of the horses, and the clanking of the scabbards were so great, when the right half squadron moved up, that many thought it the forerunner of a general charge; some mounted officer called out:

'Had we better not form square?'

'No', replied Picton; 'it is but a ruse to frighten us, but it won't do.'[18]

His judgement proved correct, because shortly afterwards the Third Dragoon Guards came up from the direction of Fuenteguinaldo to relieve the situation and drive the French away. The commander of the Third Division characteristically offered a sober account of the same testing encounter:

During this attack the other Regiments of the Division, which occupied very distant and remote Points, were completely cut off from all communication with the left by the intervention of large bodies of the Enemy's Cavalry, and had to retire across a Plain of above three miles in extent, accompanied by large bodies of the Enemy's Cavalry which hung upon our Rear and Flanks, but the movement in Close Columns was executed with so much regularity and precision that they never even dared Charge us during the whole operation.[19]

Two of Picton's greatest attributes as a general were conspicuous in this action: his steadfastness in the face of danger, which was all the more remarkable given his poor state of health at the time; and an aura of authority that derived from both his willingness to place himself in the front line of battle and his sheer physical presence. Apropos, his large frame and booming voice were decided assets.

Despite his success in this engagement, Picton remained glum about British prospects in the long term. His view was simply that numbers would prevail:

The business of Spain is, I fear, nearly brought to a conclusion. The French have all the strong places except Cadiz. We may hold out another year in this country. If we exceed that it must be in consequence of the ill conduct or false measures of the Enemy. With anything like an equality of numbers we can easily beat them: our soldiers are much better, and our officers are at least as good, but numbers, numbers will tell in the End, and there we cannot contend with them.

This deficiency could not be made up by the native Spanish force, Picton argued with some vigour, for the latter were most abominably led:

What an extraordinary Phenomenon this country presents! The Peasantry are I believe the most intelligent of their class in the whole world, showing great quickness and ability on all occasions, but the upper classes have not produced a single example of Talents or Integrity. The influence of a wretched government corrupted everything within its reach, and produced such a state of vicious degenerate effeminacy as was never equalled in any of the Eastern Courts, either of Persia or the Indies.[20]

His view of Spain as a nation of inverted strength was one which had been held by many Spaniards of liberal persuasion, including Gaspar Melchor de Jovellanos, the radical reformer. Later in the century, Prime Minister Cánovas del Castillo would give the point proverbial force: 'Todo decae en España, menos la raza.' ('Everything decays in Spain, except the common stock.')

Picton was affected by the news in November of the death, on 14 October, of his uncle and mentor, William Picton, who had given him such stalwart support when he was on trial. The news came while the army awaited the arrival of the siege train from Oporto and when Picton himself was resigned to a bout of tedious inactivity at Albergueria, twenty miles south of Ciudad Rodrigo on the Portuguese border. According to Donaldson, Albergueria had been rechristened 'the Hungry Village', since the soldiers were reduced to half rations for much of their time there.[21] Picton liked it little better, though he had fewer privations:

We are now fixt. at this place for the winter. It is a miserable Little Village, with nothing but ground Floors, except the single House of the Curate in which I live. I have a flock of excellent sheep which afford mutton fully equal to the best in Wales or Scotland. We also have abundance of good Beef and Pork, but we get no kind of Bottled Wine under five Shillings a Bottle, and, even that, in general very indifferent.[22]

Once again it was the season for horse racing, theatricality and, to the great joy of Sergeant Grattan, the singing of popular airs to the accompaniment of a violin:

Tell her I love her while the clouds drop rain,
Or while there's water in the pathless main.[23]

The Allies' idyll was interrupted by the arrival at Almeida on 1 December of the ungainly convoy of bullock carts bearing the siege train. This remarkable triumph was largely due to the tenacity of Alexander Dickson, a 34-year-old major in the Royal Artillery, whom Wellington had put in charge of the operation. Dickson, as affable as he was studious and meticulous, directed the movement of 68 pieces of ordnance, many of which weighed more than three tons, transporting them in 892 country carts drawn by 384 pairs of bullocks with the assistance of legions of horses and pack mules. At Oporto he assembled fleets of river boats in which were ferried all necessary guns, shot, soldiers and draught animals up the twisting Douro to the vicinity of Lamego. Boats were in plentiful supply thanks to the port wine trade, but much harder to negotiate was the steep climb from the Douro valley to Lamego and across to Pinhel and Almeida, on roads that tested the endurance of man and beast.

The arrival of the battering guns coincided with intelligence that Napoleon had recalled 60,000 of his best troops from the Peninsula to assist in his Russian campaign. Wellington was encouraged to believe that an assault on Ciudad Rodrigo would meet with success. Three days before Christmas Picton was writing spiritedly: 'Though we are quiet, we are in constant expectation of a sudden movement and some apprehensions of a Winter's Siege, for which we are preparing.'[24] He was more appreciative now of the effort made by Spaniards: 'Though there is no government in Spain, and consequently any thing like a regular Army, the War is carried on in a most effectual and destructive manner by the Guerillios, whose chiefs show great talents, activity and enterprise'. No doubt he had in mind the likes of Don Julián Sánchez, 'el Charro', whose ambuscades had reinforced the blockade of Ciudad Rodrigo, when he concluded: 'if we can continue the supplies necessary to keep these Independent Corps in activity, Buonaparte will have a hard task yet to accomplish in this Country'.

III

On New Year's Day 1812 Wellington issued orders to prepare for an attack on Ciudad Rodrigo. The compact fortress, standing on the north bank of the Agueda river, where it overlooked a Roman bridge, was just 800 yards across at its widest. Its square *alcázar* dated from the fourteenth century while, on its southern side, the ground fell steeply to the river from twelfth-century ramparts built by Count Rodrigo González, whose name had replaced the town's original Celtic place name of Mirobriga. Elsewhere a *fausse-braie* ('revetted earth bank') commanded a wide ditch guarded by strategically placed ravelins, beyond which the rocky glacis afforded no cover to assailants. Some 2,000 soldiers defended the town, a few hundred of whom manned the fortified convents of Santa Cruz and San Francisco and, half a mile to the north, the Redoubt Renaud that the French had built soon after taking the town two years earlier by storming the weaker north side. The new redoubt was designed to hamper siege work in that area, by dominating the two hills known as 'el Pequeño Tesón' and 'el Gran Tesón', the second of which reached a height slightly above the town's ramparts.

Wellington's plan was to knock out the redoubt and satellite convents, establish batteries on the north side and fire on the same point in the battlements which the French had breached two years before, this being clearly visible in repair work done in inferior mortar. For good measure he would open one further breach 200 yards east of the main one. Siege preparations necessitated that soldiers billeted in outlying villages to the south had to march twelve miles or more and cross the Agueda before starting their day's work. The crossing was a severe trial in early January, as Private Costello wrote:

> Pieces of ice that were constantly carried down this rapid stream bruised our men so much, that, to obviate it, the cavalry at length were ordered to form four deep across the ford, under the lee of whom we crossed comparatively unharmed, although by the time we reached the trenches our clothes were frozen into a mass of ice.[25]

The Agueda was 'much swollen', Simmons recalled. 'Our poor fellows had to cross the river nearly up to their shoulders, and remain in this wet state until they returned to their quarters, some working and some covering the working parties by firing.' As time went by, he noted, 'the enemy got the range to such a nicety that their shells were literally dropped in to our works'.[26] Grattan reported that the Third Division broke from its cantonments on 4 January, a 'dreadfully inauspicious' morning, when 'the snow on the surrounding hills drifted down with the flood, and nearly choked up the roads'. He could not remember a more disagreeable day: 'the rain which had fallen in the morning was succeeded by snow and sleet, and some soldiers, who sunk from cold and fatigue, fell down exhausted, soon became insensible, and perished'. Amazingly, an Irishwoman was 'delivered of a child upon the road, and continued the march with her infant in her arms'. Once she had reached Ciudad Rodrigo, this hardy being, like the soldiers, faced the twofold challenge of the elements and the enemy's guns: 'we had no tents or huts of any description; and the ground was covered with snow'.[27]

The French, already surprised at Wellington's decision to

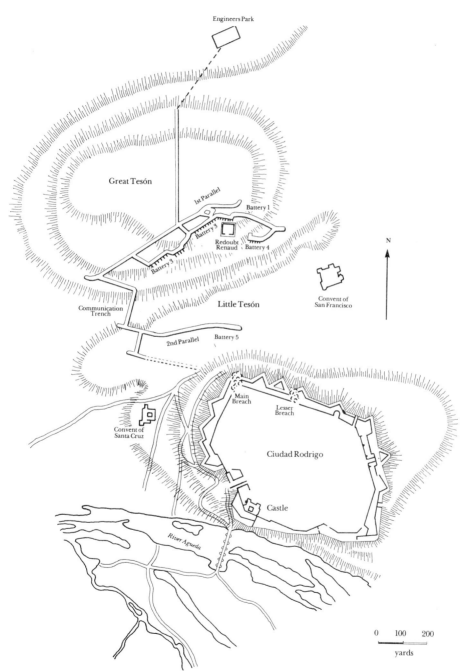

Engineers Park

Great Tesón

1st Parallel

Battery 1

Battery 3

Redoubt
Renaud

Battery 4

Battery 3

N

Communication
Trench

Little Tesón

Convent of
San Francisco

2nd Parallel   Battery 5

Main
Breach

Lesser
Breach

Convent of
Santa Cruz

Ciudad Rodrigo

Castle

River Agueda

0   100   200

yards

CIUDAD RODRIGO, JANUARY 1812

campaign in midwinter, were now astounded by the progress the Allies made as they took advantage of the long hours of darkness and put men to work in shifts through the night. The bitter weather was itself a spur, as Donaldson recalled: 'the frost was so excessive that we were almost completely benumbed, and nothing but hard working, I believe, kept us from perishing with the cold'.[28] A further inducement was the nagging recollection of what had happened at Ciudad Rodrigo in the summer of 1810 when, in Grattan's words, 'a weak garrison of Spaniards', unassisted by Wellington, defied the might of Masséna's army for twenty-five days. Tactically justifiable as their aloofness may have been on that occasion, the Allies were still shamefaced about it and keen to make amends. They also wanted to atone for the fiasco of Badajoz and show the French what they could do.

The siege got off to a rousing start. On the night of 8 January, 360 men under Colonel Colborne of the 52nd caught the French with their muskets piled, and, in ten minutes, with the loss of just six lives, took Redoubt Renaud on 'el Gran Tesón'. John Kincaid of the Rifles was amused by the French commanding officer, 'a chattering little fellow', who was indignant that the Allies had 'stormed a place without first besieging it'.[29] The French had bargained on the redoubt delaying the Allies for at least a fortnight, but the 'short, sharp action' was over by ten past eight, whereupon 1,200 men were immediately put to work with pick and shovel so that by dawn three parallels of batteries were ready to take 24-pounder guns. Next came the convents, which were well placed to annoy the sappers with enfilading fire. These were bombarded mercilessly and stormed on successive nights; Santa Cruz on 13 January and San Francisco the following night. The French made one attempt to thwart the Allies' progress with a bold sortie on the morning of 14 January when 500 infantry charged the ever encroaching batteries. Once this was repulsed and the second convent taken, work continued unhindered against the main fortress. So anxious were the Allies to storm the town before Marmont returned, they ignored enemy fire from the ramparts and put all their effort into the breaching batteries. Their own fire was ready to open on 18 January when twenty-five guns were brought to bear on the main breach and seven 24-pounders targeted the new site. The aim was generally accurate, but some roundshot cleared the battlements and smashed into the cathedral's walls, where several enduring mementos of the campaign were sculpted.

So ferocious was the battering Ciudad Rodrigo took, its ramparts collapsed within two days at both targeted points. The rubble, which came down from walls that were eight feet thick and nearly thirty feet high made a passable if steep ramp in the breaches for the Allies to scale. The storm was planned for the night of 19 January and soon after 5.00 p.m., when darkness fell, the Third Division was posted behind what remained of the convent of San Francisco. Grattan recalled how they saw men of the 43rd pass ahead of them towards the side of the lesser breach, quipping as they went, 'We'll meet in the town by and by', while the Third remained ignorant of their own duties and even feared they might be left behind.[30]

Suspense ended with the order, 'Stand to your arms', whereupon the men were instructed as to exactly how they were to carry the main breach. They listened 'with silent earnestness', wrote Grattan, then hastily prepared themselves for combat, dumping their knapsacks, lowering cartridge-boxes, unclasping stocks, oiling bayonets, and even, in some cases, 'taking leave of their wives and children'. The last scene was not so affecting as might be imagined, he adds, for the prospect of plunder animated all the family, and if there was an element of 'painful suspense' during a soldier's absence it was more than recompensed by the gaiety on his return. Should he fail to return, moreover, his place was sure to be filled by another in the company to which he belonged, and all that a British army woman risked was 'widowhood for a week'.

By 6.30 p.m. the men were ready and stood quietly to arms as the sergeants called the rolls. 'The evening was piercingly cold', Grattan recalled, 'and the frost was crisp on the grass; there was a keenness in the air that braced our nerves at least as high as concert pitch.' The call went out for a volunteer to lead the forlorn hope, to which young Lieutenant William Mackie of the 88th responded promptly. Next, General Picton appeared. He passed by each regiment, animating all with a few well-chosen words, uttered in his strong, deliberate voice. When he came to the 88th, led by Colonel Mackinnon, he said: 'Rangers of Connaught! It is not my intention to expend any powder this evening. We'll do this business with the cold iron.'[31]

No man could remain silent after such an address, Grattan affirmed, and with one 'Hurrah!' they were ready to face the enemy fire. Scarcely had their enthusiasm abated when a crack from the signal gun announced that the assault was to commence. Major-General Picton and Colonel Mackinnon dismounted and stationed themselves at a point where their troops entered the trenches, with Mackie and twenty other Connaught Rangers in the van. Companies of Portuguese were at hand, carrying bags of straw, which they were to throw into the ditch to soften the landing of the storming party. Donaldson described how he dropped down: 'each section being provided with a pick axe and rope, we advanced rank entire under a heavy fire from the garrison, to the brink of the trench, where planting the one end of the pick axe firmly in the ground, we threw the noose of the rope over the other, and then descended by it into the ditch'.[32]

In the darkness below it was easy to go wrong, as Simmons did, mistaking a traverse for the top of the breach and ascending a ladder that moments earlier some of his comrades had descended. Donaldson described the unholy scramble that ensued: 'mounting the breach, we found great difficulty in ascending, from the loose earth slipping from under our feet at every step, and throwing us down; the enemy at the same time pouring their shot amongst us from above'. At this point there was a sudden explosion: 'an expense magazine near the ramparts on the large breach blew up and ignited a number of live shells, which also exploded and paid no sort of difference to friend or foe'. Lawrence attributed the multiple explosion at the main breach to a train-man's error: 'a mine was sprung before the French were clearly off it, and both French and English were suddenly blown into the air and buried together in the ruin'.[33] Picton thought that 'the forlorn hope' had provoked the premature springing, this being precisely their function. He recorded: 'The troops immediately took advantage of the explosion, rushed forward and possessed themselves of the breach, where they were for some minutes exposed to a most destructive fire of grape and musketry, until, by scrambling over the parapets, they turned the entrenchments on both sides, and overcame all further resistance.'[34]

One who fell in the explosion was Colonel Mckinnon, whose mutilated body would be found in the breach next day. Alongside him lay soldiers of both sides, 'mangled in a most shocking manner; headless trunks, and others torn into masses of lacerated parts, which it was hard to fancy ever belonged to human beings'. But the horrific explosion served only to stiffen the resolve of the storming troops whose mood by now was irresistible. As Grattan put it, 'the *fighting division* were not the men to be easily turned from their purpose'; indeed, he detected in their faces a 'severity, bordering on ferocity' unseen in soldiers fighting in an open field.[35] The rest, as Lawrence confirmed, was straightforward: 'After the smother had fairly cleared away, our troops met with very little difficulty in mounting the breach and scouring the ramparts, the French throwing down their arms and retiring into the town itself, where after a brief contest in the streets, the whole surviving garrison surrendered.'[36]

The assault had only taken half an hour from start to finish, but the night was just beginning for soldiers hellbent on asserting their 'right of conquest'. Lawrence testified to 'all the horrors of the soldiery, excesses, riot, and drunkenness taking place on every side. Houses were plundered of their contents, cellars broken open and emptied, and many houses were even set on fire, amid the yells of the dissipated soldiers and the screams of the wounded.' Grattan saw the terrifying countenances of the pillagers: 'many with their faces scorched by the explosion of the magazine at the grand breach; others with their faces blackened from biting off the ends of their cartridges, more covered with blood, and all looking ferocious'.[37] He was also witness to numerous acts of outrage done to the *mirobrigenses*, as the townspeople were still called:

> Groups of the inhabitants half naked in the streets – the females clinging to the officers for protection – while their respective houses were undergoing the strictest scrutiny. Some of the soldiers turned to the wine and spirit houses, where having drunk sufficiently, they again sallied out in quest of more plunder; others got so intoxicated, that they lay in a helpless state in different parts of the town, and lost what they had previously gained, either by the hands of any passing Spaniard, who could venture unobserved to stoop down, or by those of their own companions, who in their wandering surveys happened to recognize a comrade lying with half a dozen silk gowns, or some such thing, wrapt about him.

Kincaid tried to explain what possessed those who stormed a town:

> The soldiers no sooner obtain possession of it, than they think themselves at liberty to do what they please. It is enough for them that there had been an enemy on the ramparts; and, without considering that the poor inhabitants may nevertheless be friends and allies, they, in the first moment of excitement, all share one common fate; and nothing but the most extraordinary exertions on the part of the officers can bring them back to a sense of their duty.[38]

No one exerted himself more than Picton to restrain the soldiers' depravity at Ciudad Rodrigo, as Kincaid, caught up in the human throng, testified:

> Finding the current of soldiers setting towards the centre of the town, I followed the stream, which conducted me into the great square, on one side of which the late garrison were drawn up as prisoners, and the rest of it was filled with British and Portuguese intermixed, without any order or regularity. I had been there but a very short time when they all commenced firing, without any

ostensible cause; some fired in at the doors and windows, some at
the roofs of houses, and others at the clouds; and, at last, some
heads began to be blown from their shoulders in the general
hurricane, when the voice of Sir Thomas Picton, with the power
of twenty trumpets, began to proclaim damnation to everybody.

Leading his officers, Picton took hold of some broken barrels
of muskets, which were 'lying about in great abundance', and,
using these as cudgels, 'belaboured every fellow most unmerci-
fully about the head who attempted either to load or fire, and
finally succeeded in reducing them to order'. Three houses in
the Plaza Mayor were burnt to the ground. But for Picton's leadership, the whole of Ciudad Rodrigo would almost certainly
have gone up in flames like Port of Spain.

At dawn, when order and a measure of sobriety had been
restored, it was time to count the cost: 105 Allied soldiers killed,
390 wounded. Besides Picton's close friend, Colonel Mackinnon,
his old rival, General Robert Craufurd, was also numbered
among the dead. The fearless commander of the Light Division
was buried with full honours at the foot of the lesser breach,
where he fell. Many fatalities were decidedly less glorious and
were caused by the wild firing inside the town after the breaches
had been carried. Without these unnecessary incidents the losses
would have been relatively meagre considering the town's importance and the fact that it was taken in just twelve days. Picton was
delighted with his Third Division, which had 'rendered itself the
most conspicuous Corps in the British Army', and whose
command he considered 'the highest Honor his Majesty could
confer upon him'. They had entered the town ahead of the Light
Division, he claimed, though this is uncertain, as is the claim by
William Mackie, leader of 'the forlorn hope', that he personally
accepted the surrender of the town from General Barrié, the new
French governor. These matters were to remain the subject of
dispute between the Third and Light divisions.

One matter that was resolved was the 'Guinea per Man' which
Picton had promised to the first corps to carry the breach. In
view of the confusion, he decided that the sum of £300 would
be 'proportionately divided amongst the British regiments of
the 3rd Division' who would do him the honour to drink to the
future success of the division. Doubtless this largesse was
prompted, at least in part, by the news that his Uncle William
had bequeathed him his entire estate, thereby finally relieving
him of financial worries. His buoyant mood can also be gauged
by a conversation that he had the morning after the assault when
he approached a group of Connaught Rangers as they prepared

to leave town for their billets. One Irishman, who was evidently still in high spirits, called out:

'Well, General, we gave you a cheer last night: it's your turn now!'

At which Picton laughed and, taking off his hat, shouted:

'Here, then, you drunken set of brave rascals: Hurrah! We'll soon be at Badajoz!'[39]

IV

Following the capture of Ciudad Rodrigo, the British government elevated Wellington from Viscount to Earl, while the Spanish Cortes recognized his achievement by creating him Duque de Ciudad Rodrigo and grandee of Spain. Never one to be burdened by honours, Wellington hurried south to Badajoz, leaving the bulk of his men in cantonments near the northern fortress, where, for six weeks, those not engaged in repairing the breaches found themselves with dangerously little to do. Some had acquired a taste for mischief after sacking Rodrigo and, as Lawrence noted, a number of sentries who were ordered to guard a supply of grog and biscuits, 'instead of guarding, they took so much rum, which being there generally carried in pigs' skins was easily got at, that they died in consequence next morning'.[40] Others were so desperate to get money for grog they sold their horse's corn, which left many a horse lamentably thin. One soldier, court-martialled and sentenced to fifty lashes, begged for mercy on the grounds that it was his first offence. His colonel replied: 'The horse's looks tell a different tale; he has long had the bitters, and you the sweet, and now it is time things should be the other way round.'

The men were glad to set off for the warmer climes of Badajoz and, from the second week in March, arrived at the Portuguese twin fortress of Elvas, where they bivouacked and prepared to invest the Extremaduran citadel a third time. It was a propitious moment to do so, with Soult busy at Cadiz, Marmont regrouping in the north, and Napoleon, furious at the loss of Ciudad Rodrigo, still bent on withdrawing Peninsular veterans for his Russian campaign. There was the usual urgency, for if the two French armies decided to converge, Wellington's force would be hopelessly outnumbered. On 16 March, therefore, a pontoon bridge was quickly thrown over the Guadiana river and 15,000 men left their bivouacs at Elvas: 'The soldiers swear we shall succeed', wrote

Wellington spiritedly, 'because we invested on St Patrick's eve, and broke ground on St Patrick's day'.[41]

Badajoz, if anything, was more daunting now than a year before. San Cristóbal, the outwork that had frustrated the Allies then, had been repaired and strengthened, while a new redoubt stood where they had formerly placed their breaching batteries. Retrenchments had been constructed behind the city's main walls, more guns were deployed on its battlements and counter-mines had been laid to the south between the Pardeleras fort and the Guadiana. Governor Armand Philippon had also maximized the defensive possibilities of water by having a *cunette* ('supplementary ditch') dug in the bottom of the main ditch, making it deep enough to drown a man, and by damming the Rivillas tributary at Fort Roque from which point a flood now stretched 100 yards upstream.

In response to these developments, Wellington devised a new plan. He would ignore San Cristóbal and concentrate instead on the south-eastern face: he would take Fort Picurina, use this as a base to establish parallels for his batteries, open two or three breaches near the bastions San Pedro and La Santa Trinidad, then launch his human missiles. He had better artillery now to shatter the stout curtain walls, which reached forty feet above the uneven ground. True, he had not risked bringing his siege train from Ciudad Rodrigo, for the rough terrain and poor communications would have made it easy pickings in any counter thrust by Marmont. Instead Dickson had obtained twenty 18-pounder guns from Admiral Berkeley's ships on the Tagus. Since they were of Russian origin and made for use at sea, they presented problems of windage and accuracy, but twenty of them splendidly complemented the sixteen 24-pounders already at Badajoz.

For a week preparations were hampered by torrential rains: 'our soldiers were working in the trenches nearly up to their hips in water', Grattan reported.[42] The Guadiana became so swollen that on 22 March the pontoon bridge was swept away in its flood. Three days before this the French had tried to take advantage of the Allies' discomfort by making a bold sortie. Grattan, detecting a bustle in the town, had forewarned his own men, but was amazed nonetheless at the audacity of the French when, shortly after noon, 1,500 blue-coats, with bayonets fixed, charged through a thin fog into the besieging masses. The trenches near Picurina suffered considerable loss of life as workmen were caught unawares with only pickaxes and shovels to defend themselves. Yet they fought back fiercely and before the covering parties arrived the parallels had rallied and repulsed the French by weight of numbers.

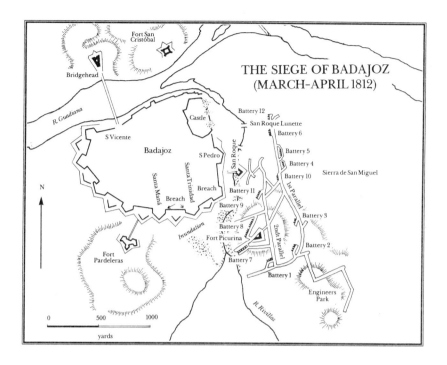

THE SIEGE OF BADAJOZ
(MARCH-APRIL 1812)

The general on duty in the trenches that day was Picton, who, as Grattan reported, was fast upon the scene:

> General Picton soon arrived in the battery where I was stationed, and seemed to be much alarmed for its safety, not knowing, in the confusion of the moment, which was great, that the enemy had attacked it, and had been driven back; but when he learned from me, that the workmen alone had achieved this act, he was lavish in his praise of them, and spoke to myself – for him – in flattering terms.

Yet Grattan, still suspecting that his commander was ill-disposed towards the Connaught Rangers, could not resist adding that Picton showed an 'austerity of demeanour' even as he gave praise: 'the caustic sententiousness with which he spoke rather chilled than animated'.[43]

Without blaming Picton, Grattan attributed the loss of more than 100 lives to 'the superlative neglect of our people'. Indeed, the British learned a salutary lesson from the episode and henceforth posted observers on the high ground of Sierra del Viento, while a squadron of cavalry and a troop of artillery were kept in constant readiness at the engineer park one mile to the south-east. Among those who died in the action of 19 March was Cuthbert, one of Picton's most valued aides-de-camp, who was, besides, genuinely popular with the men: 'I had yesterday a most severe loss in my own family', wrote Picton on 20 March, 'that of my first 1st Aid de Camp, Capt Cuthbert, who was killed close to my side by a 24^{lv} during a Sortie from the Town.'[44] In fact, as Picton had stood speaking to the men, Cuthbert remained in his saddle and, Grattan reported, 'in the act of giving directions to some of the troops, he was struck in the hip by a round shot, which killed his horse on the spot, leaving him dreadfully mangled and bleeding to death'.[45] More fortunate was Colonel Fletcher, the Chief Engineer, who, thanks to a silver coin in his pocket, survived being hit in the groin by a musket ball. Subsequently confined to his tent, he was visited each morning at 8.00 a.m. by Wellington, who there planned the day's action with him.

The atrocious weather continued to hamper progress for several days, as Captain MacCarthy, assistant engineer in the Third Division, noted: 'the heavy rains inundated the trenches and decomposed every shovelfull of earth as it was thrown up, so that the embankments could not retain their consistency'.[46] At length the rain abated and two dry days enabled the workmen to finish the parallels. On the morning of 25 March an assort-ment of 24-pounders, 18-pounders and howitzers opened fire on the outposts of Fort Picurina and San Roque. Ammunition for the assault, to Kincaid's mirth, was brought laboriously by Portuguese militia from Elvas, twelve miles distant: 'each man carrying a twenty-four pound shot and cursing all the way and back again'.[47]

Effectively, Picurina was a detached bastion, having on its two front sides a ditch and a partly revetted rampart with *fraises* ('rows of sharpened stakes'), which protruded horizontally; to its weaker rear lay a simple gorge, or open stretch, by which the defenders might escape towards the town over the Rivillas inun-dation via a makeshift bridge of planks on trestles. Picurina was reduced to a state of ruin by the afternoon of the first day's bombardment when it had 'more the semblance of a wreck than a fortification', wrote Grattan, 'its parapets crumbling to pieces from each successive discharge from our guns'.[48] Yet appear-ances were deceiving, as Grattan noted, for when Major-General Sir James Kempt, commanding a brigade of the Third Division, attempted to storm the fort that night 'a violent fire of musketry opened upon the assailing columns' and they were repulsed several times, both to the front and rear. To Kempt, who lost 80 men in the assault, it came as a great relief when the defenders suddenly and inexplicably withdrew by way of the half-demolished trestle bridge where, MacCarthy recounted, 'many French soldiers drowned in their panic to regain the Town, their bodies left floating in the water'.[49]

From 26 March batteries could be sited before and alongside the dilapidated Picurina and trained on Badajoz itself, notably on the bastions of La Trinidad and Santa María. Work proceeded briskly on establishing new parallels, for word had come that Soult was stirring in Sevilla, nine days' march away. The work itself was monotonous, as Kincaid mused: 'One day's trench-work is as like another as the days themselves; and like nothing better than serving an apprenticeship to the double calling of grave-digger and game-keeper, for we found ample employment for both the spade and the rifle.'[50] Picton, too, was bored: 'These Sieges are damned disagreeable things,' he wrote on 20 March, 'one is worse than half a dozen Battles, and I have reason to be tired of them, as this is my third in one year.'[51] Having been obliged to quit Badajoz the previous year when in sight of victory, he was well aware that the success of a siege was coldly determined by factors of poundage, distance and time: 'It is an affair of calculation this time also, and if Lord Wellington is as accurate in his arithmetic as he was at Ciudad Rodrigo we shall succeed: but it is accompanied with difficulties which nothing but laborious perseverance can get over'.

To combat tedium the men sometimes amused themselves by taking risks, raising their hats to taunt marksmen on the battlements, or even their heads if they believed they were outside the range of accurate fire. MacCarthy told of one engineer who would pace out the ground, oblivious to the fire aimed at him, then ostentatiously lift his coat tails, challenging the French to improve their aim. Shelling from the battlements became ever more precise, and MacCarthy recalled looking up on one occasion to see a missile approaching 'like a cricket ball to be caught'.[52] Fatalities in the trenches were plentiful, especially when workmen changed shift and, as sometimes happened, a relief shift entered before the old one left. This practice ended after one horrendous incident witnessed by Sergeant Lawrence:

> One night as I was working in the trenches near this place, and just as the guard was about to be relieved, a shell from the town fell amongst them and exploded, killing and wounding about thirty. I never saw a worse sight of its kind, for some had their arms and legs, and some even their heads completely severed from their bodies.[53]

It was vital to keep up a steady fire at night to discourage the enemy and hamper their reparations in the breaches. But when Picton came on duty at first light on 1 April it was clear this had been neglected and, after giving the men a piece of his mind, he reported the matter to Wellington, who issued an order threatening dire consequences if officers were not more assiduous in the hours of darkness.

On 3 April, as MacCarthy recalled, the Commander of the Forces inspected the trenches: 'Lord Wellington, with an officer, came from the breaching batteries, gently walking in the trenches, where shot and shells were flying, as tranquilly as if strolling in his own lawn in England.' Wellington exchanged pleasantries and accepted a field-glass from one of the officers to inspect the progress at the breaches. He placed the glass in a scollop of earth that an enemy roundshot had made in the edge of the bank and proceeded with his observations. At that moment, perhaps having seen cocked hats, the enemy fired: 'the shot hummed as it passed over Lord Wellington's head', MacCarthy wrote, 'he smiled, but made his inspection, and returned the glass'.[54]

Wellington must have been delighted to see the damage Dickson's artillery was doing to Badajoz's tough masonry and he confidently expected to launch his assault on the night of 5 April. Yet Philippon continued to conduct expert defensive operations, having the parapets repaired with sandbags and the breaches cleared of debris each night to keep the slopes difficult. On 5 April, at the final inspection, Wellington was advised by Colonel Fletcher, now sufficiently recovered to leave his tent, that although the breaches were practicable the enemy's retrenchments behind them were so formidable that the proposed assault would entail a massive loss of life. He determined to delay the attack twenty-four hours, intending in the meantime to open a third breach between Santa María and La Trinidad. Picton, doubtful of success at the breaches, proposed that the Third Division be allowed to attempt an escalade of the towering Moorish Alcazaba at the same time as the breaches were stormed. Wellington acceded to this, but, to judge from the brief mention in his orders, he very likely saw the escalade as little more than a feint.

By mid-afternoon on 6 April a heavy cannonade had opened a third breach in the curtain wall and Philippon had to withdraw soldiers from the fortress to defend it. By 5.00 p.m. ladders had been apportioned to the storming parties and there was nothing for the men to do but wait. Many had been frustrated by the twenty-four hour delay, their extreme eagerness to risk life and limb being attributable, in Grattan's view, to a number of factors: the previous unsuccessful sieges, the supposed hostility of the inhabitants to the British and, not least, an unwholesome desire for plunder. Kincaid detected a strange anxiety in the men that stemmed not from thoughts of death, but rather 'fear that the place should be surrendered without standing an assault',[55] for pillaging was only permissible after resistance and bloodshed. 'So great was the rage for passports into eternity', Kincaid added, 'even the officers' servants insisted on taking their places in the ranks.' Lawrence noted that men in his division 'knew the town perfectly well', having been quartered there after Talavera, 'and so understood the position of most of the valuable shops'. He admitted ingenuously to having volunteered for 'the forlorn hope' on hearing that 'there was to be three hours' plunder' following a successful assault, and even to having arranged to meet with friends inside the walls at a silversmith's they knew.[56]

Late in the afternoon the men were busy with their preparations, choosing flints, oiling bayonets and tucking their ragged shirt-tails and trouser legs in. They looked fearsome, with bronzed, whiskered faces and tattered jackets that were barely recognizable after weeks in the trenches. For a while the playing of music was to be heard on this Easter Sunday and, amongst the Connaught Rangers, the singing of Irish airs. At 8.00 p.m., when the deep note of the town clock tolled the hour, a deathly hush came over the place as the men assembled and waited for darkness to fall. Grattan describes the slow passing of time as the soldiers counted the minutes until 10.00 p.m., the hour fixed for the assault:

> A thick and dusky vapour, issuing from the Guadiana and the Rivillas, hung above the heads of the hostile forces; the batteries on both sides were silent, as if they reserved their efforts for the approaching struggle; and, except for the gentle noise which the rippling of the Guadiana created, or the croaking of the countless frogs that filled the marshes on each side of its banks, everything was as still as if the night was to be one of quiet repose.

In the same vein Donaldson recalls: 'It was dark and gloomy, not a single star showed its head; the air was still, not a sound could be heard, but the noise of the field cricket and the croaking of frogs; every word of command was given in a whisper.'

Darkness would create its own problems, especially for Picton's division which had much ground to cover before it reached the foot of the Alcazaba. At 8.00 p.m. Picton had met with Major-General Kempt, Major Burgoyne and other officers in the Third Division, to whom he gave his orders and then, according to MacCarthy, dispatched with the words: 'Some people are of the opinion that the attack on the Castle will not succeed, but I will forfeit my life if it does not!'[57]

He had then superintended the allocation of ladders, pick-axes and grass bags to the duty soldiers. This done, he inquired of Burgoyne who was to show him the way, whereupon the major presented Captain MacCarthy. Informed by Picton that he needed to collect the bulk of his men, MacCarthy then observed the commander ride off:

> I followed and soon lost sight of him in the dark, but pursuing the same direction I fortunately arrived at the Division, which was drawn up in column between two hills, at the distance, I supposed, of three miles, and quite out of sight of Badajos. General Picton having addressed each of the Brigades, he returned to the head of the Division, ordered the 'march', and said to me, 'Now, sir, which way are we to go?'
>
> We proceeded a considerable distance, and again came within sight of the Fortress; the lights of which were altered and much extended. I was to conduct to a certain point in the trenches to meet Major Burgoyne, and thence to the escalade; and naturally felt the weight of the charge. I several times ran ahead to ascer-tain the correctness of my guidance; the General inquiring each time if we were going right, I confidently answered in the affir-mative and informed the General that it was necessary to incline to the right; and, coming to the side of the Talavera road, the column descended into it. Here General Picton, dismounting, sent away his horse, and headed his Division on foot.
>
> The firing of the enemy's musketry becoming brisk, increased the General's anxiety to be as contiguous as possible. When I had again advanced some distance, to discover Major Burgoyne, and returned, General Picton, emphatically expressing himself, said that I was blind, he supposed, and going wrong; and, drawing his sword, swore he would cut me down.[58]

The urgent terms in which Picton addressed the junior officer at this critical moment resonate even now, though the cause of his bizarre behaviour remains a mystery. Was it panic, brought on by the darkness and his feeble eyes? Had he indulged too heartily earlier in the evening, in an attempt to shore up courage? MacCarthy was more charitable: 'I explained, and he was appeased. I was fully sensible of the high responsibility the General felt for the success of his own proposition of escalading the Castle.' Indeed, while he lamented his Commander's 'unnecessary precipitancy', MacCarthy adds that he could not repress 'an involuntary admiration of his ardour!' as he looked upon 'the interesting picture of the General, sword-in-hand, and myself before him assuring him of my correctness'.

V

Picton's altercation with MacCarthy had taken place shortly before 10.00 p.m. at a point near the Rivillas flood and the San Roque fort. At that moment the Fourth Division, under orders to take San Roque before storming the Trinidad breach, had opened fire and begun to escalade the outpost, which in turn provoked a response of gunfire from the main fortress. Arriving on the scene precisely when San Roque was stormed, Picton was very likely disorientated by the crossfire and only realized his error when the main fortress lit the scene with a shower of fire-balls. It must also have been unnerving to find his entire division, 3,000 strong, plainly visible from the ramparts of the fortress in the resulting glare. Grattan reported that:

> The soldiers, finding they were discovered, raised a shout of defi-ance, which was responded to by the garrison, and in a moment afterwards, every gun that could be brought to bear against them was in action; but, no way daunted by the havoc made in his ranks, Picton, who just then joined his soldiers, forded the Rivillas, knee-deep, and soon gained the foot of the castle wall, and here he saw the work that was cut out for him, for he no longer fought in dark-ness. The vast quantity of combustible matter, which out-topped this stupendous defence, was in a blaze, and the flames which issued forth on every side, lighted, not only the ramparts and ditch, but the plain that intervened between them and the Rivillas.[59]

Major-General Kempt was badly wounded at the Rivillas mill-dam where, at one point, the whole division had to negotiate a passage in single file with the French looking down their barrels at them: 'On this place the enemy had brought their guns to bear', Donaldson wrote, 'and they kept up such a fire of grape and musketry on it, that it was a miracle any of us escaped.'[60] Those who made it across found themselves impeded by a palisade, but the quick-thinking MacCarthy shouted 'Down with the paling!' and, helped by many hands to rock the fence, he succeeded in making an opening by which the entire division entered. Fire now poured down on the assailants as Picton himself led the way, entering the ditch and heading for the bastions of San Pedro, San Antonio and the Alcazaba. Here it was Picton's turn to be struck in the groin. Like his Chief

Engineer, however, he escaped serious injury because, as he later recalled, 'a bundle of papers in my Breeches pocket prevented the ball from penetrating, and I was merely stunned for the time'.[61]

During the twenty minutes or so he was *hors de combat* the assault on the fortress proceeded without proper direction and at an appalling cost in lives. Donaldson, for one, believed he had reached comparative safety in the shelter of the ditch, but was soon undeceived when the enemy 'opened several guns from angles which commanded the trench and poured in grape shot upon us from each side, every shot of which took effect, and every volley of which was succeeded by the dying groans of those who fell'.[62] Kempt's leaderless brigade, in utter confusion, placed their ladders against the curtain wall instead of the fortress proper, which was 100 yards further north. Grattan gave a precise account of what the men faced:

> A host of veterans crowned the wall, all armed in a manner as imposing as novel; each man had beside him eight loaded fire-locks; while at intervals, and proportionately distributed, were pikes of an enormous length, with crooks attached to them, for the purpose of grappling with the ladders; the top of the wall was covered with rocks of ponderous size, only requiring a slight push to hurl them upon the heads of our soldiers; and there was a sufficiency of hand-grenades and small shells at the disposal of the men that defended this point to have destroyed the entire of the besieging army; while on the flanks of each curtain, batteries, charged to the muzzle with grape and case shot, either swept away entire sections, or disorganized the ladders as they were about to be placed, and an incessant storm of musketry, at the distance of fifteen yards, completed the resources the enemy brought into play, which, as may be seen, were of vast formidableness.[63]

When a hobbling Picton was sufficiently recovered to rejoin the fray he quickly saw the error of Kempt's brigade, now caught in the crossfire between the fortress and the neighbouring bastion. He directed the men north with their ladders, each of which required four of them to carry, and these were dragged laboriously into the ditch, as Grattan recalled, there to be 'planted against the lofty battlements that domineered above his soldiers' heads'. Now the escalade began in earnest: 'Each ladder, so soon as placed upright, was speedily mounted, and crowded from the top round to the bottom one; but those who escaped the pike-thrusts, were shattered to atoms by the heavy cross-fire from the bastions'. The chaos of limbs and sheer horror of this slaughter was captured by the Scot, Donaldson:

When the ladders were placed, each eager to mount, crowded them in such a way that many of them broke, and the poor fellows who had nearly reached the top, were precipitated a height of thirty or forty feet, and impaled on the bayonets of their comrades below; other ladders were pushed aside by the enemy on the walls, and fell with a crash on those in the ditch; while more who got to the top without accident were shot on reaching the parapet, and tumbling headlong, brought down those beneath them.

As the Third Division struggled in vain for more than an hour at the Alcazaba, the main onslaught of some 10,000 men had no more success at the breaches. At Santa María the carnage was prodigious, and Harry Smith of the Light Division described his comrades' heroic but futile attempts to carry it in stark terms: 'the more we tried to get up, the more we were destroyed'.[64] Kincaid thought the scene was 'as respectable a representation of hell itself as fire, and sword, and human sacrifices could make it'.[65] The picture was no different at La Trinidad breach, the Fourth's target, where again the retrenchments were wholly effective. The third, newly opened breach that stood between them might have provided easier ascent, but access to it was made difficult by the deep *cunette* in the flooded ditch before it. Within a short time the assault had degenerated into what Kincaid described as 'gallant but hopeless attempts on the part of individual officers, forming up fifty or a hundred men at a time at the foot of the breach, and endeavouring to carry it by desperate bravery'.

What ultimately thwarted these reckless hordes was the chilling defensive barrier known as the *chevaux de frise*, which consisted of beams of wood with sword-blades bristling at lethal angles. The beams were chained, as Grattan says, 'boom-like, across the breach',[66] so that if an assault party managed to survive raking musket fire and gain the upper part of a breach, they were greeted by these inhuman sentries, which were spaced sufficiently far apart to allow tiers of riflemen to fire through from the retrenchments behind. Lawrence recalled the welcome he and his comrades got when urged by their commanders up the slopes of rubble:

We hastened to the breach, but there, to our great surprise and discouragement, we found a *chevaux de frise* had been fixed and a deep entrenchment made, from behind which the garrison opened a deadly fire on us. Vain attempts were made to remove this fearful obstacle, during which my left hand was dreadfully cut by one of the blades.[67]

Lawrence's wound forced him to retire, and as he made his

painful way back to the ditch he found new obstacles: the bodies
of his comrades. The ladders below were:

> filled with the dead and wounded, hanging some by their feet just
> as they had fallen and got fixed in the rounds. I hove down three
> lots of them, hearing the implorings of the wounded all the time;
> but on coming to the fourth, I found it completely smothered with
> dead bodies, so I had to draw myself up over them as best I could.

Having managed at length to get out of the range of enemy
fire, Lawrence happened upon Wellington and his staff, whereupon the Commander of the Forces, after inquiring as to the
extent of his wounds, asked if any troops had got into the town.
Lawrence replied 'No', adding that he 'did not think they ever
would' on account of the *chevaux de frise* and deep entrenchments to the rear of them. No doubt this first-hand report
contributed to Wellington's decision to retreat.

At the fortress it was equally plain to Picton that the assault
had reached a critical stage and that such an unavailing sacrifice
could not long continue. Half his division were already dead or
wounded, without having struck a blow at the enemy, and the
ladders were in a pitiful state, their green rungs shattered by
rocks dropped from above. Faced with the wall, which stood as
daunting and seemingly impregnable as ever, Picton knew that
only the indomitable spirit of his men, who were laying down
their lives so prodigally, would carry the day. Yet this spirit was
perceptibly waning now. He called out to them to make one last
effort, telling them that they had never been defeated: 'If we
cannot win the Castle', he cried, 'let us die upon the walls.'[68]

Immediately, his words struck a chord. Grattan observed that
'Picton, although not loved by his soldiers, was respected by
them, and his appeal, as well as his unshaken front, did wonders
in changing the desperate state of the division.'[69] Soon fresh
ladders were raised and placed at greater intervals against different parts of the battlement where hundreds rushed to scale
them. Led by Lieutenant-Colonel Ridge of the 5th, Lieutenant
Canch, the commanding officer of his grenadier company, and
Connaught Rangers Richard Martin and William Mackie of
Rodrigo's 'forlorn hope', this surge proved irresistible. The
French, exhausted by their slaughterhouse exertions, con-
founded by the resolution, not to say downright manic
stubbornness of the yelling, cursing British, were finally swept
aside. As Picton later wrote: 'They poured on and bore one
another up until at length the wall was gained; nothing could
resist them. Yet I could hardly make myself believe we had taken
the Castle.'[70]

Donaldson was amongst the first to set foot on the battlement and live to tell the tale: 'a few having made a landing good on the ramparts, at the expense of their lives, enabled a greater number to follow. When about a company had thus got collected together, we formed and charged round the ramparts, bayoneting the French artillery at their guns.'[71] There ensued a 'general rush to the ladders', wrote Grattan, when all hell broke loose:

> The dead and wounded, that lay in the ditch, were indiscriminately trampled upon, for humanity was nowhere to be found. A frightful butchery followed this success; and the shouts of our soldiery, mingled with the cries of the Frenchmen, supplicating for mercy, or in the agonies of death, were heard at a great distance. But few prisoners were made. [72]

There was no time for niceties, in fact, as Philippon had already ordered a counter-attack to regain the strategically vital fortress, which, in addition to commanding the town, was also the main storage centre for food and ammunition. This counter-attack was comprehensively repulsed, though it cost the life of Ridge, among others, a colossus moments earlier in the taking of the Alcazaba.

Picton, forced by injury to stay at the foot of the ladders and exhort his men from below, now sent his aide-de-camp, Captain Tyler, with news of the escalade's success to Wellington. Having already ordered the retreat to be sounded at the breaches, the Commander of the Forces had no better hope or intention at that moment than to resume the whole gory business in the morning, a prospect that appalled many of his staff. Wellington's relief when he heard Tyler announce the Third Division's triumph can hardly be imagined. Joyously exclaiming, 'Then the place is ours!',[73] he at once sent Tyler back with the order to hold the fortress at all costs, though by the time this reached Picton the counter-attack had already been repulsed and Philippon had fled across the Guadiana to Fort Cristóbal where, six hours later, he would formally surrender.

With the fortress safely in the hands of the Third Division by midnight, the opposite side of the town was escaladed by the Fifth Division under General Sir James Leith. Storming the now less heavily manned bastion of San Vicente, they secured a landing and fought their way south along the ramparts, clearing the bastions as they went. When their bugles sounded the advance of four regiments to the rear of the French who still guarded the breaches, the latter, much alarmed, dispersed, whereupon the Fourth and Light divisions scrambled up the slopes heaped with their dead comrades, dismantled the dreaded *chevaux de frise*, and entered the prized town.

Grattan movingly described the scene he witnessed at dawn on the morning of 7 April 1812:

> The shattered remnant of Picton's invincible soldiers stood in a lone group upon the ramparts of a spot that, by its isolated situation, towering height, and vast strength, seemed not to appertain to the rest of the fortifications. Nevertheless, triumphant and stern as was their attitude, it was not without its alloy, for more than five-sixths of their officers and comrades either lay dead at their feet, or badly wounded in the ditch below them. All their Generals, Picton amongst the number, and almost all their Colonels, were either killed or wounded; and as they stood to receive the praises of their commander, and the cheers of their equally brave companions in arms, their diminished front and haggard appearance told, with terrible truth, the nature of the conflict in which they had been engaged.[74]

Lieutenant MacPherson, one of those who distinguished themselves in the assault on the fortress, offered Picton the *tricolor* that he had taken from the flagstaff the night before, leaving in its place, as an improvised emblem of conquest, his own red coat. Picton, however, declined to accept the flag from the young officer, saying: 'Take it to Lord Wellington, and show him what the Third Division can do.'[75]

That the losses weighed heavily with Picton is beyond dispute. Very likely too, as MacCarthy later testified, he was less than impressed by Wellington's strategy, there being nearly 1,000 dead and 4,000 wounded among the British, while French losses did not reach three figures. Whereas in the letters that Picton wrote from Portugal there are many laudatory references to the Commander of the Forces as a defensive strategist so parsimonious with his soldiers' lives, there is a corresponding dearth of comments on the victor of Badajoz. It has been suggested that Picton's friends destroyed the letters he wrote after Badajoz for fear that their outspokenness might do him damage. The questions they may have raised, others have since asked: Why did Wellington delay the assault until 10.00 p.m., giving the French garrison two hours of darkness to cover the breaches with harrows, crow's-feet and *chevaux de frise*? Why was more care not taken in the preparations? Would it have been insuperably difficult, for instance, to reduce and make more negotiable the walls in the ditches where so many died, or burst the Rivillas dam to drain the inundation?

That Wellington's army stood precariously between Soult and

Marmont explains the need for urgency without justifying the sacrifice. By the same token, the fact that Wellington wrote soon afterwards to the prime minister, urging the formation of a new Corps of Sappers and Miners to provide a more scientific approach to siege operations, shows the wisdom of a man who learnt from experience, just as it tends to confirm the suspicion that he may have been too hasty at Badajoz. Picton, for his part, may not have found it wholly edifying to hear Wellington say that the 'Third Division had saved his honour and gained him Badajoz',[76] for it was a devastated body of men that was cheered when they entered the town the following day. In fact, on seeing the full extent of the fatalities for which he was responsible, Wellington lost his customary composure, as Picton wrote: 'our Chief, when I waited upon him next morning, shed as copious a torrent of Tears as any woman could have done on the occasion, and appeared most profoundly affected by our loss.'

Wellington's Welsh general also noted that: 'military reputation is not to be Purchased without blood, and ambition has nothing to do with Humanity'.[77]

VI

Badajoz was soon the victim of another type of inhumanity, which the pillaging of Ciudad Rodrigo had only mildly presaged.

The rites of plunder had begun in earnest by 6.00 a.m., when, as Lawrence put it, 'our troops found the city illuminated to welcome them'.[78] First it was the turn of the spirit stores to be ransacked: 'Casks of the choicest wines and brandy were dragged into the streets', wrote Grattan, 'and when the men had drunk as much as they fancied, the heads of the vessels were stove in, or the casks otherwise so broken that the liquor ran about in streams.'[79] Donaldson saw men running from a large spirit vault in the centre of the city 'with their hat-caps full of it, and some, it was said, were actually drowned in it. Farther on a number of those who had visited the spirit store were firing away their ammunition, striving to hit some bells in front of a convent.'[80] Lawrence, who arrived late on account of his wounds, met an advanced state of debauchery:

> Next morning I hobbled as well as I could into the town and there sure enough I found a pretty state of affairs. Pipes of wine had been rolled into the streets and tapped by driving the heads in, for any one to drink of them who liked, and when the officers tried to keep order by throwing all of these over that they could, the

men that were in a state of drunkenness lay down to drink out of
the gutters, which were thus running with all sorts of liquors.[81]

Inevitably, atrocities ensued when several thousand men,
armed to the teeth, went stumbling, mad drunk, through the
town, blowing doors open by firing down the locks, firing in at
windows, at the terrified inmates, or at each other. In this 'fine
city', observed Grattan, 'amongst which may be reckoned a
proportion of the most beautiful women that Andalusia, or
perhaps the world could boast of', it was not surprising that
hardly a house and hardly a woman escaped the attention of a
mob that for two days and nights rampaged at will, or that the
booty, though plentiful, gave rise to quarrels:

> Men were killed, in endeavouring to carry away some species of
> plunder, by the hands of those who, but a few hours before, would
> have risked their own lives to protect those they now so wantonly
> sported with: then would they turn upon the already too deeply
> injured females, and tear from them the trinkets that adorned
> their necks, fingers or ears! and, finally, they would strip them of
> their wearing apparel.[82]

Trains of pack animals and carts loaded with plunder were
taken off to camp by ragamuffin soldiers who forced unfortunate Spaniards to drive or carry their ill-gotten wares at bayonet
point. In camp the soldiers' wives became guards, stockpilers
and shopkeepers while their men went back for more. 'The
camp during that day', Donaldson wrote of 8 April, 'was like a
masquerade, the men going about intoxicated, dressed in the
various dresses they had found in the town; French and Spanish
officers, priests, friars, and nuns, were promiscuously mixed,
cutting as many antics as a mountbank.'[83] News that the camp
was glutted with saleable goods reached far and wide and from
early morning on 9 April people poured in seeking bargains and
turning the camp into a vast *mercado*. Some soldiers cleared a
thousand dollars in the day, according to Grattan, but what he
found offensive was the noisy bartering that took place alongside the suffering of the wounded, the dispatching of
merchandise in one direction and of corpses simultaneously in
another.

The insensitivity and selfishness which the sacking of Badajoz
provoked was most apparent in the neglect of the wounded.
Many were left in the breaches, bleeding or thirsting to death,
while the delinquent rabble of their comrades marauded inside
the city walls. Donaldson, sickened by the depravity, exited via
the breaches which he found much changed from the heroic

scene of hours before: 'all was comparatively silent, unless here and there a groan from the poor fellows who lay wounded, and who were unable to move'. Amidst the rubble and mangled bodies the morning light revealed the pathetic profile of a woman bent with a child at her breast rocking backwards and forwards over a bleeding corpse. The neglect continued for days. On the third day Kincaid tells how he came upon two fellows who had each lost a leg and, though no more than 300 yards from their regiment, had been left to starve by comrades 'from whom they could obtain nothing but promises'.[84]

That the men were desensitized by alcohol, lust or plain greed is certain. Wellington's famous comment that his army consisted of 'the scum of the earth' who had all enlisted for drink finds its definitive illustration in the aftermath of Badajoz. Yet it would be remiss not to reflect on what these men had been asked to do in storming the citadel, for violence was perhaps the supreme desensitizer and numbness a requisite state of mind in any man who faced the walls or breaches. In the circumstances, it is not surprising that the men were no longer harrowed by the sight of blood, brains and mutilated limbs, or that they should guffaw at such tales as the one Lawrence told of a cannonball taking a man's head clean off, which fact was concealed by the night from the soldier who carried the body a good mile back to camp, slung over his shoulder, only to deliver a headless trunk to a perplexed doctor. Nor, finally, is it entirely remarkable that some held as cynical a view of their superiors and of the whole business of warfare as the one Grattan espoused, though he wisely voiced it in the comical brogue of one of his countrymen, a certain Paddy Aisy:

> 'Well!' said he, 'now ids all past and gone, and wasn't it the divil's own dthroll business, the taking that same place; and wasn't Long-nose (meaning the Duke of Wellington) a quare lad to sthrive to get into it, seeing how it was definded! But what else could he do, afther all? didn't he recave ordhers to do it; and didn't he say to us all, 'Boys', says he, 'ids myself that's sorry to throuble yees upon this dirty arrand; but we must do it, for all that; and if yees can get into it, by hook or by crook, be the powers, id 'ill be the making ov yees all – and ov me too!' and didn't he spake the thruth?'[85]

The fact is that the men's making lay in what they could pillage and that pillaging was accepted by them and tacitly condoned by their superiors as the final act in the ritual execution of a siege. This was stated, artlessly, by all. Donaldson: 'When the town surrendered, and the prisoners were secured, the gate leading into the town was opened, and we were allowed to enter the town for the purpose of plundering it.'[86] Grattan saw pillaging as 'necessary; for if such latitude was not allowed to the soldiery, I believe that few fortresses would be carried by assault'.[87] Kincaid pointed to the officers' complicity: 'The greater part of the three divisions were, by this time, loose in the town; and the usual frightful scene of plunder commenced, which the officers thought it prudent to avoid for the moment, by retiring to the camp.'[88]

The same reluctant compliance may be detected in Wellington, who once said that the next greatest calamity to losing a battle was winning one. His orders on 7 April are couched in a language that suggests resigned acquiescence: 'It is now full time that the plunder of Badajoz should cease.'[89] Next day, having sent in men to fetch out stragglers only to find that they too became infected by the fever of pillage, he mildly announced: 'The Commander of the Forces is sorry to learn that the brigade in Badajoz, instead of being a protection to the people, plunder them more than those who stormed the town.' In time his patience wore thin, but the measures he took were lenient in the face of the excesses committed, more restraining than punitive: he ordered that rolls be called in camp at every hour; that a pass be required from a field officer to enter Badajoz; that the ladders on the escarpments be removed and that the gates and breaches each be guarded by fifty men 'to prevent soldiers from entering the town, or from quitting it with bundles of any description'. At length gibbets were erected in the Plaza Mayor, but while several men were flogged, none, wrote Grattan, was executed. In effect, the Saturnalia was allowed to run its course and only burnt itself out from sheer exhaustion.

A number of individual officers did their best to curb the mayhem, and one or two paid for it with their lives. Some had success, notably Harry Smith, a brigade major in the Light Division, who rescued two sisters he found with their ears bleeding after their earrings had been ripped off: one, the beautiful Juana María, who was fourteen at the time, would become his wife and was so highly respected that, years later, the town of Ladysmith in South Africa was named after her. At Badajoz, however, no one of sufficient stature took on the challenge of riot control as firmly as Picton had at Ciudad Rodrigo. Unfortunately his injury kept him outside the walls in the early stages of the havoc, though it is a matter for speculation whether even a fit Picton would have prevailed at Badajoz. The town was so much larger, richer and better defended, while there was also the factor of animosity: the British felt unwelcome in Badajoz after Talavera and an odour lingered over the Spaniards' surrender of the fortress to Soult without a fight in 1811. The British were *rubios* ('fair- or red-headed'), and, as Wellington later pointed out, *rubio* also implied heretic, for Judas Iscariot, curiously, was always depicted with red hair, he said, and 'we had this additional claim to be called *rubios*, that we wore red coats'.[90]

Wellington, an Irish Protestant, may have overstated the religious difference, but, in general, Spaniards had more in common with their French neighbours than with the British. That there was a more divisive issue than religion can be inferred from the remark of Wellington's that preceded the scathing opinion of his men, cited above: 'the French system of conscription brings together a fair sample of all classes; ours is composed of the scum of the earth'.[91]

Indeed, the fact that the French army was drawn from a wider spectrum of the population and did not consist so heavily of impoverished, brutalized recruits, explains in large part why French attitudes on matters of dress, food, wine and even women were better appreciated by Spaniards. In contrast, as Picton knew full well, British soldiers were an unruly lot, and if Grattan was wont to complain that the Connaught Rangers were an 'unrewarded tribe', this was likely attributable to the intractable marauding spirit of his 'brave ragged rascals'.

What Picton thought of the aftermath of Badajoz is not to be found in print and, in any case, was probably unprintable. The shameless rapacity may have contributed as much as the horrific slaughter to his deepening ennui and to his earnest desire to return home. Ironically, the severity of the losses could only delay his departure, as he dutifully accepted two days after the assault: 'I meant to have visited England immediately after the conclusion of this Siege, but so many general officers are hors de Combat in consequence, that I must postpone the Voyage until the conclusion of the Campaign.'[92] On 8 May he wrote more hopefully to Flanagan from Penedono, near the Portuguese Douro, where the army had moved to eject Marmont: 'I think, upon the whole, that I may now be allowed to retire. I have little, I may say no ambition to bear the weight of these cares.'[93] He was disappointed, however, in his plan 'to profit of this movement and visit Oporto', whence he hoped to take his passage to England. Instead, with General Colville insufficiently recovered from his wound and, therefore, unable to take over command of his division, Picton was obliged to press on with the army in pursuit of Marmont to Salamanca. There, on 24 June, he wrote to Marryat: 'I am perfectly tired with the continual movements and fatigue of this unceasing kind of warfare, in a country where we are exposed to every kind of privation, and, I may almost say, want. I mean to take my interest, for someone to succeed me in the command of the Third Division.'[94]

By now he was quite seriously ill and, at the time of the Battle of Salamanca on 22 July, he was confined to bed. The recurring bouts of Walcheren Fever, of which his streaming eyes were but one depressing symptom, had reduced him to a sorry state of mind as well as body. Indeed, when a subaltern entered his tent unannounced and saw the commander's white, emaciated head rise from the pillow supporting a huge nightcap, the young man was unable to contain his mirth, something that Picton understandably took amiss. However, he was cheered by the victory of Salamanca and especially by the thought that his name was now the subject of eulogy at home, his conduct at Badajoz having been singled out for praise by Lord Liverpool in a speech at the House of Lords on 27 April. In the presence of two great French armies, with double the number of veterans, an Allied force of 40,000 men had taken Badajoz, and Picton had played the key role.

It would not be 'the Tyrant of Trinidad' who returned home.

SIX

FROM VITORIA TO TOULOUSE

Shere Hard Fighting

I

On 22 July 1812, shortly after Wellington defeated Marmont at Salamanca, Picton returned home. He took the waters at fashionable Cheltenham Spa and then retired to Wales, where, in the autumn of 1812, he steadily recovered his health.

By November he was well enough to accept an invitation to stand for Parliament and canvass as prospective Tory member for the Pembroke boroughs: 'Mr Owen's Interest was offered me in so handsome and wholly unconditional a Manner', he wrote on 14 November, 'that I had no plea for holding back.'[1] Indeed, for the Owens of Orielton the Peninsular hero was an ideal choice to steal a march on rival gentry in the county, notably the Philippses of Picton Castle, Haverfordwest, and the Campbells of Stackpole. No doubt Picton saw the offer as a civil approbation that would finally lay his Trinidad ghost to rest. The last word on the Calderón affair had been pronounced in January when Lord Ellenborough ruled that the recognizances of the plaintiff, Mrs Marianne Fullarton, were 'to be respited until further order'. Fullarton's loyal widow was advised that should she press on and obtain a verdict against Picton, the punishment would probably be so slight as to bring little credit to her or the prosecution. In all, justice would be best served, said Ellenborough wearily, 'by suffering the case to remain where it is'.[2] Lord Liverpool's accolade in April had smoothed the last furrow from Picton's brow.

As for the election, at first he anticipated a 'warm contest', but soon realized that resistance was token as the big-spending Owen family had the majority of burgesses in their pocket: 'The Adverse Party are merely making a show to give us some trouble, as they are perfectly aware that they cannot stand the poll against so decided a superiority of numbers.' Nonetheless, he found canvassing repugnant: 'I have been going through a great deal of Mummery and making puppet show triumphal entries into Haverfordwest, Carmarthen, &c. I have pitied others in similar situations, and I am ashamed of myself: but those who become candidates for Popularity don't know how far the torrent may carry them, or they would never undertake the Voyage.'[3]

Prior to the election he was busy with property matters. He sold a farm to raise £2,000 to advance his young friend, Lewis Flanagan, who had been duped out of a similar sum by a sharp London barrister. Flanagan wrote at length about the latter's 'long and dark designs' on him, which were of a complexion he was 'horrified to give a name to', while he spoke of Picton, by contrast, as 'no Ordinary Man', but a soldier of independent mind who had fought every inch of his way 'to Public Distinction and Respect'. Picton, who had reproved Flanagan for his 'facinorousness' little more than a year before, advising him to treat other men's wives as 'prohibited Game', now trusted that the money he sent would enable the trainee lawyer to get over his 'Embarrassment' and complete his studies without further interruption. Flanagan was effusive in his gratitude, though his ink-spattered scrawl must have sorely tested his benefactor's eyes. Next, Picton negotiated to buy a stately pile with much land attached on the Towy estuary south of Carmarthen: 'I have been at Iscoed', he wrote at the end of November: 'It is certainly one of the most beautiful Places in the Principality: combining all the advantages of wood, water and diversified scenery: but the House is a mere shell, and will require very considerable repairs before it will be habitable. It is very beautiful, but very dear.' Indeed, the estate would cost him all of £30,000.[4]

At the more modest Poyston residence, with his brother the Revd Edward, he had time to reflect on events as he convalesced. The first year of the Regency had seen unparalleled success in the Peninsula, which induced a mood of optimism about the war. The triumphs at Ciudad Rodrigo, Badajoz and Salamanca had been crowned by the raising of the siege of Cadiz and by Wellington's entry into Madrid on 12 August after King Joseph – el Intruso to Spanish patriots – fled the capital. For Picton it must have been galling to miss an occasion when soldiers in his own army and his own division were, as Kincaid wrote, 'hailed as liberators, with the most joyous acclamations, by surrounding multitudes, who continued their rejoicings for three successive days'.[5] Yet October saw the disastrous siege of Burgos, in which Wellington, unaccountably eschewing his heavier cannon, sought to take a garrison of 2,000 with a mere 700 soon-dispirited men. Retreat was followed by the evacuation of Madrid, as Joseph menacingly regrouped, and withdrawal to winter quarters on the Portuguese border. Prudent as it was, the retreat looked like humiliation to the public, and Picton was no doubt glad to be out of it. His own reputation remained intact, while Wellington's grudging admission of culpability was indirect praise: 'The fault of which I was guilty in the expedition to Burgos was, not that I undertook the operation with inadequate means, but that I took there the most inexperienced instead of the best troops. I left at Madrid the 3rd, 4th and Light Divisions, who had been with myself always before.'[6] Picton very likely consoled himself with the thought that he and his talismanic 'fighting division' would have made all the difference at Burgos.

On the home front too there was growing unease. The Luddite Riots had begun towards the end of 1811 and quickly spread from Nottingham to other manufacturing cities where it was feared frames would reduce the demand for labour. The rioters found an ally in the 24-year-old George Gordon Byron, sixth Baron Byron, who, in his maiden speech in the Lords on 27 February 1812, evoked the distressing conditions that drove the labouring poor to such desperate acts as framebreaking and, as an Opposition peer, spoke out against the government's bill to punish such acts with death. Nonetheless, large bodies of militia were stationed in the disturbed counties to maintain the public peace. Also during that winter of 1811–12 a series of horrific murders took place in Wapping, which gave rise to tension in the capital and led to talk of establishing a police force. The Nightly Watch was now scarcely adequate to patrol a metropolis whose huge growth had been matched by a doubling in the number of criminal acts in the last five years. On Monday 11 May 1812 a state of lawlessness appeared to be confirmed when the Prime Minister, Spencer Perceval, was shot in the Commons lobby by a half-crazed bankrupt. The assassin, John Bellingham, who had a grievance over Russian trade restrictions, was hanged a week later, two days after Perceval's funeral. To some observers it seemed that civilization itself was under threat of extinction as the Continent lay ravaged by war and Napoleon advanced towards Moscow. Many would have agreed with Madame de Staël that Europe was now as decadent as the pre-Christian Roman Empire.

Such an impression was hardly contradicted by the example of the Prince Regent, who was famed for more than his architectural excesses at Carlton House and the Royal Pavilion, Brighton. In March 1812, barely twelve months after being sworn in, he was vilified in *The Examiner* as 'a libertine over head and ears in debt and disgrace, a despiser of domestic ties, the companion of gamblers and demireps', for which radical eloquence Leigh Hunt, the newspaper's editor, spent two years in jail and received a £1,000 fine. Amongst Hunt's Newgate visitors were Shelley, Keats and, inevitably, Lord Byron, while in the spirit of poetic solidarity, Charles Lamb, inspired by his future sovereign's seventeen stone, penned 'The Prince of Whales':

> Not a fatter fish than he
> Flounders round the polar sea.
> See his blubbers, at his gills,
> What a world of drink he swills...
>
> Every fish of generous kind
> Scuds aside or slinks behind;
> But about his presence keep
> All the Monsters of the Deep.

Gouty, obese and more frilled than Beau Brummell, Prinny was meat and drink to satirists like Gillray and Cruickshank, who crammed their cartoons with this royal paradigm of self-indulgence. The Prince's domestic strife had been wretchedly public and had occupied a great deal of parliamentary time ever since, seven years earlier, 'the Delicate Investigation' of his estranged wife, Caroline of Brunswick, for 'high treason by the foul crime of adultery'. Indeed, the vulgar, scatter-brained Princess of Wales had been forbidden, from fear of contamination, to see her daughter, Charlotte, except at regulated intervals, though moral high ground was hardly at stake in the interminable dispute.

Not that such matters weighed heavily with Picton when he was summoned to the second levee of the season at Carlton House on Monday 1 February 1813. For some time his thoughts had been gravitating towards the prospect of honours. Two years earlier he had claimed, somewhat piously, to be 'actuated by no other motive than a Sense of public Duty', while at the first siege of Badajoz he had protested, perhaps too much, 'I am neither ambitious of a R. Ribbon or any other Distinction, and therefore can easily make up my mind to the insipid walks of private life'. By the second siege, however, he had been allowing himself to participate in an open speculation, telling Flanagan with some hauteur: 'Forbes you may recollect, in one of his Moments of Prophecy, predicted that I was destined for a pair of Gilt spurs. Though I do not hold our friend to be one of the Inspired, his prediction may eventually be realised.'[7]

Amongst the serried ranks of royalty and aristocracy at

Carlton House that Monday was Lord Liverpool, soon to complete the first of fifteen stolid years as prime minister, and Frederick, Duke of York, who, in 1809, had been forced to resign as Commander-in-Chief after a London demirep by the name of Mary Anne Clarke had publicly implicated him in her criminal trafficking in commissions while she was his mistress. She was as vexatious to the Duke of York as Princess Caroline was to his elder brother, the Prince Regent, which prompted Colonel Torrens to remark in a letter to Wellington: 'I wish both these *amiable women* were hanging at any of your outposts'. After the levee the Prince presided at a Chapter of the Knights of the Bath, at which Picton, sponsored by Lord Cochrane and General Sir Thomas Graham, was, with fitting ceremony, created a Knight of the Order. It is difficult to imagine two persons less compatible than the Prince and Picton, the one as wasted by private pleasure as the other by public service. Perhaps the Prince inquired urbanely after the health of the throaty general and, with the aid of the Duke of York, Lord Liverpool or General Graham, inspired thoughts of an early return to unfinished business in the Peninsula.

Two weeks later, on 19 March, Picton duly became a Member of Parliament. 'I have been returned without a dissenting voice', he wrote from Pembroke: 'The Enemy saw us so well fortified as to be deterred from any attempt, and I have just gone through all the Mummery of Chairing.'[8] Within ten days he was back in town at his Edward Street residence when thoughts of the Peninsula rather than Parliament prompted him to put on a brave face: 'By constantly taking large doses of Bark I succeeded in keeping the Fever off, & I am now perfectly well', he informed Flanagan. On 8 April he boarded the frigate *Pomone* at Portsmouth, requesting his friend to send on items that he had left behind in his hurry: military memoranda, maps, hunting shot, 'a couple of good Razors and a Strop', and twelve boxes of Seidlitz Powders to continue the Cheltenham diuretic. 'The wind is at length become fair', he wrote, 'and we shall sail before 12 o'Clock with the prospect of a favorable passage.'

II

After 'a remarkably fine and agreeable passage out' he landed in Lisbon on 18 April. There he was met by his plump and affable aide-de-camp, Tyler, who, with his 'usual good Appetite and bad Memory', Picton quipped, 'cares as little about what is going on in the World as any man in it'. With the mules and horses 'all in readiness and good order', they left Lisbon inside four days and reached Castelo Branco a week later. Picton quickly assessed the situation:

> The French are drawing towards the Douro, having abandoned Madrid, Toledo, and nearly everything south of Avila. They are making dispositions to dispute the Positions on the above mentioned River, but a movement we are making through Trazosmontes will probably determine them at once to retire behind the Ebro, where they will make their Chief stand. This will give the Spanish an enlarged theatre to act upon, and if they show any corresponding Energies or Cooperation equal to the means they will become possest of, I really think we ought to clear the Country before the commencement of 1814.[9]

He was right about where the French would make their stand. The Allies' two-pronged thrust, with the main body under Wellington heading directly for Burgos and the other under Graham sweeping north through Tras-os-Montes, would drive Marmont back behind the Ebro faster than Masséna had been ejected from Portugal two years before. Picton's eight months at home soon became a distant memory in the trackless wastes of Tras-os-Montes, but he was delighted to be back with the Third Division, who gave him a rousing welcome, and happy to serve under Graham, whom he had last met in the more sumptuous surroundings of Carlton House. Above all, he was favourably impressed by the state of the troops: 'Our Army is generally more healthy than at any period during the War, and we shall certainly take the Field in considerably greater numbers than last year, not far from 80,000.' No effort had been spared to provide Wellington with the recruits he needed and the army showed a welcome blend of fresh faces and those inured to the hardship of campaigning. The sense of well-being also owed something to Napoleon's disastrous Russian campaign in the winter of 1812, when the evacuation of Moscow was followed by a decimating retreat. Amongst its other consequences, this would surely lead to further depletion of French forces in the Peninsula, if not their total withdrawal.

Picton had his reservations about the Spanish troops, who would now have to fight as an army rather than in guerrilla bands. In this he was in agreement with Wellington, who had been critical of their low discipline and high desertion rates, attributable mainly to the fact that they had not been paid for months, or, in some cases, years. The Cortes of Cadiz, whose 184 *diputados* all signed the historic liberal constitution of 18 March 1812, had made Wellington *Generalísimo* of the Spanish forces on 22 September, following his triumphant entry into Madrid in August. By December, however, Wellington was moved to write: 'I certainly was not aware till very lately of the real state of the Spanish army, or I should have hesitated before I should have charged myself with such a Herculean labor as its command.'[10] His running battle with the Spanish Minister at War, Don Juan de Caraval, whom he called 'that greatest of all blackguards', was consistent with his long-held view that Spain was leaderless – 'this lost nation', he complained, 'with nobody to excite them to exertion' – though his verbal offensive may also have been designed to pre-empt criticism after Burgos.

If Wellington spoke all too pointedly about the need for discipline in his address to the Spanish Army at Cadiz on 1 January, he was no less blunt in his advice to *diputados* on constitutional matters later that month, when the Allies intercepted a letter from Joseph to his brother Napoleon Bonaparte. The Commander of the Forces elaborated with scarcely concealed pleasure on the usurper's theme that: 'Les habitans prefèrent aux théories des Cortes les ordres d'un souverain de votre maison.'[11] Not that the House of Napoleon was preferable to the theories of the Cortes, said Wellington shrewdly, but 'it is so far true that the people do not like those theories'. In this he recognized the mood of common citizens who, when Fernando returned as absolute monarch, would gleefully drag the *Piedra de la Libertad* ('Stone of Liberty') from the Cortes, shouting '*¡Vivan las caenas!*' ('Long live chains!'). Wellington's advice to the *liberales* in the spring of 1813 was nearly as reactionary: they should repeal half the articles in their new-fangled Constitution, establish a regency, with powers placed in the hands of one royal personage, and create a second chamber along the lines of the British House of Lords, 'an assembly of the great landed proprietors'.

Picton would doubtless have agreed on all counts with the Commander of the Forces, whom the Prince Regent had created Marquess in September and a Knight of the Garter in January. The person with whom he had a celebrated disagreement at this time was Wellington's butler. The incident occurred when the two wings of the Allied army had joined together as the French retreated behind Burgos, blowing up its fortress. Picton, eager to press the Third on in their pursuit, found his road blocked by headquarters baggage, which traditionally enjoyed privilege on the road. When the butler refused to give way, a fuming Picton charged up on his cob and beat the devoted servant about the head with his trusty umbrella. Presumably Wellington accepted this type of behaviour from his irascible Welsh general who was prone to such episodes. Indeed, within weeks, Picton would have another highway altercation, this time with General Alten, who had succeeded Craufurd as commander of the Light Division. On this second occasion he came up behind a group of men, led by George Simmons, who had been collecting wood:

'Well, sir', said Picton testily to Simmons, 'you have got wood enough for yours and my Division. I shall have it divided. Make your men throw it down. It is a damned concern to have to follow. You sweep up everything before you.'[12] Whereupon General Alten arrived on the scene and was none too pleased with Picton for interfering with Simmons in the performance of his duty. The latter, for his part, wisely slipped away with his men and the firewood, leaving his superiors to argue the case.

Between these two intramural incidents came the rather weightier confrontation with the enemy at Vitoria. First, on the morning of 13 June, the French blew up Burgos, the tremendous explosion at 6.00 a.m. sounding as music in the ears of Allied soldiers who, as Simmons observed, 'would much sooner have a fair field to fight on, than storm a town'. Two days later, in hot pursuit, the Allies crossed the Ebro river at Puente Arenas and approached Vitoria, the capital of the Basque province of Alava, where Joseph, whose force of 50,000 men was much inferior to the Allies', felt obliged to make a stand if only to cover the evacuation of the loot he had collected in five years as King of Spain. He had the advantage of the position which, by coincidence, was the one on which the Black Prince, in 1367, had fought for Pedro I, 'el Cruel', against Henry of Trastamara, a rival for the throne of Castile. This ground stood a few miles west of Vitoria near the Zadorra river and was protected on two sides by a bend in the river and to the south by the rugged heights of La Puebla. Even here Joseph was less than astute, for the river was little more than a fast-flowing mountain stream, fordable in various places, while the undulating ground allowed Wellington vantage points from which to assess the strength and dispositions of his enemy.

This he duly did on 20 June when he formed a plan to attack in four columns: General Sir Rowland Hill would approach with his Second Division and General Pablo Morillo's Spaniards by the south-west over the Puebla high ground; Graham, with British, Portuguese and Spanish divisions, would make for the extreme east and attempt to cut the enemy off close to Vitoria itself; finally, in the centre, the main thrust would come from General Sir Galbraith Lowry Cole, with his Fourth Division and

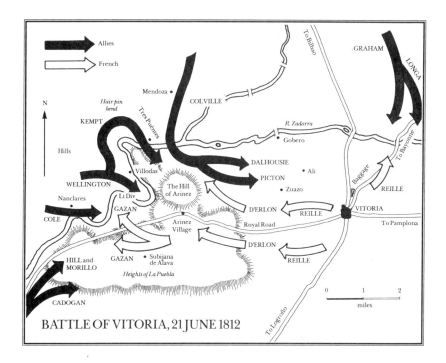

BATTLE OF VITORIA, 21 JUNE 1812

the Cavalry, and, further east, from General Lord Dalhousie's Seventh and Picton's Third. The main drawback was the extended nature of the Allied front, with resulting problems in communication. This would be largely offset by decisive action, not least on Picton's part.

The battle began early on 21 June when Hill advanced on the enemy's left flank and was warmly resisted on the crest of La Puebla. In the centre, Kincaid observed, Kempt's Riflemen approached the Zadorra soon after dawn and saw the French on the hills opposite 'while the spires of Vitoria were visible in the distance'.[13] By mid-morning Picton's Third was in position near the river at the village of Mendoza, but Dalhousie, unaccountably, had not yet arrived. With all but Hill's division inactive, the troops became impatient, and Picton, who even suspected Wellington had forgotten him, fumed in frustration, jerking the bridle of his long-suffering cob. Just then a staff officer came by with news that Kempt's brigade had crossed the Zadorra by one lightly defended bridge. He also had instructions for the missing Dalhousie, who was to cross immediately in pursuit. Picton needed no further invitation. Within minutes the Third Division was on the French side of the river.

They quickly overhauled Kempt's brigade, as Kincaid reported: 'We had not been many seconds there before we observed the bayonets of the third and seventh divisions glittering above the standing corn.' In fact, Dalhousie had arrived shortly after Picton took it upon himself to carry out Wellington's order, but the Seventh were thereafter obliged to follow in the Third's bold steps as they thrust into the centre of the French position. This proved to be the key action in the battle, at least in Picton's view:

> The 3rd Division was closely Engaged, from 12 o'Clock until dark, when the French Army was entirely routed. I may say with a safe conscience that the 3rd Division had the principal share in the brilliant achievement, and that we were opposed by at least five times our numbers and 50 pieces of Cannon, which never once checked us in our rapid Career. We were so situated that the whole Army had its Eyes upon us, and express their Admiration at our Exploits.[14]

This is borne out by rifleman Kincaid, who was one such admiring observer: 'Old Picton rode at the head of the third division, dressed in a blue coat and round hat, and swore as roundly all the way as if he had been wearing two cocked ones.'[15]

The Third forced the French back to the village of Zuazo where they attempted to resist. Coming up behind, Kincaid recalled 'a wall at the entrance of a village', where the French held their line, though this was promptly overcome: 'The French fled from the wall as soon as they received a volley from a part of the third division, and we instantly dashed down the hill, and charged them through the village, capturing three of their guns.' While this confrontation and numerous others like it took place on the plain between the river and the heights, General Dalhousie pushed further east to assist Graham, who had been held up at Gamarra Mayor. His arrival there with the Seventh Division completely dispirited the French, who fled in confusion, having lost the battle.

The Third had suffered badly in the centre of the action, as Picton reported: 'Great things are not to be purchased at so small Expense, our loss was equal to our exertions, out of 5600 men we lost 1800.'[16] He was full of praise for the Portuguese under him, who 'fully equalled the English during the whole day', and had a good word for the Spaniards, many of whom 'fought in a manner becoming the Castilians'. What most decidedly did not please him was Wellington's subsequent report of the battle, which, he said indignantly, 'like most of the

despatches of the noble Marquis, is anything but a correct likeness of the Event it purposes to relate'. In Picton's view the
Commander of the Forces wrongly attributed 'to combination
and manoeuvre alone what was really effected in part by hard
fighting'. He observed that it was not so much a question of
deep strategy, or of the French weakly capitulating at the centre:

> The fact is that they obstinately disputed every foot, & were driven
> back by shere hard fighting by the 3^d Division from a succession
> of strong Positions, occupied by a numerous well served Artillery,
> and as Proof of the hard work we had from one o'Clock till 5 in
> the Evening, we lost in killed and wounded 89 officers, 71
> sergeants, & 1475 Rank and File, being more than one third of the
> Casualties of the whole Army, and equal to one third of our own
> numbers. Yet it does not appear, in the official account, that we
> were at all engaged except Genl. Colville's Brigade.

Picton was clearly angry that the meritorious effort made by
the Third Division had not received special commendation.
There was some difference of opinion as to how hard the French
fought at Vitoria, at least in the centre of their position, which
is reflected in individual accounts. On the one hand, Sergeant
Lawrence wrote, 'Once on the other side of the river and
formed into a line we were up and at them in spite of a murderous fire which they kept up from their cannon.'[17] Yet George
Simmons gave a different emphasis: 'In the afternoon the
enemy to our front began to make less opposition, and only
seemed determined to get out of our clutches as fast as possible.'[18] Whatever the truth, it is likely that the level of French
resistance at the centre would have been higher had they not
neglected to blow up the Zadorra bridges, for this in turn would
have enabled them to use their artillery to more damaging
effect. Yet Picton's casualty figures tell their own story and, if a
hounded army is likely to be less than wholly resolute, it would
be harsh to undervalue the efforts of those who risked or gave
their lives in bearing the brunt of the attack.

The most disappointing feature in the victory was that it was
not pressed home. Once again, plunder proved to be the British
undoing. Picton wrote: 'Night covered the routed Army, and
they saved themselves by abandoning Every thing and dispersing to the mountains from whence they are Endeavouring to
make their way back to France.' Kincaid was more pointed: 'Had
a single regiment of our dragoons been at hand, or even a
squadron, to have forced them into shape for a few minutes, we
must have taken from ten to twenty thousand prisoners.' As it
was, the French beat a hasty retreat to Vitoria and, finding the

main road to France blocked by Graham's Division, took the one
road left open to them, that of Pamplona. It was not open long,
however, as Kincaid related:

> For their fugitive army, and their myriads of followers with
> baggage, guns, carriages, &c., being all precipitated upon it at the
> same moment, it got choked up about a mile beyond the town, in
> the most glorious state of confusion; and the drivers, finding that
> one pair of legs was worth two pairs of wheels, abandoned it all to
> the victors.[19]

It was 6.00 p.m. when the victorious but weary troops fell on
wagonloads of claret, champagne and brandy, not to mention a
veritable emporium of comestible delicacies which invited
immediate gorging. The highway, strewn with carriages and
unwieldy baggage trains, soon looked like the scene of a comic
masquerade as inebriated soldiers and their women bedecked
themselves in the finest robes and most precious jewels that ever
French courtiers lavished on themselves and their powdered
mistresses. Dumped, too, were chests crammed with plate, gold
and specie, amongst which the soldiers in their revelry
rummaged by torchlight. Picton estimated that the loss to the
French 'must amount to between three and four millions sterling', and Wellington thought that a good million had probably
fallen into his soldiers' hands. It was the greatest treasure ever
found on the open road and it bought Joseph's return passage
to France.

III

The French scrambled to their Pyrenean fastness, skirting the
well-garrisoned fortress of Pamplona, which covered their
retreat. Once in France, Joseph was ignominiously relieved of
the command of his now shambolic army, which one bitter
veteran dubbed 'un bordel ambulant'. In his place Napoleon
charged Marshal Soult with the task of regenerating morale in
readiness for a counter-attack. Wellington, raised to the rank of
Field Marshal following his strategic triumph at Vitoria, which
had seen him march a vast army 400 miles in 40 days, was not
inclined to pursue the French onto their own soil: besides
Pamplona, San Sebastián also remained in enemy hands, as did
Tarragona on the Catalan coast. He preferred to wait and see
what kind of treaty Napoleon would make with the Austrians,
Prussians and Russians, deeming it more prudent to hold the

natural frontier of the Pyrenees and concentrate on what was left of the French in Spain.

The Allied army was soon stretched laterally over some forty miles, from San Sebastián in the west, where General Graham began siege operations, to Pamplona in the east, which from 17 July was blockaded by Spaniards under the Conde de Abisbal. Between these extremities stood forces under Generals Hill, Campbell, Cole and Byng, which guarded the three main valleys in the western Pyrenees, namely the Baztan, Baigorry and the Carlos with its famed pass of Roncesvalles. Wellington placed his headquarters at Lesaca, where he might keep an eye on proceedings at San Sebastián, while Picton and the Third were kept in reserve at Olaque, due north of Pamplona, ready, at least in theory, to assist wherever Soult chose to attempt a breakthrough. On 26 July Picton wrote: 'We are now amongst the Pyrenees covering the Siege of St. Sebastian and the Blockade of Pampeluna. Soult has taken the Command of this discomfited Army, and is close on the Frontier; but not, I think, in sufficient force for offensive operations. If Pampeluna and St. Sebastian surrender we shall be tolerably secure on this side, and then we must turn our minds towards Catalonia and Souchet.' He was suffering badly from his recurring complaint and was blind to the stunning scenery: 'My Eyes continue very weak and inflamed; from its long continuance I fear it is becoming chronical. If I can I certainly intend withdrawing after this campaign.'[20]

His letter was written a day after the abortive first attempt to storm the isthmian fortress of San Sebastián, when General Graham, seeking to take advantage of low tide, but against Wellington's advice, attacked before dawn and paid a heavy price in terms of lives lost in the confusion. This calamity followed General Sir George Murray's worse example of incompetence at Tarragona, where, on learning that Marshal Suchet was advancing from Valencia, he raised the siege and took to his boats with unseemly haste, leaving the guns that had once breached Ciudad Rodrigo to fall into enemy hands without a fight. As if this were not enough, the news came that Soult had mobilized a large force, which was moving upon Wellington's right to relieve Pamplona. The physical barrier of the Pyrenees had clearly hindered military intelligence, for Wellington expected Soult to try to relieve San Sebastián before Pamplona, while he still had little idea of French strength. In response, Wellington sent word to Cole, who commanded the Fourth Division, and to Picton, whose Third was now close by, instructing them to 'support Major-General Byng in the defence of the passes in front of Roncesvalles', adding, in his next message, that these passes 'should be maintained to the utmost'.[21] Owing to poor communications in the mountains, however, the messages of 23 and 24 July were not received in time, as Picton explained to Wellington in a letter sent from Zubiri on the evening of 26 July: 'If I had known your Lordship's intentions sooner, I would have joined Sir L.Cole before he had retired from the passes.'[22]

To his credit, Cole had retired from the heights only when darkness came on 25 July, after having fought long and hard throughout the day in support of Byng and against overwhelming numbers which he put at more than 30,000. Picton had withdrawn far from the passes and met with Cole on 26 July, when he stood against the French at Zubiri. Picton reported to Wellington:

> When I joined Sir Lowry Cole he had taken up a position about two miles in front of Zubiri, where he was attacked about half-past three by a very superior force. The enemy was not able to make any impression on the post, though he drove in our sharpshooters, and extended himself much to our right and left, particularly to our right, which was easily turnable.

This encounter again finished at nightfall, when Picton, the senior officer, noted that he and Cole were agreed they should leave such an exposed area and retire further towards the Vitoria road.

Next day, 27 July, with Picton at Huarte and Cole at Sorauren, it was again the Fourth Division that attracted Soult's attention. To the unexpected pleasure of Cole's troops, Wellington himself arrived on the scene, having covered a considerable distance at speed on his thoroughbred, much of it unaccompanied. The suddenness of the field marshal's appearance must have surprised Soult, whose response was to defer his attack for twenty-four hours. When it came, the action was fierce enough, but the superior French forces were repulsed in such a short space of time as to suggest that, perhaps as a result of under-nourishment, they were too fatigued to scale Cole's well-chosen ground, or else they had not truly recovered their spirits after Vitoria. What is certain is that Sorauren marked the end of Soult's interest in relieving Pamplona and by the end of the month his army had crossed into France in a very sorry state with nothing to show for their efforts but losses of 13,000 men.

Picton and his Third had taken no part in the Battle of Sorauren, other than protecting Cole's right from attack by virtue of their simple presence on that side. Indeed, they had seen little action at all in the Pyrenees, their function being strictly supportive. There is no reason to doubt that Wellington's order to resist 'to the utmost' at Roncesvalles reached Picton too late, but his operation in this brief campaign does seem excessively cautious, more so than at Almeida, where his refusal to assist Craufurd accorded precisely with Wellington's instructions. The most likely explanation for Picton's passivity is, quite simply, his eyes, which not only discomforted him but would have been a severe handicap in the field, especially in such alpine terrain. The lingering effects of Walcheren Fever must have undermined his confidence and sapped his spirit. Besides, after Vitoria, where he felt his efforts had not been properly appreciated, he was increasingly susceptible to dark moods.

A period of relative inactivity followed Soult's withdrawal into France as the Allied army continued its blockade of Pamplona and prepared for a fresh assault on San Sebastián. Availing himself of heavier breaching guns brought in through Pasajes, Wellington used volunteers in place of Graham's floundering Fifth and, overcoming both the tide and fierce French resistance, succeeded on 31 August in taking San Sebastián. Pamplona, the capital of Navarra, surrendered on 30 October, by which time Picton had long since returned home to attend to his health and personal affairs.

His letter, written in London on 10 September, to senior officers in the Third Division shows that he had left Spain in some distress: 'In the extreme weak state to which I was reduced, previous to my leaving the Peninsula, my Feelings were too powerful for my Spirits, and it was not possible for me adequately to Answer the kind Letter of the General Officers Commanding Brigades, from the Valley of Baztan, on the 27th of August last.'[23] He continued by expressing his sense of indebtedness to the Third for the honours that had been bestowed on him and for the way he had 'risen in the service'. He wrote in a vein that suggested that he felt it unlikely he would see military action again:

> The Period of my Life, to which I shall always recur, with the greatest satisfaction, is that which was passed at the Head of the 3rd Division, where I always experienced such a spirit of unanimity and Heroism as never have failed to have success in any of the difficult Enterprises we were Employed upon. Though I may never again have the honour of Commanding so distinguished a Corps, I shall ever feel myself identified with the 3 Division in all its Operations, and shall retain as strong an Interest in its success as I ever did whilst I had the honor of Presiding at its Head.

His main wish now was to take his seat in the House of

Commons, barely a stone's throw from Westminster Hall, whose corridors he had once paced so anxiously. The Pembroke by-election earlier in the year had come about when John Owen was elected to the county seat in October 1812, for this obliged Owen to relinquish his boroughs seat, which he promptly invited Picton to contest. Owen, who had since been made a baronet, spent more than £10,000 securing victory over John Campbell in the hard-fought October election, which saw nearly 3,000 cast their vote. Most of this went on 'treating' the electorate, though transport, lodgings, cockades and ribbons all had to be paid for. After inheriting the Orielton estate by maternal line in 1809 when he took the Owen name, he was understandably keen to prove himself and continue the tradition of a family, which in 200 years, sent no fewer than fourteen proud if rather mute members to Parliament. No doubt he would have supported Picton to the hilt, if necessary, in the interest of extending his hold. So open-handed was he in his campaigns and so profligate in his investments that the entire Orielton estate would eventually have to be sold to pay his debts.

Flush when Picton knew him, Owen was a lawyer who would have regarded the sums he laid out as a necessary investment to safeguard his seat of patronage, a fair price to pay for the privilege of monitoring legislation on turnpikes, enclosures, fisheries and the like. As it happened, the issue of electoral reform and of pocket boroughs was much in the spring air of 1813 when a bill on malpractice at the recent Weymouth election was debated in the House. It appeared that 'gross abuses' had been committed 'by persons claiming and exercising a right to vote upon nominal reserved rents', one such person having acquired eight votes on a rent of two pence! Though Picton's election would surely not have been besmirched by such practices, it is nonetheless unsurprising that it did not go to a poll for the Pembroke boroughs electorate consisted almost entirely of the freemen of Tenby and of Pembroke itself, both of which towns lay in the south Pembrokeshire, property-based stronghold of the Owens of Orielton.

Also controversial at this time was the religious issue, for the question of 'Catholic Relief' was raised in the Commons in March, while in June the House debated the matter of the illegal Orange Lodges whose sole purpose was the maintaining of the Protestant Ascendancy. The Owens of Orielton had always fought under the orange colour and indeed the previous Member of Parliament, Sir Hugh Owen, had been a champion of the Protestant cause. However, to his credit, his cousin and heir, Sir John, voted on 2 March 1813 in favour of Catholic

Emancipation, though he later lost his nerve under Tory pressure and abstained, when the bill was defeated.

On the morning of Thursday 11 November 1813 Picton went with Sir John to take his seat and, before the full House, was welcomed by the Speaker in the most glowing terms:

> Lieutenant-General Picton, in this House your name has been long since enrolled amongst those who have obtained the gratitude of their country for distinguished military services; and we, this day, rejoice to see you amongst us, claiming again the tribute of our thanks for fresh exploits and achievements. Wherever the history of the Peninsular War shall be related, your name will be found amongst the foremost in that race of glory; by your sword the British troops were led on to the victorious assault of Ciudad Rodrigo; by your daring hand the British standard was planted upon the castle of Badajoz; when the usurper of the Spanish throne was driven to make his last stand at Vitoria, your battalions filled the centre of that formidable line, before which the veteran troops of France fled in terror and dismay; and by your skill, prudence, and valour, exerted in a critical hour, the enemy was foiled in his desperate attempt to break through the barrier of the Pyrenees, and raise the blockade of Pamplona.[24]

The Speaker ended by delivering the House's unanimous and repeated thanks, most notably on this occasion for his contribution at Vitoria, which must have deeply pleased the recipient. It was to resounding applause that Picton rose and, with no little difficulty, began his reply, having been strongly moved by the Speaker's address. In a few words, uttered in a low tone, he expressed his humble awareness of this recognition, having always regarded the Thanks of the House of Commons as one of the greatest honours a British officer could receive. His troublesome eyes probably added to his self-consciousness as he acknowledged the heroism which made the corps he had proudly commanded 'truly invincible'. He concluded with appropriate modesty: 'It would be unfortunate indeed if we failed entirely to reflect some of the rays of the great luminary that directed us.'

At Carlton House at 2.00 p.m. that same day Picton attended the Prince Regent's first levee of the season. Amongst the guests were General Sir Thomas Graham, recently returned from the Peninsula, and Sir Thomas Hislop, the governor of Trinidad, with whom Picton had corresponded in 1806. Hislop and Picton may well have compared notes on the island colony, for the ex-governor would surely have been interested to hear how Port of Spain had been rebuilt after the fire, as well as to have news of old planter friends, if not of Rosetta and the children. But the

topic on everyone's lips ever since the Prince Regent opened
Parliament a week before, was Napoleon's defeat at the Battle of
Leipzig and the ensuing treaty that his enemies had struck with
him. Euphoria at the crushing of the Corsican had quickly given
way to outrage over the leniency of the terms. Had the nation
suffered the horrors of war for no purpose? Was the perpetrator
of all this suffering to be held a hero? One angry correspondent
wrote to *The Times*: 'For what have we toiled, and bled, and
famished? Is it that we should seize no compensation for what
we have lost? Is it that we should end as we began?'

Picton was also kept busy at this time by persons seeking
favour from him in his newly influential capacities as Member of
Parliament, Knight of the Bath and authentic military hero. One
such inquiry came from Sir William Garrow, the Fullartons' wily
prosecutor, who sought for a young friend, Chambers, a posting
in the Peninsula, ideally on Picton's personal staff. The latter
replied that although he had 'long since been engaged three
deep' with such applications, he would do what he could, taking
the trouble to assure Garrow that he bore no grudge towards
him and had 'no recollection of the past'.[25] He was as good as
his word, for he took Chambers with him when he next left
England and, after the first serious action, wrote to say that
Chambers was unscathed, telling Flanagan: 'Be so good as to let
Sir W. Garrow know that his protege is a most promising young
man and cannot fail to do well.'[26]

It is doubtful whether Picton returned to the House in the
latter part of 1813, for his health and personal affairs kept him
out of town. It appears that he made a speedy recovery from the
Walcheren Fever for, on 30 November, he sent a note to
Flanagan from Molloy's, his favourite coffee house: 'I am again
under the necessity of taking a running Leave of you, being
suddenly called upon to Embark on board the *Porcupine* Frigate.'
With ultimate victory over the French in sight, it was natural he
should want to have a part in it: 'after all the fatigues of the
chase', he wrote shortly from France, 'it would not be decorous
to be thrown out at the Death'.[27]

IV

Picton enjoyed a 'quiet and agreeable passage' out from
Portsmouth to St Jean de Luz which took ten days. In contrast,
Tyler, who had accompanied him home but returned with the
horses on a different boat by way of the deeper Pasajes harbour,

had the misfortune to experience 'a most miserable voyage', as he was quick to complain. Increasingly, the aide-de-camp's portly figure and cavilling banter cast him as a Sancho Panza to Picton's gaunt Don Quixote, and he had the same endearing appeal to his superior: 'Mr Tyler is as fat and good humoured as ever, and amongst the Portuguese of the Division he universally goes by the name of the *Adjutanta Gordo* or the fat A.D.C.: but as long as he is well fed he does not care a farthing for the gibes and jokes.'

Before leaving England Picton had been offered command of the Army of Cataluña when General Murray was censured and removed for his feebleness at Tarragona. To Wellington's satisfaction, he turned down this chance of an independent command, admittedly of a mixed bag of soldiers, and chose instead to rejoin his Third at the heart of the action: 'I have given up all idea of Catalonia on finding that the state of the Force in that quarter did not give any Hopes of actual operations. I have therefore, with the approbation of the Marquis, determined to resume the Command of the old 3rd again.'[28] It must have been a special pleasure to tread French soil and share the sense of victorious momentum that his troops enjoyed. Kincaid of the Rifles described the uplifting prospect that the view of France offered from La Rhune mountains when they finally penetrated the Pyrenean mists:

> On our left, the Bay of Biscay lay extended as far as the horizon, while several of our ships of war were seen sporting upon her bosom. Beneath us lay the pretty little town of St. Jean de Luz, which looked as if it had just been framed out of the Lilliputian scenery of a toy-shop. The town of Bayonne, too, was visible in the distance; and the view to the right embraced a beautiful well-wooded country, thickly studded with towns and villages, as far as the eye could reach.[29]

Affairs were quiet on Picton's arrival: 'it is almost impossible to carry on operations in the actual state of the weather and Roads, which are all but impassable, being up to the Horses shoulder every step'. Nursing a 'severe cold', he had time to appreciate the area's greater comforts, while the inhabitants impressed him as 'a much more civilized race than in any part of the Peninsula'. He noted that they were well disposed towards the Allies:

> The French generally appear glad to see us, and are remarkably civil. They talk of their old masters with regret and affection, and, I think, would be delighted to have them back. When they speak of Buonapart they shake their Heads and draw the forefinger

across their Throats, intimating, I suppose, that he is a Cut Throat
or something as execrable.

Wellington, as always, insisted that his troops treat the locals
courteously, but this was less easy for Spaniards who had experienced six years of French tyranny, as General Hope reported
from Boucaut: 'I am sorry to say that the Spaniards spread
dismay by their conduct wherever they move.'[30] Many would
soon be sent home, for Wellington preferred to fight with inferior numbers rather than antagonize the local people. By
contrast, Napoleon berated his nation for not repelling the
armies that were now closing in on him and, as Picton observed
in the south: 'Senators and Generals were sent by the Emperor
to raise the *Loi du Mass* and irritate the people of the country
against us, but they completely failed, as we are every where
received in the most friendly and hospitable manner.'[31]

Towards the middle of February 1814, when the weather
improved, the troops broke up winter quarters and, once mobilized, pushed the French eastward across the series of rivers that
run down from the Pyrenees in a north-westerly direction,
namely the Nive, the Bidouze, the Gave d'Orloron and the Gave
de Pau, at each of which Soult orchestrated defensive manoeuvres and blew up key bridges. Picton wrote on 4 March:

> We had three considerable rivers to pass and it was important that
> the Enemy should be ignorant of the points where we meant to
> pass them. We fully succeeded in every instance, and on the 26th
> of February the 3rd Division Forded the Gave de Pau, about 4
> o'Clock p.m., drove in the Enemy's advanced Posts, and took up
> a Position within four miles of the then main Army, which Marshal
> the Duke of Dalmatia had concentrated, on a strong commanding
> ground of very difficult access in Front of the Town of Ortes.[32]

With Soult – to British soldiers, the Duke of Damnation –
clearly determined to make a stand at Orthez, Wellington
formed a plan of attack which was strikingly similar to that used
at Vitoria. Both flanks of the enemy would be pressed while a
central thrust would be timed for the right moment: the Fourth
and Seventh divisions would occupy the French right near the
village of St Boes; Hill would take his corps in a wide outflanking movement to the east and cut in at the village of Orthez;
finally, the Third would combine with Sir Henry Clinton's Sixth
and, as Wellington instructed, 'direct their attacks against the
centre of the enemy's position by the tongues of land which orig-
inate from the ridge on which the French were posted'.[33]
Fighting was to have begun on the morning of 27 February, but
poor roads delayed the Seventh's approach, and 'it was nearly

one o'Clock', Picton noted, 'before the attack commenced on the Enemy's right'. In fact, the Fourth Division began the attack on their own, and, though they twice carried the ground, which consisted of 'strong ridges of live growth on an elevation of considerably difficult access', ultimately they were 'overpowered by numbers and obliged to abandon it'. Wellington then sent in the Light Division, which he had held in reserve on that flank, and, when they were joined by the Seventh, who had at last arrived, they began to drive the enemy back. Picton reported that:

> During this operation seven Bat[ns] of the 3[d] Division moved upon the Enemy's centre, and three (two Portuguese and one British) turned his left Flank and carried a strong position on which it rested. As the Enemy had a numerous Artillery on this point, which might be considered as one of the keys of his Position, the resistance was obstinate, and our loss in storming it very considerable.[34]

In fact, he put the Third's losses at 825, which included his acting aide-de-camp, Captain Parker of the Engineers, 'killed by a cannon shot within a few yards of me'. Nevertheless, the Third had again found the soft underbelly of the French and, 'very well supported by Sir H. Clinton and the Sixth Division', as Picton readily acknowledged, had driven them back remorselessly. With Hill also making progress near Orthez, Soult feared his road to Toulouse would be cut off and he consequently ordered a general retreat. This was at first executed with great regularity, Picton observed, 'but as the night advanced they fell into great disorder and made off in perfect confusion, dispersing and making the best of their way, and by that means escaped us, as they had formerly done at Vitoria'.

This time there was no booty for the Allies, and it was sheer exhaustion that made them give up the chase: 'We were so fatigued with moving up the mountains and over the Ravines during the Operations of a long day, that we were unable to pursue them any further', said Picton, who was no doubt glad of the respite himself even if it meant the enemy would reach the safety of Toulouse. It was clear now that the French were a beaten force, which, despite superior numbers, was only able to fight on the defensive. Besides, the Allies needed to gather their provisions, which was not difficult in such well-farmed country, and tend their wounded, among them Wellington, who, at Orthez, had been struck in the thigh by a spent ball. Picton was briefly worried: 'We cannot afford to lose such a Man at such a time', he wrote.[35] As for himself, he looked forward to the end of hostilities when, 'after the example of Pyrrhus', he told Flanagan, he would 'sit down and drink good Wine'.

George Simmons thought that the French had fought 'very obstinately' at Orthez, much better than usual, though he added: 'every cock ought to fight better upon its own dung-hill'.[36] He spoke for most of the troops when he called Soult 'a persevering fellow', for the Marshal's manoeuvres had become damnably frustrating to the Allies: 'Though thrashed every time we come in contact with him, still he moves to another position, making it as strong as possible, and waits till we move up and thrash him out of it.' This prolongation irritated veterans who had had six years' hard fighting and, with the war effectively won, simply wished to return home. Yet they could not be released until an armistice was signed, not even if they had completed their turn of service and had refused the sixteen guineas offered those who signed for life.

Soult continued to play for time throughout March, as Napoleon defended in the north with brilliant ripostes against the invading Prussian–Austrian–Russian army. Wellington stalked him cautiously, sending Beresford with a force to Bordeaux, but refusing to overreach: 'I have always found that we lose more men in a pursuit than in a general action', he wrote on 8 March.[37] There were bridges to rebuild, supplies to be brought up and the peasantry to consider. There were partial engagements too, at Vic en Bigorre on 19 March and at Tarbes the next day, when it seemed Soult intended drawing the Allies back into the Pyrenees. But, strong and elevated as his position near Tarbes was, Soult again chose to withdraw during the night, this time definitively towards Toulouse.

By 29 March the Allies had reached Toulouse and stood facing the city across the River Garonne. The curve of this broad and rapid river, together with the fortified bridgehead of St Cyprien, protected the city's west side. To the north and east lay another liquid barrier, the Languedoc canal, while further east stood the high ground of Calunet beyond which lay the River Hers. Faced with this challenging topography Wellington's options were by no means obvious. First he sent Hill across the Garonne, via a pontoon bridge placed four miles south of the city, to see if access was possible on that weaker side. Hill reported that it was not, owing to the vast number of streams in the area, and he recrossed to the west bank on 1 April. By 4 April Wellington had repositioned his pontoon bridge twelve miles north of the city, sending three divisions across under Picton's command. As it happened, heavy rains fell before all the troops had crossed and, with the Garonne rising and the bridge having to be dismantled,

Picton found himself dangerously exposed on the eastern side for some days. Soult, however, was too disinclined to offensive action to take any advantage and, by 10 April, when the weather had cleared, the Allied troops were ready to carry out Wellington's plan.

Picton's Third, together with the Light Division, were to cross the Languedoc canal and make a series of feint attacks on the city's northern side; Hill was to make similar demonstrations against St Cyprien to the west, while Beresford, who had taken the bulk of the army to skirt unseen behind the heights of Calunet, was to make the main assault on the eastern quarter. The operations started well on 10 April, which was Easter Sunday, with Hill and Picton engaging the enemy warmly. But Picton grew concerned when he realized that Beresford had not appeared to the east, where, unsurprisingly perhaps, heavy mud alongside the Hers had held him up. Soult took advantage of the delay to reinforce that side and, in the north-east, drove back General Manuel Freire's Spanish troops in complete disarray. At this point, fearing the worst, Picton decided to take matters into his own hands and change what was supposed to be a feint into a committed assault.

Sir George Murray's memorandum clearly stated that the operations of the Third and Light divisions were meant 'more as diversions than as real attacks, it not being expected that they will be able to force any of the passes of the canal which covers Toulouse'.[38] Picton had other ideas. Perhaps the thought of Badajoz went through his mind, for the assault on that city seemed to have floundered until he lifted the Third to one last supreme effort. Perhaps he wished to atone for his passivity in the Pyrenees, knowing that this was his last chance to go out in a blaze of glory. Whatever the truth, on this occasion he made the wrong decision. As Murray's memorandum indicated, the redoubts covering the Jumeaux bridge over the canal were formidable and not to be taken by infantry supported by a mere two guns. The three charges that Picton made, before finally ordering the troops to withdraw, were all repelled with considerable carnage.

Because Wellington had to wait to be resupplied with ammunition, the battle could not be rejoined the following day. During the night of 11 April, Soult, fearing that the road to Carcassonne might be cut off, slipped out of Toulouse at the head of his army. Perhaps he had heard that in Paris on 4 April, Marmont had declared against Napoleon. Within an hour of his taking possession of the city on 12 April 1814, Wellington was greeted with news, brought from Bordeaux by Colonel

Frederick Ponsonby, that Napoleon had abdicated. He was to be banished, with an income of six million livres, to the island of Elba. On 18 April Soult signed an armistice and, at last, the troops could go home. The Battle of Toulouse was one that need not have been fought. With Allied casualties of 4,500, compared with the French 3,200, it had been the closest run thing of the Peninsular War.

SEVEN

THE ROAD TO WATERLOO

Charge! Hurrah! Hurrah!

I

A ball in Wellington's honour was held at the Hôtel de Ville in Toulouse on 20 April 1814, by which time the dispersal of the Allied army was already well under way as recruits headed for Bordeaux to embark for home and sixteen-guinea men sailed out to the war in America. With few exceptions, the women who had attached themselves to British soldiers in the Peninsula also had to find their way home, some with babes in arms, their men lacking the wherewithal to buy their passage to England.

Picton is likely to have been amongst the first to reach a now festive London, where the Allied Sovereigns were honoured guests at lavish entertainments to mark the peace. The newly restored Bourbon King Louis XVIII of France had to depart early, on 24 April, taking his leave of the Prince Regent at Dover, whence he crossed to Calais to make his triumphant entry into Paris on 3 May. His place was filled by Tsar Alexander I, who was fêted at the Guildhall on 18 June as the leader who had summoned Russia to a holy war against Napoleon, the enemy of the orthodox faith. If Picton read *The Times* on Tuesday 3 May he would have been delighted to see his own name listed among those of six generals who were expected to be raised to the peerage. His return also coincided with the happy news of his friend Flanagan being called to the Bar on 5 May, which must have warranted a celebration of its own. On 10 May the Prince Regent announced in the Lords that he was conferring on Wellington the title of Duke and granting him £500,000 for the purchase of a suitable estate, plus an annuity of £10,000. Several other pecuniary awards were proclaimed and acclaimed in the euphoric spring of 1814.

However, a disappointment awaited Picton. Conspicuous by his absence at the Carlton House levee on Wednesday 11 May, he was not, after all, to be elevated to the peerage. His name was omitted from the list of six so confidently predicted the week before, and which now read Beresford, Graham, Hill, Cotton and Hope. That same day, as if by way of mitigation, the Duke of Norfolk informed the House of Lords that 'a greater number of peers had been made in the present reign than had been created in any reign since the Revolution'. This did not appease those who felt Picton had been unjustly excluded and, on the Friday, a letter appeared in *The Times* asking its editor to satisfy 'the curiosity of thousands' by answering the following question: 'What is the reason that Lieut-General Sir Thomas Picton has not been created a Peer of Parliament, as well as those distinguished officers whose names have appeared in the *Gazette*?'

The correspondent, who signed himself 'An Old Soldier' and who was doubtless an officer of rank, said he was continually being asked this question as he went about London but had no reasonable answer to give. It was not that he objected to any who had been made peers, but it was clear to him that Picton's claim was at least as strong as Sir John Hope's and Sir Stapleton Cotton's. He continued:

> I am told, and indeed it is the only attempt at an answer which I have heard, that the reason is, because the honours were thought to be due to those officers only who had the good fortune to have had, at some time or another of the Peninsular War, what they call *distinct commands*, by which I presume they mean, commanding corps at a certain distance from the Chief, although not moving without his orders.

Yet this argument was implausible, he contended, for it applied only to three of the five named, not to Hope and Cotton, whose merits he assessed in turn:

> The first was, on Sir T. Graham's leaving the army in the Peninsula, considered nominally or *titularly*, as some classes would call it, second in command. He has been but a few months with the army, was left a few weeks at Bayonne, to superintend the siege, and taken prisoner there. Sir Stapleton Cotton has commanded the cavalry. This is the sum of his good fortune. I assert that it is no more than the mere command of a division of the army; that it is straining too hard for a distinction, to endeavour to support it by calling it a *distinct command*.

The theory of a distinct command was specious, 'words instead of reasons' to justify Picton's exclusion. If Picton himself accepted the argument, well and good, the whole army would be contented; but since this was not likely, the correspondent concluded, 'I assert without fear of contradiction, that by thus excepting him, a positive injustice and insult have been offered to him.'

This was probably the majority view, both inside and outside the army. Picton's contribution in the Peninsula had been immense and, on more than one occasion, decisive in the most dramatic fashion. His name was better known than any of those who had been honoured and it was even popularly held that, in the event of his own death in the Peninsula, Wellington had arranged for the command to fall to Picton. It is true that he could be faulted in the Pyrenees, a phase that Wellington recalled years later when speaking to Stanhope: 'In France Picton came to me and said: My Lord, I must give up. I am grown so nervous, that when there is any service to be done it works upon my mind so, that it is impossible for me to sleep at nights. I cannot possibly stand it, and I shall be forced to retire.'[1] This testimony, if accurate, has to be considered in context: the man was in the grip of a demoralizing illness in the Pyrenees and therefore his conduct contradicted everything that he had done before. In short, it is inconceivable that the commander of 'the fighting division' would have been excluded on the ground that he lacked courage, surely his greatest attribute. Picton's own view of the matter was that: 'If the coronet were lying on the crown of a breach, I should have as good a chance as any of them.'

That recognition was not based solely on merit may be inferred from the circumstances of the five soldiers honoured, each of whom was well connected. In particular, Hope was the second son of Sir John Hope, the second Earl of Hopetoun, while Stapleton Cotton – who, with the peerage, received an annuity of £2,000 for his own and two succeeding lives – was the second son of Sir Robert Cotton, the fifth baronet of Combermere. An old Etonian himself, Wellington naturally preferred the company of aristocrats to that of 'a rough foul-mouthed devil' who came from the backwoods of Wales, though this does not mean he was blind to ability. In the final analysis, it is probable that between Picton and a coronet there fell the shadow of *el Tío*, 'the Tyrant of Trinidad', and the ex-governor may well have sensed the flourish of a dress sword.

On 16 May the press again erred in forecasting that he was to command new troops destined for America. Either their source was unreliable or plans had changed, for in the event, on 25 May, the command was taken by Sir Rowland Hill. Picton would hardly have wanted it, given his age, health and recent disappointment, which was all the harder to bear in the jubilant capital. One can only guess at his reaction to the series of trivializing festivities that purported to celebrate the deliverance of Europe from tyranny. Frivolity was apparent too in the daily diet of royal bickering paraded in epistolary instalments in the press: the Prince Regent to the Princess of Wales expressing his intention never to meet with her again in public or in private; the Queen to the Princess saying she was no longer welcome in her drawing-room for fear of an indelicate meeting with her estranged husband; the Princess expressing her deep hurt in language that matched Pope's *Rape of the Lock* for hyperbole. But there were better options for literary diversion, if Picton felt the need: Kemble was giving sepulchral voice to the political infighting of *Coriolanus* at Covent Garden, while Kean was playing Othello at Drury Lane, where the pangs of jealousy suffered by Shakespeare's tragic hero may well have resonated with another 'much abused' soldier.

Very likely Picton was disenchanted with the whole London scene and anxious to retire to Cheltenham and Wales. This he seems to have done soon after 24 June when, with what must have been mixed feelings, he received from the Speaker the Thanks of the Commons for the seventh time. He thus escaped the culmination of festivities in the metropolis, which came a month later. At Carlton House on 21 July the Prince Regent held his grandest fête yet, at which Wellington, resplendent in his red field marshal's uniform, was hailed by more than 2,000 guests. Threading its way through covered promenades, marquees and the vast Polygon Room, the fashionable throng encountered a specially built Corinthian temple, in which was displayed, to everyone's astonishment, atop a *verde antique* column, a bust of the Duke newly executed in marble by Turnelli. On 1 August it was the turn of the people to salute the hero at vast open-air festivals in the Royal Parks. Many wore 'Old Nosey' masks as they circulated the booths or watched the antics of jugglers, tumblers, dancers and, towards evening, displays of Congreve rockets and fireworks. This public-relations exercise was conceived by the Prince Regent, whose round Royal Booth bore the inscription 'Peace restored under the Regency'. The splen-did Temple of Concord in Green Park was upstaged by the Chinese Pagoda in St James's Park, which was set alight, proba-bly by an errant Congreve, with the unfortunate consequence that its five upper storeys collapsed into the bridge below, and a workman was killed when he threw himself from its height to escape the flames.

Picton would not have regretted missing such events. The ageing bachelor was ill-suited to London social life, having

nothing in common with the dandies who rode out daily in
Hyde Park at five, nor with those who risked their fortunes into
the small hours at White's, Boodles' or Brooks'. On 5 September
he wrote from his new home at Iscoed to tell Flanagan he had
just completed three weeks at Cheltenham and would have
stayed longer had it not been for the sudden arrival of his
brother from India, 'whom I was anxious to meet on his way into
Wales'.[2] The retired Major-General John Picton, whose duelling
had sorely tried Wellington's patience in India nearly twenty
years before, spent what must have been a delightful fortnight
with his elder brother at Iscoed. To encourage Flanagan to pay
him a visit, a re-invigorated Picton elaborated:

> We are about half a mile from the Banks of the River Towey, with
> an extensive view of the Bay of Carmarthen and the Islands off
> Tenby. The opposite Bank of the Towey is equally beautiful, and
> affords a rich view from the House: the beautiful village of
> Llanstephan, a very handsome seat with the grounds beautifully
> laid out, and the magnificent ruins of an old Castle, on a
> commanding knoll, projecting into the River. The River affords
> plenty of the finest Eels, Salmon and Salmon Trout, and the neigh-
> bouring sea cockles, muscles, soals, mullets, small Turbots, and
> various kinds of flatfish.

An added attraction was Carmarthen market, 'one of the most
plentiful and moderate in the kingdom', which could be
reached by road or sea: 'there is a boat which attends the market
constantly (indeed every Tyde), which exempts you from the
inconvenience of sending a Horse & Man to market: as I merely
send my market book, to the Passenger, the day before, with the
market Basket, which is returned by the Boat on the following
Day'. Picton eagerly anticipated the pleasure of field sports,
once harvesting was over, and with some insistence he invited
Flanagan to take advantage of 'the general salubrity of the
Cambrian air'. It seemed that the just reward for his years of toil
was within his reach. Yet, remarkably, a sadness had entered his
life, which left him a changed man: 'I discover that my disposition has undergone a considerable revolution', he confided in
Flanagan, 'and that these tame appeals to the Senses have but
little amusement for one who has been habituated to scenes of
more distraction and Interest.'

As the days shortened and the weather turned inclement he
spoke with moving irony about his solitary existence: 'The winds
are, as usual, musical, and the storms appear to have set in good
earnest, so that you can have no difficulty in forming an idea of
the amusing life I lead in this absolute seclusion from living and

dead Society.' Picton was no pupil of the Romantic school as might derive sustenance from nature. On the contrary, he was a practical man who saw all too clearly that the estate he had bought was a poor business proposition: 'I am fully aware of the consequences of Farming, and that I must pay, I hope not too severely, for my Amusement: but living in the country is becoming a matter of necessity, and I want to make it bear as lightly as possible.' He asked Flanagan to inquire of a mutual friend, Dr Coventry, if he could send him a bailiff or 'factotum' to run Iscoed, believing that his enterprise would 'go on miserably without some experienced person to attend regularly to its operation'. By 7 December he had resigned himself to not finding anyone suitable, for the man Coventry had in mind was 'one of too high qualifications for the smallness of my undertaking'.[3] A week later he was lamenting that he had ever bought Iscoed: 'I should be glad to dispose of this expensive concern, which cost me originally £30,000, and between two and three since, and before the end of next year will stand over at least £36,000. I would willingly dispose of it for £30,000, but I cannot sell for below that sum, and must therefore make the part of a bad bargain.'

Picton did not visit his constituents until late September, his tardiness suggesting a limited interest in local affairs. Returning from Pembroke on 11 October, he complained of being 'heartily tired with Corporation Hospitality', which, if the haughty remark of one who had been a guest more than once at Carlton House, was also a way of telling Flanagan he could expect better at Iscoed. He was late too in taking the field to shoot partridge, having been annoyingly let down: 'My gun case has not yet arrived from France, though it was entrusted to an Officer of my Regiment', he wrote in September. Three months later he was still complaining: 'I have as yet been able to bagg but one solitary woodcock. They were never known to be so scarce in the County as this Season. I walked all day yesterday without killing a single bird, and the Parson, who is down with me, was equally successful.'

He would have enjoyed seeing his elder sister, Elizabeth, a spinster who lived frugally at Rudbaxton near Haverfordwest, and he was delighted to receive Flanagan for a few days in November. For company, however, he relied mainly on visits from his brothers, the intellectual Revd Edward, and the worldly Major-General John, who might have shown off his skill at cards if a reasonable school could be mustered for an evening's diversion. In one unusual respect John's life paralleled Picton's own: he had never married but had taken a common-law wife in

Mauritius, an Indian woman who bore him a son. No doubt the two soldiers compared notes on their experiences and perhaps Thomas, at fifty-seven, envied John the greater number of years he had shared with his companion. His five years in the West Indies with Rosetta, the mother of his four children, must have seemed very remote from his present solitary mode of existence in West Wales.

The newly blossoming affection between the two brothers was cut short when John suddenly took ill and died at Poyston in the New Year: 'I have been engaged in the melancholy business of Interring my poor Brother, the Major-General, who was found dead in his bed without any previous illness', Picton wrote to Flanagan from Haverfordwest on 9 January 1815:

> It was a great shock to us all, I believe you did not meet him when you were at Iscoed. He was a most even tempered amiable man, and deservedly beloved by everyone. His long residence in the East Indies had certainly undermined his constitution, though we had no Idea that it could lead to so sudden a dissolution.

Picton's dwelling on the merits of his brother – whose 'independent principles' made him 'rich in respectability if not money' – shows the regard in which he held him, but his death also marked the end of what little company he had, giving, as he said, 'the *Coup de Grace* to my rural attachments'. He determined to sell the 'encumbrance' of Iscoed, even at a loss, if he could find a purchaser who was, as he put it, 'as great a fool as myself'. To that end he tried to make the estate a more attractive proposition: 'I have been purchasing a couple of contiguous Farms, consisting of above 180 acres, as a kind of make weight to assist in the disposal of the others: but I must wait some time before I shall find any one disposed to purchase beauty at so dear a rate.'

He was now more isolated than ever and, though Molloy's shipped him pipes of the best wine from London, he lamented: 'I don't think wine drinks well by one's self what ever the quality of it may be.' To his surprise, he had been unable to adapt to Iscoed, where he felt the lack, especially, of female company: 'I find after all that I am in want of those valuable acquirements which, to use the expression of Cicero, *pernoctant nobis cum peregrinantur rusticantur* ('These studies stay with us, through the night, they roam, rusticable'), and without which a Country life is very little amusing'.[4] The quotation was apt for one who, after years of travel, was now finding the quiet country nights long. That he took a healthy interest in the opposite sex is confirmed by Wellington's recollection of his comment when General Cole announced he was going to get married:

Sir Lowry explained his views by saying that he did not think he
was going to do a very imprudent thing, for that the lady was not
very young – and so on; Sir Thomas, who was present, and
between whom and Sir Lowry there had always been a little
rivalry, suddenly broke in with, 'Well, when I marry I shall do a
damned imprudent thing, for I mean to marry the youngest tit I
can find![5]

His search appears to have been fruitless in West Wales.

During the winter nights of 1815, as the westerlies whipped
across the Towy from Llansteffan's ruins and rattled the windows
of Iscoed on its exposed height, Picton must have ruminated wist-
fully on his situation. True, he had appeared in the New Year's
honours list when he was made Knight Grand Cross of the Bath,
the highest of the three divisions into which the Order was now
reformed. But this cosmetic promotion brought him no nearer a
peerage and, if anything, must have sharpened his sense of injustice. Nor was there much joy to be had in the course of political
events, at home or abroad. In France, the flames of discontent
were again being fanned by Jacobins as hordes of discharged
veterans and their generals grew restless. In Rio de Janeiro the
Royal Family showed no sign of returning to their impoverished
kingdom of Portugal. In Spain the restored King Fernando VII
had repudiated the Constitution of 1812 and with it the whole
notion of parliamentary democracy. This development had been
encouraged by Wellington's poor view of the liberal reformers
and by his counselling of generals Freire, Anglona and Elío to
obey the King. Francisco Elío, Captain General of Valencia,
where Fernando landed in the spring of 1814, was able to
engineer what proved to be the first in a long series of *pronunci-
amientos*, partly because the area between Valencia and Madrid
was held by troops under General Whittingham, who was himself
in close contact with Wellington. Picton would not have been a
solitary cynic had he wondered whether the return of absolutism
in Spain suited the British Government.

II

There was little cause for cheer on the domestic front either.
Frame breaking continued to make news, but political agitation
took a new turn in March 1815 when mass demonstrations were
held in the capital against the Corn Bill, which had led to bread
shortages and suffering among the poor. MPs who supported
the bill had their windows stoned until eventually the military

were brought in to guard Mayfair streets and the House of
Commons. Picton is unlikely to have sympathized with the
rioters, to judge from the way he described his own philosophy
for Flanagan's benefit. Admonishing the young barrister for his
altruism, he wrote:

> You put me in mind of the worthy K^t of La Mancha, who was always
> on the look out to redress real or imaginary Grievances, and was
> generally left to pay the piper. Romantic Ideas of General benevo-
> lence, where the Individual sinks his own Interests in promoting
> those of Society, is a very beautiful dream, but I have never known it
> succeed in practice.... a man's own interest is his nearest concern
> ... I do not carry any sentiments of Philanthropy to the romantic
> extent that some do. There are evils, and not trivial ones too, which
> I shall never volunteer to redress, but leave to those whose duty it is
> more particularly to watch over the execution of the Laws.[6]

This may seem a narrow view of the law and a passive attitude
towards society for an MP to hold, but it was probably not
extreme for its time. Coming up to London in the last week of
February, Picton had little time to ponder the ethics of social
unrest, which culminated on 9 March with the deployment of
vast numbers of cavalry in the metropolis. He must have been as
shocked as Lord Castlereagh, who returned from a weekend
parley with King Louis in Paris only to find his house in St
James's Square under attack. However, the sight of mobs in
London's most fashionable quarter was quickly forgotten when
the appalling news broke that Napoleon had escaped Elba and
landed in the South of France. *The Times* reported on Saturday
11 March:

> Early yesterday morning we received by express, from Dover, the
> important but lamentable intelligence, of a civil war having again
> been kindled in France, by that wretch Buonaparte, whose life was
> so impoliticly spared by the Allied Sovereigns. It now appears that
> the hypocritical villain, who, at the time of his cowardly abdica-
> tion, affected an aversion to the shedding of blood in a civil
> warfare, has been employed during the whole time of his resi-
> dence at Elba, in carrying on secret and treasonable intrigues with
> the tools of his former crimes in France. At length, when his plots
> were ripe, he sailed from Elba, with all his guards, between 12 and
> 1300 in number, on the night of the 28th ult. and landed near
> Frejus, in France, on the 3d instant. Some accounts state that a
> considerable number of military were collected on the coast await-
> ing his arrival, and immediately joined him, and that he advanced
> at their head upon Lyons.

After Elba the Emperor was intent on extending his

dominion and redressing the insult he believed he had suffered. Louis XVIII had proclaimed Napoleon and all his adherents traitors, but *The Times* was near the mark in anticipating that the disaffected in France, including both the disbanded and the embodied soldiery, would rally to the standard of their old hero. Generals Soult, Ney and Murat all deserted the Bourbon monarchy and, by 20 March, Napoleon was at the gates of Paris with a new army and Louis fled. Wellington returned from the Congress of Vienna via Brussels, where he began coordinating the Allied force. In the House of Lords, on 12 April, he urged caution: having conceded Napoleon an over-generous peace, they must not compound the error by rushing into war with him, which was precisely what 'the decollator of Europe' wanted. The Duke underestimated Napoleon, hoping that he might come unstuck without Allied intervention. But he also knew that the Allies were unready: the massive Austrian army was weeks away, as were Field Marshal Count Barclay de Tolly's Russians, while the only forces at hand were Blücher's Prussians and his own clutch of untried Dutch and Belgians plus a British contingent decidedly inferior to those disbanded a year before. No doubt Wellington also sensed that a swift victory was all Napoleon needed to restore his credibility and focus French minds.

High on the list of generals Wellington called upon was Picton, who, before agreeing to serve, required personal assurance that he would be employed directly under the Duke with no other officer his superior in rank. This was not pique at lack of recognition, but the precaution of an old campaigner who was not going to be told what to do by a novice like the Prince of Orange. The new confrontation was already one more than he had bargained for, and, if it was to be his last, he wanted things in their place. Besides, his months of solitary brooding had induced a morbidity that prompted him to confide to friends his belief that he would not survive the campaign. One evening shortly before his departure, when out walking with Sir John and Lady Owen, they came upon a freshly dug grave. Picton, on an impulse, jumped into it, stretched himself out on the earth, and said: 'Why, I think this would do for me.' Naturally, his horrified companions took it as a fatal presentiment.[7]

He had sufficient time to put his affairs at Iscoed in order and on 16 May wrote to Flanagan saying that he had at last found a bailiff: 'Mr Anderson appears to suit me perfectly well, & is a plain labourious kind of Man without any thing like coxcombry or pretension.'[8] Ten days later he instructed Tyler: 'You must get ready as soon as you can; and you will be so good as to communicate to Captain Chambers and Price that I have received orders for Flanders. Look out for some active horses, not above fifteen hands.'

When the party was assembled in London in early June, Chambers introduced to Picton his friend, Rees Howell Gronow, a 21-year-old guardsman from Ewenny in Glamorgan, who very likely knew Picton's elder brother, Richard, a resident of Ewenny. Gronow had fought briefly in the Peninsula three years before and now, desperate to see action in Flanders, was frustrated by orders to stay in London. In his *Reminiscences and Recollections* Gronow recalled the meeting with Picton and his aide-de-camp Tyler:

> Sir Thomas said, 'Is the lad really anxious to go out?' Chambers answered that it was the height of my ambition. Sir Thomas inquired if all the appointments to his staff were filled up; and then added with a grim smile:
> 'If Tyler is killed, which is not at all unlikely, I do not know why I should not take my young countryman: he may go over with me if he can get leave.'

Gronow was 'elated' at this development but he was also very short of funds for his new position with 'the great general' and resolved to go to Cox and Greenwood's to seek credit:

> I there obtained £200, which I took with me to a gambling-house in St James's Square, where I managed, by some wonderful accident, to win £600; and, having thus obtained the sinews of war, I made numerous purchases, amongst others two first-rate horses at Tattersall's for a high figure, which were embarked for Ostend, along with my groom.

At Ramsgate, on Saturday 10 June, the well-groomed Gronow, along with Chambers, caught up with Picton, who had spent the previous night in festive company at the Fountain Tavern in Canterbury. 'We remained there for the Sunday', Gronow recalled, 'and embarked on Monday in a vessel which had been hired for the general and suite. On the same day we arrived at Ostend, and put up at a hotel in the square; where I was surprised to hear the general, in excellent French, get up a flirtation with our very pretty waiting-maid.'[10]

The old general was evidently making up for lost time and, linguistic skills apart, his physical presence impressed Gronow: 'Sir Thomas Picton was a stern-looking, strong-built man, about the middle height, and considered very like the Hetman Platoff'. His supposed lookalike was none other than the ferocious Cossack leader, Count Matvei Ivanovich Platov, six years Picton's senior, who had pitilessly pursued the French in their retreat from Moscow in 1813 and accompanied Tsar Alexander on his visit to England the following year. Gronow continued with a description of Picton's attire: 'He generally wore a blue frock-coat, very tightly buttoned up to the throat; a very large black silk neckcloth, showing little or no shirt-collar; dark trousers, boots and a round top hat.' It was in this very attire that he would shortly fight at Quatre Bras, having been obliged to hurry to the scene of action before his uniform arrived. This, no doubt, was also his apparel at the Hotel d'Angleterre in Brussels when, as Gronow reported, he was summoned by Wellington that Thursday morning:

> While we were at breakfast Colonel Canning came to inform the general that the Duke of Wellington wished to see him immediately. Sir Thomas lost not a moment in obeying the order of his chief, leaving the breakfast-table and proceeding to the park, where Wellington was walking with Fitzroy Somerset and the Duke of Richmond. Picton's manner was always more familiar than the duke liked in his lieutenants, and on this occasion he approached him in a careless sort of way, just as he might have met an equal. The duke bowed coldly to him, and said, 'I am glad you are come, Sir Thomas: the sooner you get on horseback the better: no time is to be lost. You will take the command of the troops in advance. The Prince of Orange knows by this time that you will go to his assistance'. Picton appeared not to like the duke's manner; for when he bowed and left, he muttered a few words, which convinced those who were with him that he was not much pleased with his interview.[11]

As the oldest general in the British army, Picton perhaps felt he deserved better, but Wellington's peremptory instructions reflected the urgency of the situation as Napoleon marched on Brussels at the head of 125,000 men. The Anglo–Dutch army had grown from 40,000 in April to 92,000 by the eve of hostilities and it now formed an extended front stretching south and west of the Belgian capital. With Blücher's 84,000 Prussians to the south-east, they were ready to concentrate and outnumber the French wherever the Emperor chose to strike. Yet their success depended on the speed with which they could converge from cantonments spread laterally over ninety miles. To the west at Ninove stood 9,000 cavalry under Lord Uxbridge; south of this, at Ath, Lord Hill's 28,000 infantry anticipated a French thrust from Mons; more centrally, from his headquarters at Braine-le-Comte, the Prince of Orange's 30,000 troops reached down towards Charleroi; finally, from their front at Sombreffe, Blücher's Prussians spread eastward in four corps as far as Liège. Picton had been told to remain with Wellington in a reserve of

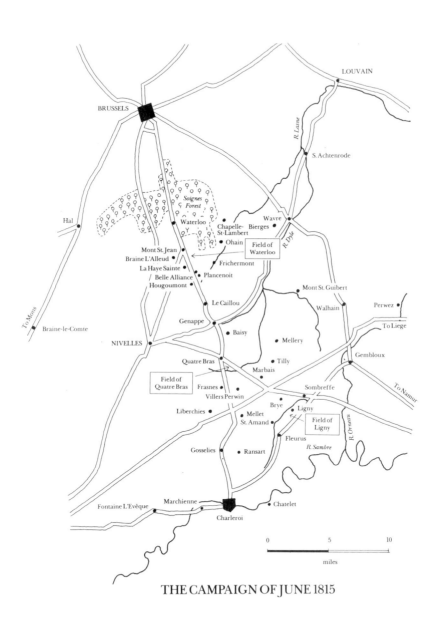

THE CAMPAIGN OF JUNE 1815

22,000 men at Brussels, from which point he would be ready to assist the Prince of Orange or move anywhere that circumstances dictated. He commanded the Fifth, a fine division, which consisted of British brigades under generals Sir James Kempt and Sir Denis Pack, together with one Hanoverian brigade under Colonel Von Vincke and a mixed British–Hanoverian battery, some 7,000 men in all.

Wellington doubtless chatted with ducal civility to the Lords Somerset and Richmond once Picton had taken his sour leave of them in the park. Richmond may have inquired whether, under the circumstances, he should not tell his wife to cancel the ball she had planned for that evening. Amazingly, Wellington was keen to let it go on: a ball would send the right signal to Francophile Belgians and help keep the city calm. He saw no reason to change his mind when news came that Napoleon, contrary to expectations, had moved on Charleroi with the bulk of his army, the attack on Mons to the west having been a feint. It was clear now that the Emperor meant to drive a wedge between the Anglo–Dutch and the Prussian armies and then smash through to Brussels. Let him come, said Wellington: there would be time enough for the Duchess to have her ball and for his officers – conveniently gathered under one roof – to head south at dawn.

III

The French crossed the Sambre at Charleroi on 15 June and drove off a Prussian force at Gosselies five miles north of the town. The Allies had respected the frontier and awaited government sanction of an invasion, but Napoleon had seized the initiative and made a concerted thrust at his scattered enemy.

Meanwhile, in a coachmaker's dépôt next to the house of the Duke and Duchess of Richmond in the Rue de la Blanchisserie, in Brussels, 'there was the sound of revelry by night/And Belgium's capital had gathered then/Her beauty and her Chivalry' for what was to become, through the medium of Byron's poetry, the most famous ball in history.

Amidst bemedalled dignitaries and bejewelled aristocrats, gallant young officers and elegant young women began arriving at the Richmonds' splendid house around 9.00 p.m. and soon made their way to the specially decorated ballroom to the rear. Hung with drapes, ribbons and magnificent chandeliers, this imposing room, some 120 feet long, comfortably held 300 guests together with troupes of musicians and servants. No expense had been spared for the entertainment, which was the Richmond style: they had lived regally when he was Lord Lieutenant of Ireland, and she was said to be so free with money as often to leave it carelessly on gaming tables. Among the first to arrive was the Prince of Orange, who had to get back to his troops at Braine-le-Comte. The late entrance of Wellington, for all his legendary sang-froid, served to remind his officers of the task ahead. Outside there was such a commotion in the streets that Kincaid was unable to snatch an hour's sleep on the pavement as the nervous citizens of Brussels kept stumbling over him in the dark or pestering him about the need to remain vigilant.

Just before supper Wellington received news that the Prussians had been repulsed from Fleurus, north-east of Charleroi. He at once advised the Prince of Orange to return to his headquarters and scribbled instructions for one or two officers before joining the other guests. Within minutes the Prince returned, whispered something in Wellington's ear and then left, while the Duke, apparently unconcerned, remained at the table. When some time had elapsed, the Duke announced he would retire and, almost off-handedly, asked his host if there were a decent map in the house. Richmond accompanied Wellington to his study, where the Prince of Orange's whispered message was repeated. The alarming news was that the enemy had pushed up the Brussels road as far as Quatre Bras, at which place Prince Bernhard of Saxe-Weimar, with greatly inferior numbers of Nassauer troops, was holding off Marshal Ney. For the benefit of the generals now gathered in the study, Wellington took the map and scratched it with his thumbnail at a point between Quatre Bras and Waterloo. It was nearly 2.00 a.m. and there would be a major confrontation later that day. Some might have to get there in their dancing pumps.

Picton, who had scarcely been in Brussels twenty-four hours, was told to take his Fifth Division directly to assist the Prince of Orange, who had himself left early to bring his men to Quatre Bras. As day broke on Friday 16 June, Picton inspected his troops in the park in Brussels and shortly after 4.00 a.m. had them marching out of the capital down the broad road to Charleroi. Seldom can an army have gone to war with its officers so bleary-eyed. Wellington wisely snatched a couple of hours' sleep before leaving the city and overtook Picton near Waterloo, then a village of less than 2,000 inhabitants, where the men were allowed to breakfast. Kincaid reported:

Lord Wellington joined us about nine o'clock; and, from his very particular orders to see that the roads were kept clear of baggage, and everything likely to impede the movements of the troops, I have since been convinced that his Lordship thought it probable that the position of Waterloo might, even that day, have become the scene of action.[12]

Indeed, had Marshal Ney realized that he had a three to one advantage at Quatre Bras on the morning of 16 June, the French would surely have brushed all opposition aside at the hamlet crossroads by noon and drummed their way on towards the capital. In the event, Ney allowed himself to be persuaded by his staff officers to stand off, because Quatre Bras, they said, with woods and high-standing rye in place of the customary reverse slope, was a defensive position typical of Wellington, for it concealed his true strength.

Having reached Quatre Bras by 10.30 a.m., Wellington was pleased to find the area quiet. He pressed on to Ligny, where, around 1.00 p.m., he held a brief parley with Field Marshal Blücher. As he observed the main French army from the vantage point of the windmill at Bussy, he suddenly spotted Napoleon, who, with his own field glass raised, was evidently studying him. For a moment the two generals stood looking at each other: the Duke, with his plain cocked hat worn 'fore and aft', and the Emperor, with his own famously square, accentuating his squat figure. Napoleon's force of 80,000 men at Ligny was more than matched by Prussian numbers, but Wellington was horrified to see Blücher's army arrayed on the bare forward slopes with no cover from French cannon. He advised his 73-year-old ally that such a deployment was less than ideal and, having pledged to support him later, if at all possible, made off back to Quatre Bras. When he regained the latter ground at 2.30 p.m. he could hear the first salvos of Napoleon's cannon firing upon the Prussians behind him and was just in time to witness Ney's belated but devastating thrust at the crossroads.

Quatre Bras, a virtually enclosed position, was flanked to the west by the thick Bois de Bossu, where six of the ten Nassau battalions were posted, and, to the east, the gently sloping fields of rye were crowned by the Hutte wood. Wellington witnessed the feeble resistance of the combined Dutch and Belgian troops at the centre where they soon conceded the crossroads, and was informed by the 23-year-old Prince of Orange that the Bois de Bossu, though stoutly defended by Nassauers, could not be held much longer. Almost immediately he was heartened by the arrival of Picton's battalions, seen marching, one behind the other, along the Genappe road. They were dispatched to the east

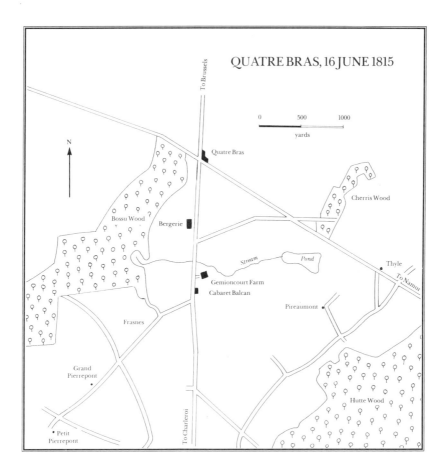

to keep open communications with Blücher, while the Brunswickers, coming up last, were sent to the northern end of the Bossu wood.

Ney reacted by launching his cavalry east, parallel with the Namur road, where, between the crossroads and the small wood of Cherris, they were repulsed repeatedly by steady fire from Picton's infantry whose squares held firm. At one point, with the enemy descending upon his 28th battalion on three sides, Picton, mounted on his cob, roared: 'Twenty-eighth, remember Egypt!',[13] a stirring reference to the Battle of Alexandria, in 1801, when they had performed outstandingly under the command of the late Sir John Moore, fighting off combined attacks on their front and rear. Ney, as stubborn now as he had earlier been cautious, persisted in sending waves of cavalry at Picton, Kempt and especially Pack, whose exposed position was decidedly not one their Commander-in-Chief would have chosen freely. Throughout their long ordeal the Fifth Division stood defiant in the face of these charges and constant *tirailleur* fire; consequently enemy horses and their riders were reduced to milling around helplessly or else collapsed in heaps before them. But at length, despairing of relief from Uxbridge's distant cavalry and seeing his own casualties steadily mounting, Picton took matters into his own hands, as Kincaid reported:

> The forward movement of the enemy's cavalry gave their infantry time to rally; and, strongly reinforced with fresh troops, they again advanced to the attack. This was a crisis in which, according to Buonaparte's theory, the victory was theirs, by all the rules of war, for they held superior numbers, both before and behind us; but the gallant old Picton, who had been trained in a different school, did not choose to confine himself to rules in those matters: despising the force in his rear, he advanced, charged, and routed those in his front, which created such a panic among the others, that they galloped back through the intervals in his division, with no other object in view but their own safety.[14]

Picton's bold stroke of ordering his infantry to charge enemy cavalry changed the course of the battle and, after five hours' fighting, foiled Ney on that side. West of the crossroads the French continued to have their moments. When Friedrich Wilhelm, Duke of Brunswick, the Prince Regent's brother-in-law, led his cavalry in a daring counter-attack, he temporarily succeeded in taking possession of a farm 200 yards south of the crossroads, but, in trying to form a line of resistance, the duke received a fatal ball in his stomach, after which his men were soon ejected. Seeing this, the Prince of Orange rallied the Hussars and, countermanding Picton – newly transferred to that side and whose authority he much resented – the young Prince foolishly ordered the 69th battalion to form a double line, which he then saw crushed by French cavalry. Finally, in the thickness of the Bois de Bossu, Saxe-Weimar's Nassauers were hard pressed throughout and, after sustaining heavy casualties, many of them melted away until only a presence was held at the wood's northern edge by virtue of Brunswicker support.

Despite these successes in what was a furiously fought and largely disorderly battle, Ney's cause grew steadily more hopeless as the day wore on. The telling factor was the continued reinforcements that the Allies received – Picton's arrival at 3.00 p.m. was followed by Alten's Third Division around 5.00 p.m.

and Cooke's British Guards at 7.00 p.m. – while Ney waited in vain for his. The last straw for the French Marshal came when the promised support from Comte d'Erlon and his 20,000 men was redirected to assist Napoleon at Ligny – though they never fired a shot there either – and all Ney received was the terse imperial order to finish matters off at Quatre Bras and swing over to Ligny to attack Blücher's rear. He had begun the day with 20,000 veterans against 7,000 Nassauer and Dutch–Belgian raw recruits, but by late afternoon the Allied force had swollen to 36,000, which, Ney could see with his own eyes, were not the phantoms his advisers had counted in the morning.

When Ney, discouraged, finally withdrew, the Allies, exhausted, bivouacked on the field of battle as night fell. Many, like Kincaid, were uncertain how they had come off, for their losses were, in fact, greater than those of the French. At least they had the satisfaction of knowing that the ground on which they had fought was still theirs. Wellington had also achieved his objective of taking pressure off his Allies, though when the boom of firing from Ligny ceased around 9.00 p.m. he had little idea how Blücher had fared. Not before early morning did Alexander Gordon bring news that the Prussians, including their intrepid leader, had been 'damnably mauled'.[15] French cannon had done its work: 16,000 Prussian casualties, half as many again put to flight, and the mustachioed Field-Marshal Blücher, who had lost his horse and been ridden over twice, all bandaged up and anaesthetized with gin.

The bulk of the Prussians had retreated on Wavre, which took some finding on the map. Wellington was relieved to see it was not on their direct route home, but east of Waterloo, the area he had reconnoitred the previous August. Mont St-Jean, three miles south of the village of Waterloo, was the spot he had scratched on Richmond's map and it was there that he would defend Brussels. If Blücher, who was as tough as old boots, could be patched up, and if his men had the stomach for it, the Allies might yet get a corps or two out of them. Wellington sent an urgent message to Wavre and, as the rain poured down on the morning of the 17th, he ordered his army to retreat north from Quatre Bras.

Fortunately for the Allies, Napoleon was unwell and made a late start on Saturday morning. Brooding on the events of the day before, he sensed a missed opportunity that took the shine off his victory at Ligny. He had caught Wellington napping, split him and Blücher asunder, according to plan. Yet the d'Erlon fiasco had ruined it. Had d'Erlon come to Ligny, as ordered, the Prussians would have been routed once and for all. Then he would have taken on Wellington separately, according to plan. All

Ney had to do was hold him at Quatre Bras. But Ney, the irresolute and lethargic Ney, had called d'Erlon back to Quatre Bras for no purpose at all. Now the Emperor would have to ensure the enemy armies were kept apart. But where had Blücher gone?

Napoleon's information was that they had run to Gembloux, on their homeward route east. Inspecting the Ligny battlefield at 10.00 a.m. next day, he determined to send Marshal Grouchy after them, with 33,000 men, to ensure they would not re-enter the fray. Unaware that Blücher and most of his troops had regrouped at Wavre, Napoleon miscalculated in thinking he could afford to place so many of his men out of the main theatre of action. In the event, Grouchy would lead his men to Gembloux and, blind to other possibilities, keep them out of harm's way in his Emperor's hour of need.

Deciding on this course of action, Napoleon swung the main body of his troops north and reached Quatre Bras by 1.00 p.m. on 17 June. There he was alarmed to find that Ney had remained passive throughout the morning despite his imperial order – ambiguously phrased as it was – to engage Wellington. The latter had slipped away virtually at his leisure and the Emperor, beside himself with frustration, announced gravely to Ney and d'Erlon: 'On a perdu la France'. Things might have been different had he been in the saddle earlier that morning. Now, try as he may, he could not catch Wellington whose retreat was covered by Uxbridge's cavalry to the rear and, providentially, by a stupendous storm above. On Saturday 17 June continual bursts of thunder and lightning replaced the rumble of cannon and the crack of musket fire, but if the constant downpour reminded Wellington of an Indian monsoon it left Napoleon up to his armpits in quaking mud.

IV

Picton was also unwell and had spent the night of 17 June in severe pain at lodgings in Waterloo village. Besides exhaustion from a long day's fighting at Quatre Bras, which followed a night without sleep, he had two broken ribs and internal bleeding caused, in all probability, by a blow from half-spent grape shot. At Quatre Bras the action had been so fierce he had forgotten his pain and had even confided in Tyler: 'I shall begin to think that I cannot be killed after this.'[16] The battle over, Tyler strapped him up as best he could, but his discomfort increased during the rain-soaked retreat on the 17th when both general and aide-de-camp had to borrow troop horses, their own having been shot from under them at Quatre Bras. That night Howell Gronow, newly restored to his Guards, ran into Chambers, Picton's young aide-de-camp, and was invited back to the general's quarters for supper. Gronow recalled:

> I accompanied him thither, and after groping our way into the house, for it was very dark, we passed the door of a room in which Sir Thomas himself was lying. I heard him groan from the pain of the wound he had received at Quatre Bras, but did not of course venture to disturb him, and we passed into a small hall, where I got some cold meat and wine.[17]

Picton had sworn Tyler and his 'family' to secrecy about his wound, his one thought being to keep going long enough to lead his division into a last, decisive battle. For him this could not come soon enough, and he would gladly have done without the twenty-four hour lull after Quatre Bras, during which his condition must have worsened considerably. Very likely it was pure impatience that caused him to denounce Mont St-Jean as a position to stand against Napoleon. He had apparently recon-noitred the area on the nine-mile retreat from Quatre Bras, although, given the state of the weather and his own health, his inspection can hardly have been more than cursory. Certainly he was ill-advised to voice his misgivings within earshot of Wellington next morning when the latter crustily responded that he had studied the position in detail a year before and Picton's fears about Soignes Forest to the north were groundless for its trees were well enough spaced to allow a speedy retreat should such a necessity arise.

The men had spent a miserable night in the exposed position near the crossroads at Mont St-Jean, where, Wheeler reported, they showed remarkable endurance:

> Being close to the enemy we could not use our blankets, the ground was too wet to lie down, we sat on our knapsacks until daylight without fires, there was no shelter against the weather: the water ran in streams from the cuffs of our Jackets, in short we were as wet as if we had been plunged over head in a river. [18]

With no other consolation than the knowledge that the enemy were in the same plight, they greeted the dawn in a sorry state: 'The morning of the 18th June broke upon us and found us drenched with rain, benumbed and shaking with the cold.' Kincaid was equally miserable: caked in mud and unable to rub the fog from his eyes as he searched for his wayward horse, he needed a brew of strong tea to bring him back to sorts. Wheeler, for his part, tended to look on the bright side if he had liquor to fortify him, and, this being the case, he soon saw the weather as a good omen: the eve of battle had been invariably foul in the Peninsula, he reasoned, and the Allies had never come off second best there. He was right too, though he was not to know it, for the sloughy conditions underfoot would cause a crucial delay in Napoleon's attack.

Remarkably, the weather changed and provided excellent visibility. Gronow recorded that 'the sun shone most gloriously, and so clear was the atmosphere that we could see the long, imposing lines of the enemy most distinctly'.[19] Shortly after 6.00 a.m. the guardsman had the pleasant surprise of seeing Wellington and his large suite ride towards him in a cavalcade from the direction of Waterloo. Among those accompanying the Duke were the Prince of Orange, General Alava, Baron Vincent, Lord Fitzroy Somerset, the Duke of Richmond and his 15-year-old son, Lord William Lennox, an aide-de-camp of Wellington's. 'They all seemed as gay and unconcerned as if they were riding to meet the hounds in some quiet English county', a heartened Gronow observed. Wellington was in good spirits, for only hours earlier, at 2.00 a.m., he had received word that Blücher would bring as many as four corps to the battlefield that day.

Contrary to Picton's opinion, Mont St-Jean was as good a position to defend Brussels as could be found in the area. Its main feature was that it rose to the north in 'a sort of ridge, very favourable for artillery', as Gronow noted, 'from which all the movements of the French could be discerned'. This ridge, running east–west and parallel with the Ohain-Braine L'Alleud road, screened the bulk of Wellington's forces, leaving the enemy to guess where their greater concentration lay. The position was admittedly not ideal for the ridge was low and, as Kincaid saw from his location near Picton just east of centre, consisted only of 'gently rising ground, presenting no obstacle at any point, excepting the broken hedge in front of our division; and it was only one in appearance, as it could be passed in every part'.[20] In compensation the position offered the potential strong points of farms, which Wellington garrisoned heavily in the manner of bastions. From his command post of an elm tree at the centre crossroads he looked south-west to Hougoumont farm, directly ahead to La Haye Sainte farm 400 yards down the Quatre Bras road, and east to Papelotte and La Haye farms. Of these, Hougoumont and La Haye Sainte would have significant bearing on the day's outcome.

Those like Kincaid who were positioned on the crest of the ridge had the dubious benefit of watching 'the grand and

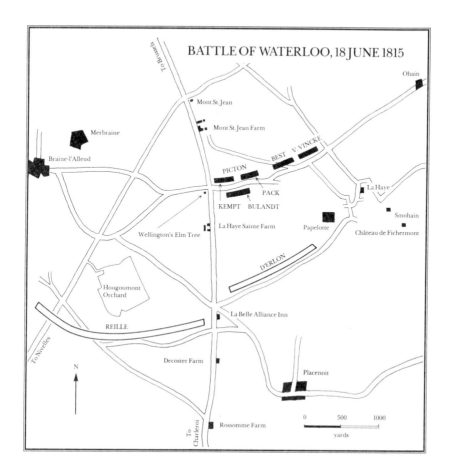

BATTLE OF WATERLOO, 18 JUNE 1815

imposing' scene take shape as the French assembled their might 1,300 yards to a mile away: 'innumerable black specks were now seen taking post at regular distances' in what had previously been an innocently undulating and empty plain. These Kincaid recognized as 'so many pieces of artillery', which, experience told him, 'were unerring symptoms of our not being destined to be idle spectators'. Into these few Belgian fields of rye, so soon to be trampled, would be crammed, in all, some 140,000 men, 30,000 horses and 400 cannon. The scale of military power that unfolded made Gronow, for one, feel a sense of awe: 'as you looked along our lines, it seemed as if we formed a continuous wall of human beings'.[21]

The French appearance on the field of battle was sheer

spectacle. First the plumed Lancers, Chasseurs and Hussars assembled; then the steel-helmeted Cuirassiers, brilliant white Carabiniers and bearskinned Grenadiers took their appointed place in front of the dark blue of the prized Imperial Guard who would evidently be kept in reserve. Only then did Napoleon, with an exquisitely theatrical sense of timing, make his grand entrance to inspect his army. As Kincaid described it: 'We saw Buonaparte himself take post on the side of the road, immediately in our front, surrounded by a numerous staff; and each regiment as they passed him, rent the air with shouts of *Vive l'Empereur!*' Long after passing their hero the French continued to erupt in raucous noise with the thunder of artillery, the rub-a-dub of drums and the tantara of trumpets, all of which, Kincaid noted, was in 'singular contrast to the stern silence reigning on our side.'[22]

This strutting show was Napoleon's way of flexing his gladiatorial muscles and intimidating his enemy. Parading his veterans in their proven glory, he also displayed his numerical superiority – around 74,000 French against 67,000 Allies – and invited novice components in the Allied army to stand in awe or even, in the case of uncertain Belgians, desert. So eye-catching was the Emperor on his white horse British officers unwittingly caught their breath and raised field-glasses to spy him. In contrast, wrote Gronow, Wellington appeared 'perfectly composed' astride his chestnut stallion Copenhagen, 'dressed in a gray great-coat with a cape, white cravat, leather pantaloons, Hessian boots, and a large cocked hat *à la Russe*'.[23] He too made himself visible along his troops' entire line to hearten spirits and harden resolve. Indeed, if Napoleon's theatre was intended to raise adrenaline prior to an irresistible charge, Wellington's calm demeanour was no less calculated to inspire unwavering resistance.

The deliberateness with which the French took the field owed something to conditions. Napoleon, breakfasting off silver plate with his generals at Caillou at 8.00 a.m., had been advised by Ney to postpone his attack so that the ground might dry and provide firmer footing for his cavalry. Lieutenant-General Comte Reille supported this by venturing to suggest that British infantry were resolute in the face of direct assault and manoeuvre was vital. As for Soult, his worry was the distant Grouchy, who should be recalled, he felt, even if it took time. Against the tenor of these observations Napoleon's youngest brother Prince Jérôme arrived with a report that Blücher, now at Wavre, had pledged to help Wellington and time was of the essence. Unimpressed by the points put to him, Napoleon found it especially hard to believe that the Prussians could have made such a swift recovery from their mauling at Ligny. Nonetheless he sent a message to

Grouchy and, conceding Ney's point about the ground, delayed his cannonade until 11.30 a.m. and his first major assault until 1.00 p.m. He was thus able to devote the greater part of the morning to a military fanfare, the main purpose of which was to make the enemy quake in their boots.

Doubtless many did, when the cannons broke upon them in a peal of thunder and, as Wheeler put it, 'grape and shells were dupping about like hail'.[24] They would have quaked again on hearing 'the rapid beating of the *pas de charge*', which, wrote Gronow with engaging understatement, 'few men, however brave they may be, can listen to without a somewhat unpleasant sensation'.[25] The long French cannonade shred the air with smoke and tested Allied morale to the limit, but heavy as its toll was it proved less destructive than at Ligny for the ridge now provided a shield against all but the most accurate fire. So loud was the cannon that Marshal Grouchy heard it as he made his way towards Wavre in response to his Emperor's latest message. But Grouchy did not grasp that the purpose of his ambulations was to stop the Prussians rejoining the fray, an end that would have been best achieved by crossing the Dyle and intercepting them somewhere between Wavre and the point west that was erupting with the unmistakable sound of battle and where, even now, the blue sky was being stained by clouds of black smoke. Marshal Grouchy was not good at reading signs.

At Mont St-Jean the first point of attack was Hougoumont farm. This solid manor house, with its walled orchard, banked hedges and rectangular buildings, proved a stout fortification. In it and its grounds Wellington placed 6 light companies, 300 Hanoverian riflemen and 1 Nassau battalion from Saxe-Weimar's brigade. Crack shots were posted at windows, hedges and gates, behind walls, ditches and parapets, and in the upper levels of buildings stripped in places of their lower floors. Napoleon had conceived the attack on Hougoumont as a diversion, a way of provoking Wellington into weakening his centre and revealing the distribution of his men behind the ridge. But resistance was so resolute that for Prince Jérôme, at least, who led Comte Reille's westernmost division in the assault, the taking of Hougoumont became a matter of personal honour. Ever more men were sacrificed in a series of desperate but unavailing attacks, which, in the course of the day, saw an Allied garrison of 3,500 keep 14,000 French veterans at bay.

'Never was a place more fiercely assaulted, nor better defended', Wheeler observed from the ridge.[26] At one point the manor house was all but taken when the French forced the north gate and entered the inner courtyard. Amazingly, the garrison commander, Colonel James Macdonell of Glengarry, with the help of four men, managed by sheer dint of effort to close this huge gate and replace its bar before proceeding to incapacitate every French intruder, a stirring achievement which drew Wellington's comment: 'The success of the battle of Waterloo depended on the closing of the gates of Hougoumont.'[27] The slaughter was dreadful, and French losses were particularly severe. When Gronow visited the scene next morning he found the orchard strewn with the dead, 'not less than two thousand men had there fallen', with all its apple trees, 'riddled and smashed', looking more like willows.[28]

At 1.00 p.m. Wellington was sufficiently encouraged by what he had seen of Hougoumont from the ridge to return to his command post at the elm tree. From there, he spotted on the horizon to the east a black line: surely the vanguard of Bülow's Prussian Corps. Napoleon saw it too, from his vantage point at Rossomme, and his response was threefold. He sent a last message to Grouchy which, though clear enough, was half a day too late. From his centre at the rear he despatched troops under Comte de Lobau to his right wing to neutralize Bülow, a necessary redeployment but one that disturbed the symmetry of his army and tied up more men. Finally, he ordered Comte d'Erlon's 18,000 infantry to strike at the heart of the Allied line, the brunt of which attack would fall on Picton's Fifth Division to the east of the crossroads.

At 1.30 p.m. eighty French guns prefaced this onslaught with a murderous half-hour bombardment. It was not long before Picton detected an increasing unsteadiness in the Dutch–Belgian light brigade in front of him. When his aide-de-camp, Captain Tyler, remarked that he was sure they would run, the general replied: 'Never mind; they shall have a taste of it, at all events.'[29] The softening up over, d'Erlon's splendid troops marched forward in three phalanxes with upwards of 200 men in each rank and 24 ranks deep. Eager for glory after missing out at Ligny, they stamped up the ridge to the constant drumming of the *pas de charge*, but though their intrepid head-on assault tested Allied nerve it was also seriously flawed in that only the first few rows of the French could fire muskets while the huge, close-ranked columns offered an invitingly deep target to those on the ridge. In the course of their advance, part of d'Erlon's troops stormed La Haye Sainte farm, driving the defending King's German Legion into its buildings, where they resisted fiercely. The French passed by, avoiding Prince Jérôme's error at Hougoumont and leaving the Germans isolated to their rear as they ascended the ridge. Kincaid wrote:

When the heads of their columns showed over the knoll they received such a fire from our first line, that they wavered, and hung behind it a little; but, cheered and encouraged by the gallantry of their officers, who were dancing and flourishing their swords in front, they at last boldly advanced to the opposite side of our hedge, and began to deploy.[30]

To the extreme east Prince Bernhard's Nassauers were quickly driven out of the lesser bastions of Papelotte and La Haye farms. In the centre, Bijlandt's Dutch–Belgian light brigade, having taken a pounding from French artillery in their forward position on the ridge, were now so appalled at the prospect of hand-to-hand fighting with French veterans that they fired only token shots before they turned and fled, running a gauntlet of abuse as they went back through Picton's ranks. With no impediment, the mighty columns now rapidly approached the crest of the Allied position and the French batteries behind gradually suspended their fire. This partial break in the thunder was followed by loud shouts from the columns of 'Vive l'Empereur!' and exhortations of 'En avant! En avant!'

At this critical moment Picton ordered his Peninsular generals Sir Denis Pack and Sir James Kempt to advance their brigades and fill the gap. Pack's Gordon Highlanders, Black Watch and 44th, reduced by Quatre Bras to barely 1,400 men, burst through the hedges and launched themselves with fixed bayonets into the French masses, who outnumbered them four to one. Seeing them swallowed up by the sheer weight of enemy ranks, Picton gave his last commands astride his cob at the front of Kempt's brigade: 'Charge!', he bellowed, waving his sword, 'Charge! Hurrah! Hurrah!',[31] which was answered by a tremendous shout and surge from his followers. Then, uttering the words 'Rally the Highlanders!', he plunged into the thick of d'Erlon's troops. There, a bullet pierced his hat near the junction of crown and brim, killing him instantly.

This breath-taking counter-attack against overwhelming odds stopped the French in their tracks and held the Allied line precisely when defeat seemed certain. Moments later an overexcited Lord Uxbridge ordered a charge of heavy cavalry by the Union and Household Brigades, the one under Sir William Ponsonby on the left and the other under Lord Edward Somerset, Fitzroy's brother, on the right. Clearing the hedge like steeplechasers, they turned the French on their heels and sent them scampering down the slippery ridge. Kincaid reported:

Next moment the Cuirassiers were charged by our household brigade and the infantry in our front giving way at the same time, under our terrific shower of musketry, the flying Cuirassiers tumbled in among the routed infantry, followed by the Life Guards, who were cutting away in all directions. Hundreds of the infantry threw themselves down, and pretended to be dead, while the cavalry galloped over them, and then got up and ran away. I never saw such another scene in all my life.[32]

But so great was the momentum of Allied cavalry they over-reached themselves riding headlong until, as Gronow wrote, 'they came upon a masked battery of twenty guns, which carried death and destruction through our ranks'. Ponsonby and many hundreds more paid with their lives for Uxbridge's exuberance. Wellington was 'perfectly furious', Gronow recorded, for Uxbridge had acted on impulse, without his Commander's orders.[33] Yet d'Erlon's first and heaviest assault had been repulsed and the Allied line along the Ohain road had held. Five hours later, at 7.00 p.m., Blücher would come down that same road and effectively end the battle. By that time, Captain Tyler had long since reclaimed the body of another veteran.

V

That afternoon saw successive French attempts to take the smoky bastions of Hougoumont and La Haye Sainte. All the while Napoleon kept the ridge under cannonade and musket fire: 'For the two or three succeeding hours there was no variety with us', wrote Kincaid, 'but one continued blaze of musketry. The smoke still hung so thick about us that, although not more than eighty yards asunder, we could only distinguish each other by the flashes of the pieces.'[34] At 4.00 p.m. Ney launched his cavalry between Hougoumont and La Haye Sainte upon the Allied right. But forty-three squadrons, so tightly packed they could barely advance at a trot, offered a huge target and once again, lacking close infantry support, fine French horsemen floundered on the rock of Allied squares.

With the cavalry repulsed and Lobau barely resisting Bülow to the east, Napoleon desperately needed to make ground some-where. He ordered Ney to take La Haye Sainte at all costs, which objective was finally realized by 6.30 p.m. Wellington responded by bringing every available man to shore up his centre against which Napoleon's last chance, the *Garde Impériale*, must surely strike. On they duly came, in three echelons, their bearskins rising above the ridge as they marched and drummed through the confusion of smoke, the ground under their feet churned

by hooves to liquid mud. But the Allied resistance continued
undaunted until, around 8.00 p.m., the *Garde* finally recoiled in
disarray while Blücher's First Corps under General Zieten
pierced the north-east corner of the French line.

'It was a fine summer's evening, just before sunset', Kincaid
observed, as the smoke cleared: 'The French were flying in one
confused mass. British lines were seen in close pursuit, and in
admirable order, as far as the eye could reach to the right, while
the plain to the left was filled with Prussians.'[35] It had been a
great victory, Wellington and Blücher agreed when they met
within an hour at the inn, appropriately named La Belle
Alliance, where they determined that the Prussians would take
up the pursuit. Victory, moreover, had been won by a greatly
inferior army, discounting the Prussians – 'a very bad army', in
Kincaid's view – which consisted largely of raw militia and only
a core of Peninsular veterans. The one toast Wellington drank
that night was 'To the Memory of the Peninsular War.'

POSTSCRIPT

Tyler safeguarded the body of General Sir Thomas Picton, which, on examination, showed such severe wounds from Quatre Bras as were thought likely to have proved fatal in themselves. Picton was the most senior officer to have been killed in the campaign. His name, therefore, was the first on the list in the official report prepared by Wellington for Lord Bathurst, and, consequently, the first to be uttered by the Prince Regent in lamenting the great number of mortalities suffered at Waterloo.[1]

Brought home via Dover and Canterbury to his town house at 21 Edward Street, later renamed Picton Place, the general was buried on 3 July 1815 in the family vault in the cemetery of St George's, Hanover Square, on the Bayswater Road. There had been talk of St Paul's Cathedral, but, perhaps for a familiar reason, this came to nothing at the time. The most splendid monument in his honour was erected from public subscription in Carmarthen in 1827, though this column, surmounted by a statue of the general, became unsafe and had to be replaced by a sturdier one in 1846. Following the Duke of Wellington's death, the supreme posthumous honour was done to Picton when a sculptural group, with his bust as the focal point, together with an inscription, was placed in the north-west transept of St Paul's. The event is recorded in the copy of H.B. Robinson's two-volume *Memoirs of Lieutenant-General Sir Thomas Picton* now in the possession of the University of Birmingham, in which appears the following note, signed by T. Sotherton Estcourt:

> In 1859, being Secretary of State for the Home Department, being applied to by Sir Frederick Stovin and Mr Picton to sanction the removal of the remains of Sir Thomas Picton from the cemetery on the north side of Hyde Park to St Paul's, I obtained the assent of the Queen. The Dean of St Paul's most kindly prepared a place

in the vault wherein repose the remains of the Duke of Wellington. The Duke of Cambridge, being Commander of the Forces, furnished an escort and military bier. Some old comrades of Sir Thomas Picton attended, my private secretary followed in my carriage and the removal was accomplished to the satisfaction of all parties who took an interest in it.[2]

This reinterment came about initially through the concern of Dr D. Brewer of St George's, who wrote to *The Times* on Thursday 5 May 1859 to explain the unsatisfactory state of affairs at his church cemetery:

Sir, – In the vaults of our burying-ground on the Bayswater-road may be seen the thick chest, or oak box, in which lie the remains of Sir Thomas Picton, as they were packed up in the village of Waterloo and sent to England. It seems obvious that the body was only to have found a temporary resting-place in these vaults, as the character of the receptacle is rather that of a rude packing-case than a suitable coffin.

These vaults are just closed by order of the Privy Council, and in a few days the brickwork, which is entirely to close in the coffins, will be commenced. Are there no old companions in arms of General Picton who would be glad to do for him what the medical profession did lately for John Hunter? It would be easy to apply to the Secretary of State for an order to have these remains removed, or, if it be thought that the bodies of our great heroes are the property of the nation, surely if a representation were made to the Government they would not be unwilling to transfer so illustrious a warrior to some more distinguished mausoleum.

On the following day, John Picton, the General's nephew, took up the matter. He wrote to *The Times* to thank Dr Brewer, and added:

Most willingly would I bear the expense of the removal as a personal matter, although the public act would be more gratifying to the feelings of the family, and I believe I may add more acceptable to the public, who still cherish a grateful memory of my heroic relative.

Four days later, on 10 May, he wrote again and pressed his case by quoting as follows from a letter that the Duke of Wellington had sent to him some years before his death:

Mr Picton does the Duke justice in giving him credit for sincere regard for the person of Sir Thomas Picton, and respect for his great merit and services. He died in the ranks of the army in the performance of a great service. The Duke has never failed to express his opinion of the services of Sir Thomas Picton, and never will, particularly if referred to and so required.

A month later, on 8 June, the reinterment ceremony took place. Noticed in *The Times*, the ceremony was reported rather more fully three days later in the weekly *Illustrated London News*:

> On Wednesday morning, according to arrangement, the remains of the late Lieut.-General Sir Thomas Picton were removed from the cemetery belonging to St George's, Hanover-square, to St Paul's Cathedral. The coffin was placed in a gun-carriage drawn by eight horses. The body was followed by Mr J. Picton [the principal mourners are now listed]. Then followed the carriages of Lord Stafford, Mr Estcourt, the Home Secretary, Lord Gough, General Sir F. Stovin, Sir R. Burgoyne [etc]. The procession moved slowly through the principal streets to St Paul's Cathedral...where a vault had been constructed, not far from the tomb of Wellington, the organ playing the 'Dead March in Saul'. Followed by the old comrades of the illustrious General, the body was conveyed in the most solemn silence to the tomb, where it was received and lowered into the grave, in the presence of Colonel Vereker, J. Picton Esq., and a large number of private mourners. The cavalcade was then reformed; the carriage of the Lord Mayor, immediately followed by that of his Royal Highness the Duke of Cambridge, heading the mournful cortége.

The few Peninsular veterans who attended this ceremony, forty-four years after Picton's death, must have thought he was at last receiving the recognition that was his due. Even before Waterloo, there can be little doubt he had earned a peerage for his outstanding achievements in the Peninsular War and had he survived that final battle he would surely have been so honoured. Picton paid dearly for his errors of judgement and his overzealousness in Trinidad, especially if the political factors that terminated his governorship are taken into account. Having been asked to do a difficult job, he had done it remarkably well, only to be told that he had done the wrong job. In retrospect, Whitehall decided that it was not a firm hand that was needed after all, though anything less at the time may well have been calamitous. The situation on the ground in Port of Spain was made impossible by the absolute incompatibility of two strikingly different personalities, Picton's and Fullarton's, with the abrasive, parade-ground manner of the ex-governor forever at odds with the polished ways of the first commissioner.

That Picton was an irascible and somewhat coarse character can hardly be denied. Bred up a remote country squire and hard-bitten soldier, he was unable or unwilling to play the game according to the rules of 'society'. Thus he was no ladies' man, nor was he favoured with invitations to dine with the likes of Wellington. Indeed his associates, like the young Lewis

Flanagan, were decidedly humble. Yet his pugnacity and resolution also worked very much to his advantage, notably in the difficult defensive phase of the Peninsular campaign when a tight hold on discipline was vital both to maintain divisional morale and to avoid antagonizing the Portuguese hosts. In action, there can be no doubt of the calibre of a commander who stamped his own personality on 'the fighting division'. His courage at Waterloo, where he concealed the wounds inflicted at Quatre Bras, shows the mettle of a man who was always prepared to lead by example. At Busaco, Vitoria, Ciudad Rodrigo and especially Badajoz, his contribution was not excelled by any other general who served under Wellington in the Peninsula. It is fitting that his remains should lie so close to those of the man he called 'the great luminary'.

*   *   *

On 9 June 1815, the day before he departed for Flanders, Picton had made a new will in London. Appointing his brother, the Revd Edward, his sole executor and major beneficiary, he bequeathed £100 to his friend Lewis Flanagan, an annuity of £150 to each of his sisters, and stipulated:

> further I do hereby expressly charge my Estate in the Island of Trinidad in the West Indies with the sum of four thousand pounds in favor of my four natural or reputed children by Rosette Smith now viz. Thomas Rose, Richard Rose, Augusta Rose and _____ Rose equally to be divided between them share and share alike with lawful Interest from the day of my decease.[3]

Thomas, the eldest, became an army surgeon and, after training in London, took a post with the Royal African Colonial Corps, succumbing to remittent fever on 5 March 1824, on the voyage out to Cape Colony. It is understood that the Revd Edward, then resident at Iscoed, was not unduly aggrieved by the news. What became of Richard, Augusta and their anonymous sibling, is not known. The subsequent career of their mother, Rosetta Smith, the great love of Thomas Picton's life, would no doubt also make interesting reading.

Notes

Abbreviations

NLW MS National Library of Wales Manuscript
SPFD Schedule of Picton Family Documents, National Library of Wales
AR *Annual Register*
DNB *Dictionary of National Biography*

Chapter One

1. N.H. Coleridge, *Six Months in the West Indies,* John Murray, London, 1825, p. 61
2. The articles of capitulation are given in Gertrude Carmichael, *The History of the West Indian Islands of Trinidad and Tobago 1498–1900*, Alvin Redman, London, 1961, pp. 373–5, and in Donald Thomas (ed.), *State Trials: The Public Conscience*, Vol. II, Routledge & Kegan Paul, London, 1977, pp. 206–8.
3. Glyn Picton, 'General Sir Thomas Picton and the Pictons of Pembrokeshire', *The Pembrokeshire Historian*, Vol. I, 1959, p. 47.
4. See George Lewis, NLW MS 1409E, p. 11.
5. See B.P. Swann, 'Sir Thomas Picton: Some Unpublished Facts about his career and relations', *Dyfed Family History Journal/Cymdeithas Hanes Teuluoedd Dyfed*, Vol. I, p. 174. Dr Picton Swann cites a manuscript letter that tells the somewhat unlikely tale of the missing brother appearing amongst Picton's division years later in the Peninsula. See also SPFD 383, p. 10.
6. Louis, or Lewis, Lochée was the author of several books on military matters, including *An Essay on Military Education*, Cadell, London, 1776.
7. See H.B. Robinson, *Memoirs of Lt.-Gen. Sir Thomas Picton*, in two volumes, Richard Bentley, London, 1836, Vol. I, p. 17.
8. See Robert Howell, 'Pembrokeshire in Wartime, 1793–1815', *Pembrokeshire County History*, Vol. III, 1982, p. 402.
9. David Geggus, 'The Cost of Pitt's Caribbean Campaigns, 1793–1798',

The Historical Journal, Vol. XXVI, 1983, p. 702.

10. *DNB*, LVIII, p.169.

11. E.A. Draper, *An Address to the British Public, on the Cause of Brigadier-General Picton*, D. Jacques, London, 1806, appendices, p. 40.

12. Ibid., pp. 20–23.

13. The twenty-eight articles of the Royal Cedula on Colonization of 1783 are given in Carmichael, pp. 363–9.

14. Draper, p. 36–9.

15. P.F. McCallum, *Travels in Trinidad*, John Arden, Liverpool, 1805, p. 153.

16. Ibid., p.188.

17. Ibid., p.22.

18. See Bridget Brereton, *A History of Modern Trinidad 1783–1962*, Heinemann, Port of Spain, 1981, p. 16.

19. Robinson, *Memoirs*, Vol. I, p. 62.

20. Captain F. Mallet, *Descriptive Account of the Island of Trinidad*, W. Fadden, London, 1802, p. 2.

21. DNB, p. 636.

22. See V.S. Naipaul, *The Loss of El Dorado*, André Deutsch, London, 1969, pp. 146–7.

23. Carmichael, pp. 377–9 and Robinson, *Memoirs*, Vol. II, pp. 429–32.

24. Robinson, *Memoirs*, Vol. I, pp. 73–4.

25. NLW MS 14005E, p. 2.

26. This phrase to describe unhealthy slaves was used conventionally by Dr Alexander Williams; see *Trinidad Negroes*, 'Extracts from the Minutes of Evidence taken by the Committee of the Council of Trinidad for enquiring into the Negro Character', R.J. Wilmot Horton, Colonial Department, House of Commons, 14 June 1827, p. 9.

27. Draper, appendices, pp. 20–2.

28. Robinson, *Memoirs*, Vol. I, pp. 76–80.

29. NLW MS 21687E, p. 1.

30. McCallum, p. 145.

31. Draper, pp. 36–9.

32. McCallum, p. 163.

33. Williams, p. 69.

34. McCallum, p. 173.

35. Carmichael, p. 55.

36. Naipaul, p. 185.

37. See Robin Furneaux, *William Wilberforce*, Hamish Hamilton, London, 1974, p. 223. Another Wilberforce description was 'that greatest of all sublunary evils'; see *The Times*, 31 May, 1804.

38. Williams, p. 66.

39. Draper, appendices, pp. 43–4.

40. Thomas Picton, *Evidence Taken at Port of Spain in the Case of Luisa Calderón, with a Letter Addressed to Sir Samuel Hood*, J. Budd, London, 1806, p. xv.

41. W. Fullarton, *A Statement, Letters, and Documents, Respecting the Affairs of Trinidad*, B. McMillan, London, 1804, p. 3. Further citations of Fullarton, when not noted, are from this source.

42. Thomas Picton, *Letter Addressed to the Right Honourable Lord Hobart*, Shury and Lloyd, London, 1804, p. 30.
43. Fullarton, p. 55.
44. McCallum, p. 25.
45. In Fullarton's account he is at pains to show that he was a good match for his adversary: 'the violence with which B.G. Picton struck the rails of the gallery with his hands ... induced Colonel Fullarton to strike the rails with superior vehemence', op. cit., p. 43.
46. Ibid., pp. 9–10.
47. Ibid., pp. 47–8.
48. Ibid., p. 44.
49. Ibid., p. 13.
50. Picton, *Letter*, p. 28.
51. Ibid., p. 19.
52. Ibid., p. 91.
53. Fullarton, p. 13.
54. Ibid., pp. 66–7.
55. Picton, *Letter*, pp. 11–12.
56. Ibid., p. 14.
57. Fullarton, p. 23.
58. Picton, *Letter*, p. 82.
59. Draper, pp. 34–37.
60. Fullarton, p. 78.
61. Ibid., p. 211.
62. McCallum, p. 249.
63. Fullarton, p. 19.
64. Ibid., p. 22.
65. Picton, *Letter*, pp. 18–19.
66. 'It is impossible for me to think of going on shore', wrote Fullarton on 15 June, 'until I have fully explained to you the circumstances of insult and outrage which have been offered to His Majesty's Civil Government in this Island, by the Military Power under the orders of B.G. Picton', op. cit., p. 106.

CHAPTER TWO

1. W.S. Lewis, *Three Tours Through London in the Years 1748, 1776, 1797*, Westport, Greenwood, 1941, p. 93.
2. Thomas Picton, 'Letter to Sir Samuel Hood', in *Evidence*, p. 2.
3. Robinson, *Memoirs*, Vol. I, p. 138.
4. Ibid., pp. 142–51.
5. Picton, *Evidence*, pp. ix–xi.
6. T.J. Howells, *A Complete Collection of State Trials*, Vol. XXX, Longman, London, 1822, p. 227. See also Picton, *Evidence*, pp. xvii–xxiv.
7. Ibid., p. vi.
8. Howells, p. 232.
9. Ibid., p. 328. The proceedings and depositions in the criminal case

brought against Carlos González and Luisa Calderón in Port of Spain, 1801, are found in Exhibits A–K annexed to the proceedings of the 'Trial of Thomas Picton', Howells, pp. 327–450.

10. Ibid., p. 409.
11. Ibid., pp. 412–13.
12. Ibid., pp. 419–26.
13. Picton, *Evidence*, p. 8 and p. 15. All statements in the examinations of the Mandamus proceedings are taken from this source.
14. Ibid., p. 12.
15. Ibid., p. 37.
16. Ibid., p. 16 et seq.
17. Ibid., p. 84.
18. Ibid., p. 61.
19. Ibid., p. 69.
20. Ibid., pp. 75–6.
21. Ibid., p. 44 et seq.
22. Ibid., p. 54.
23. Ibid., p. 136.
24. Ibid., pp. 137–8.
25. Picton, *Letter*, p. 89.
26. McCallum, p. viii.
27. J.M. Beattie, 'Garrow for the Defence', *History Today*, February 1991, p. 53.
28. The following account of the trial is taken from Howells, Vol. XXX, pp. 449–540.
29. NLW MS 18428E, p. 1.
30. For Draper's trial see Howells, Vol. XXX, p. 1063 et seq.
31. NLW MS 5416E, p. 2.
32. Ibid.
33. AR (1806), p. 457.
34. Robinson, *Memoirs*, Vol. I, pp. 205–8.
35. See Howells, Vol. XXX, p. 807. The second trial is given on pp. 805–84.
36. Ibid., p. 870.
37. Ibid., p. 1087 and p. 1129.

CHAPTER THREE

1. G.C., Bond *The Grand Expedition*, University of Georgia: Athens, Ga., 1979, p. 9.
2. Edward Edwards, 'Some Unpublished Letters of Sir Thomas Picton', *The West Wales Historical Records*, Vol. XII, (1927) p. 135.
3. NLW MS 21687E, p. 7.
4. W. Wheeler, *Letters of Private Wheeler, 1809–1828*, ed. B.H. Liddell Hart, Michael Joseph, London, 1951, p. 28.
5. Edwards, Vol. XII, p. 136.
6. Anon, *Letters from Flushing*, Richard Phillips, London, 1809, pp. 30–2.

7. Edwards, Vol. XII p. 136.
8. Ibid., pp. 136–7.
9. *Letters from Flushing*, p. 40.
10. Ibid., p. 81.
11. Edwards, Vol. XII, p. 138.
12. Wheeler, p. 35.
13. *Letters from Flushing*, p. 147.
14. Ibid., pp. 150–1.
15. Edwards, Vol. XII, pp. 138–9.
16. NLW MS 21687E, p. 8.
17. *Letters from Flushing*, p. 173.
18. Harris, (ed. Curling H.) *Recollections of Rifleman Harris*, Peter Davies, London, 1928, pp. 173–4.
19. *Letters from Flushing*, p. 233.

CHAPTER FOUR

1. Edwards, Vol. XII, pp. 140–1.
2. William Grattan, *Adventures of the Connaught Rangers from 1808 to 1814*, two volumes, Colburn, London, 1847, Vol. I, p. 3.
3. NLW MS 18428E, p. 77.
4. Edwards, XII, p. 141.
5. Ibid., p. 143.
6. Grattan, Vol. I, p. 16.
7. Ibid., p. 17.
8. McCallum, p.174.
9. Grattan, Vol. I, pp. 21–2.
10. Edwards, XII, p. 144.
11. George Simmons, *A British Rifleman*, A. and C. Black, London, 1899, p. 46.
12. Edwards, Vol. XII, p. 143.
13. Ibid., p. 145.
14. Ibid., p. 146.
15. Simmons, pp. 49–50.
16. Edwards, Vol. XII, p. 147.
17. Ibid., p. 145.
18. Simmons, p. 69.
19. Duke of Wellington, *Supplementary Despatches. Correspondence of Field Marshal Arthur Duke of Wellington, K.G. Edited by his son the Duke of Wellington*, Vols. I–XI, John Murray, London, 1858–64, Vol. VI, p. 563.
20. Edwards, Vol. XII, p. 148.
21. Ibid., p. 149.
22. Simmons, p. 76.
23. Wellington, *Supplementary Despatches*, Vol. VI, pp. 563–4. It is also clear from Wellington's dispatches that Craufurd was at fault. On 20 April he had written to Craufurd completely rejecting his plan for an attack (Wellington, *Selections from the Despatches and General Orders of*

Field Marshall the Duke of Wellington, John Murray, London, p. 357). On 28 June he wrote: 'Your situation gives me a great deal of uneasiness; and it appears that, if the enemy should make their preparations to attack you before daylight ... you would find it very difficult to withdraw your corps' (ibid., p. 369). On 23 July he admonished his wayward general: 'Your own report points out clearly the variations from the original plan ... I can only say that I have never seen an attack by our troops in which similar, if not greater, accidents and mistakes have not occurred, and in which orders have not been given, from which no authority had proceeded from the Commander' (ibid., p. 371). Finally, on 30 July: 'It is very desirable that the General Officers commanding divisions should understand that the divisions under their command respectively are only parts of an army, which must be governed by system and rule; and that every departure from the system ordered, and the rule laid down, however convenient to the particular division, must be inconvenient to the army at large, and therefore detrimental to the service' (ibid., p. 396).

24. Edwards, Vol. XII, p. 149.
25. Robinson, *Mémoires*, Vol. I, p. 300.
26. Edwards, Vol. XII, p. 149.
27. Simmons, p. 83.
28. Edwards, Vol. XII, p. 150.
29. Edwards, Vol. XIII, p. 32.
30. See G.D.H. Cole, *The Life of William Cobbett*, Collins, London, 1927, p. 151.
31. Edwards, Vol. XII, p. 151.
32. Robinson, Vol. I, p. 299.
33. Baron de Marbot, *Mémoires du général Baron de Marbot*, Plon, Paris, 1891, p. 378.
34. Ibid., p. 383.
35. Ibid., p. 332 and pp. 380–1.
36. Ibid., p. 386.
37. Ibid., p. 390.
38. Sherer, pp. 107–8.
39. A.L.F. Schaumann, *On the Road with Wellington*, Heinemann, London, 1924, p. 246.
40. Grattan, Vol. I, p. 49 and p. 58.
41. Edwards, Vol. XII, p. 152.
42. Ibid., p. 153.
43. Marbot, p. 393.
44. Wellington, *Supplementary Despatches*, Vol. VI, pp. 606–7.
45. Edwards, Vol. XII, p. 154.
46. Ibid., p. 157.
47. Robinson, *Memoirs*, Vol. I, p. 331.
48. Edwards, Vol. XII, p. 155.
49. Ibid., p. 153.
50. Marbot, p. 402.
51. Lawrence, p. 69.
52. Ibid., p. 68.

53. Wellington, *Supplementary Despatches*, Vol. VI, p. 605 and p. 606.
54. Ibid., p. 607.
55. Edwards, Vol. XII, p. 155.
56. W. Lawrence, *The Autobiography of Sergeant William Lawrence*, Sampson Low, London, 1886, pp. 69–70.
57. Edwards, Vol. XII, p. 153.
58. Marbot, p. 405.
59. Edwards, Vol. XII, p. 154.
60. Wellington, *Supplementary Despatches*, Vol. VII, p. 1.
61. Ibid.
62. Lawrence, p. 70.
63. Edwards, Vol. XII, p. 155.
64. Wellington, *Supplementary Despatches*, Vol. VII, p. 4.
65. Grattan, Vol. I, pp. 72–3.
66. Edwards, Vol. XII, p. 156.
67. Ibid., pp. 157–8.
68. Simmons, pp. 111–12.
79. Marbot, p. 406.
70. Edwards, Vol. XII, p. 156.
71. Simmons, pp. 121–2.
72. Marbot, p. 417.
73. Wellington, *Supplementary Despatches*, Vol. VII, p. 2.
74. Grattan, Vol. I, pp. 74–5.
75. Ibid., p. 77.
76. Wellington, *Supplementary Despatches*, Vol. VII, p. 43.
77. Edwards, Vol. XII, p. 158.
78. Simmons, pp. 136–7.
79. Wheeler, p. 51.
80. J. Donaldson, *The Eventful Life of a Soldier*, William Tait, Edinburgh, 1827, pp. 164–5.
81. Edwards, Vol. XII, p. 159.
82. Ibid., p. 160.
83. Marbot, pp. 431–2.
84. Edwards, Vol. XII, p. 160.
85. Grattan, Vol. I, p. 86.
86. Donaldson, p. 168.
87. Marbot, p. 444.
88. Edwards, Vol. XII, pp. 160–1.
89. Marbot, p. 444.
90. Edwards, Vol. XII, p. 161.
91. Donaldson, p. 174.
92. Simmons, p. 161.
93. Edwards, Vol. XII, p. 162.
94. Ibid., p. 161.
95. Donaldson, p. 177.
96. Edwards, Vol. XII, p. 162.
97. Donaldson, p. 179.
98. Wellington, *Supplementary Despatches*, Vol. VII, p. 100, p. 106 and p. 101.

99. Ibid., p. 123.
100. Donaldson, pp. 188–9.
101. Marbot, p. 459.
102. Grattan, Vol. I, p. 96.
103. Donaldson, p. 198.
104. Edwards, Vol. XIII, p. 1.
105. Wellington, Vol. VII, p. 123.

CHAPTER FIVE

1. Donaldson, p. 204.
2. Grattan, Vol. I, pp. 103–5.
3. Simmons, p. 188.
4. Edwards, Vol. XIII, p. 1.
5. Wellington, *Supplementary Despatches*, Vol. VII, p. 134.
6. Ibid., p. 135. Wellington would become increasingly critical of Spanish soldiers: 'I do not expect much from the exertions of the Spaniards, notwithstanding all that we have done for them. They cry *viva*, and are very fond of us, and hate the French, but they are in general the most incapable of useful exertion of all the nations that I have known', 8 August 1812, *Selections*, p. 621; and 'if I could depend upon the Spaniards to do anything. But I am quite in despair of them', 23 November 1812, ibid., p. 641.
7. Edwards, Vol. XIII, p. 2.
8. Wheeler, pp. 58–9.
9. Ibid., p. 61.
10. Edwards, Vol. XIII, p. 3.
11. NLW MS 216787E, p. 10.
12. Edwards, Vol. XIII, pp. 2–3.
13. NLW MS 21687E, p. 11.
14. Edwards, Vol. XIII, pp. 4–5.
15. Ibid., p. 6.
16. Grattan, Vol. I, pp. 162–3.
17. Donaldson, p. 223.
18. Grattan, Vol. I, p. 163.
19. Edwards, Vol. XIII, p. 6.
20. Ibid., pp. 6–7.
21. Donaldson, p. 225.
22. NLW MS 5416E, p. 26.
23. Grattan, Vol. I, p. 168.
24. NLW MS 5416E, p. 27.
25. E. Costello, *Adventures of a Soldier*, Colburn, London, 1852, p. 94.
26. Simmons, p. 219.
27. Grattan, Vol. I, pp. 180–2.
28. Donaldson, pp. 231–2.
29. J. Kincaid, *Adventures in the Rifle Brigade*, Peter Davies, London, 1929, p. 25.

30. Grattan, Vol. I, p. 193.
31. Ibid., p. 195.
32. Donaldson, p. 234.
33. W. Lawrence, pp. 103–4.
34. Robinson, *Memoirs*, Vol. II, p. 67.
35. Grattan, Vol. I, pp. 198–9.
36. Lawrence, p. 104.
37. Grattan, Vol. I, p. 206.
38. Kincaid, p. 83.
39. Grattan, Vol. I, p. 216.
40. Lawrence, p. 105.
41. Wellington, *Supplementary Despatches*, Vol. VII, p. 308.
42. Grattan, Vol. I, p. 242.
43. Ibid, pp. 244–5.
44. Edwards, Vol. XIII, p. 11.
45. Grattan, Vol. I, pp. 244–5.
46. J. MacCarthy, *Recollections of the Storming of the Castle of Badajos*, Egerton's Military Library, London, 1836, p. 15.
47. Kincaid, p. 93.
48. Grattan, Vol. I, p. 257.
49. MacCarthy, pp. 17–18.
50. Kincaid, p. 92.
51. Edwards, Vol. XIII, p. 11.
52. MacCarthy, p. 23.
53. Lawrence, p. 109.
54. MacCarthy, p. 30.
55. Kincaid, p. 95.
56. Lawrence, p. 111.
57. MacCarthy, p. 38.
58. Ibid., pp. 38–41.
59. Grattan, Vol. I, pp. 271–2.
60. Donaldson, p. 243.
61. Edwards, Vol. XIII, pp. 12–13.
62. Donaldson, p. 243.
63. Grattan, Vol. I, p. 272.
64. Myatt, *British Sieges of the Peninsular War*, Spellmount Ltd, Tunbridge Wells, 1987, p. 96.
65. Kincaid, p. 97.
66. Grattan, Vol. I, p. 275.
67. Lawrence, p. 112.
68. Robinson, *Memoirs*, Vol. II, p. 111.
69. Grattan, Vol. I, p. 273.
70. Robinson, *Memoirs*, Vol. II, p. 138.
71. Donaldson, p. 244.
72. Grattan, Vol. I, pp. 273–4.
73. Robinson, *Memoirs*, Vol. II, p. 120.
74. Grattan, Vol. I, pp. 279–80.
75. Robinson, *Memoirs*, Vol. II, p. 130.
76. Ibid., p. 128.

77. Edwards, Vol. XIII, p. 12.
78. Lawrence, p. 116.
79. Grattan, Vol. II, p. 4.
80. Donaldson, pp. 246–7.
81. Lawrence, pp. 116–7.
82. Grattan, Vol. II, p. 4.
83. Donaldson, p. 252.
84. Kincaid, p. 103.
85. Grattan, Vol. II, pp. 16–17.
86. Donaldson, p. 246.
87. Grattan, Vol. II, pp. 3–4.
88. Kincaid, p. 101.
89. Wellington, *Supplementary Despatches*, Vol. VII, p. 311.
90. P.H. Stanhope, 5th Earl, *Notes of Conversations with the Duke of Wellington, 1831–1851*, John Murray, London, 1888, p. 104.
91. Ibid., p. 14.
92. Edwards, Vol. XIII, p. 12.
93. Ibid., p. 13.
94. Robinson, *Memoirs*, Vol. II, p. 150.

CHAPTER SIX

1. Edwards, Vol. XIII, p. 13.
2. Howells, Vol. XXX, p. 1129.
3. Edwards, Vol. XIII, pp. 13–14.
4. Ibid., p. 14.
5. Kincaid, p. 128.
6. Wellington, *Selections*, p. 643.
7. Edwards, Vol. XIII, p. 11.
8. Ibid., p. 15.
9. Ibid., pp. 16–17.
10. Wellington, *Selections*, p. 649.
11. Ibid., p. 659.
12. Simmons, pp. 294–5.
13. Kincaid, p. 158.
14. Edwards, Vol. XIII, pp. 17–18.
15. Kincaid, p. 161.
16. Edwards, Vol. XIII, p. 18.
17. Lawrence, p. 134.
18. Simmons, p. 290.
19. Kincaid, p. 163.
20. Edwards, Vol. XIII, pp. 18–19.
21. Wellington, *Supplementary Despatches*, Vol. VIII, p. 112 and p. 114.
22. Ibid., p. 122.
23. NLW MS 16704E, p. 2.
24. Robinson, *Memoirs*, Vol. II, pp. 247–51.
25. Edwards, Vol. XIII, p. 19. See also NLW MS 18428E, pp. 38–9.

26. Ibid., p. 22.
27. Ibid., p. 19 and pp. 22–3.
28. Ibid., 20. See also Wellington, *Selections*, p. 780.
29. Kincaid, pp. 188–9.
30. Wellington, *Supplementary Despatches*, Vol. VIII, p. 615.
31. Edwards, Vol. XIII, p. 22.
32. Ibid., p. 21.
33. Wellington, *Supplementary Despatches*, Vol. VIII, p. 599.
34. Edwards, Vol. XIII, p. 21.
35. Ibid., p. 23.
36. Simmons, p. 343.
37. Wellington, *Supplementary Despatches*, Vol. VII, p. 627.
38. Ibid., p. 745.

CHAPTER SEVEN

1. Stanhope, p. 69.
2. Edwards, Vol. XIII, p. 24.
3. Ibid., p. 27.
4. Ibid., p. 29.
5. Stanhope, p. 323.
6. Edwards, Vol. XIII, p. 26 and p. 27.
7. Robinson, *Memoirs*, Vol. II, pp. 361–2.
8. Edwards, Vol. XIII, p. 30.
9. R.H. Gronow, *Reminiscences and Recollections of Captain Gronow*, (ed. J. Grego), Nimmo, London, 1889, p. 65.
10. Ibid., p. 66.
11. Ibid., pp. 66–7.
12. Kincaid, p. 232.
13. Major A.F. Becke, *Napoleon and Waterloo*, Kegan Paul, London, 1936, p. 80; also Elizabeth Longford, *Wellington: The Years of the Sword*, Weidenfeld & Nicolson, London, 1969, p. 430.
14. Kincaid, pp. 237–8.
15. Longford, p. 433.
16. Robinson, *Memoirs*, Vol. II, p. 377.
17. Gronow, p. 141.
18. Wheeler, p. 170.
19. Gronow, p. 68.
20. Kincaid, p. 247.
21. Gronow, p. 68.
22. Kincaid, pp. 248–9.
23. Gronow, p. 69.
24. Wheeler, p. 171.
25. Gronow, p. 142.
26. Wheeler, p. 172.
27. Longford, p. 459.
28. Gronow, p. 72.

29. William Siborne, *The Waterloo Campaign, 1815*, Fourth Edition, Archibald Constable & Co., London, 1895, pp. 396–7.
30. Kincaid, p. 249.
31. Robinson, *Memoirs*, Vol. II, p. 384.
32. Kincaid, pp. 250–1.
33. Gronow, p. 74.
34. Kincaid, p. 255.
35. Ibid., pp. 256–7.

POSTSCRIPT

1. See Wellington, *Selections*, p. 859 and p. 873; also AR, (1815) p. 177.
2. Glyn Picton, p. 47.
3. SPFD, p. 40.

Bibliography

1. Manuscript Sources

A. *Picton's Letters:*

Fifty of Picton's letters were collected in 1927 by Edward Edwards, 'Some Unpublished Letters of Sir Thomas Picton', *The West Wales Historical Records*, Vol. XII, pp. 133–66 and Vol. XIII, pp. 1–32. These deal mainly with the Peninsular years and are taken from the original letters in the possession of the National Library of Wales. In quoting from them, I have compared them with the originals, and made a few amendments where it seemed to me Edwards had erred in deciphering what Picton himself called his 'miserable scrawl' (Robinson, *Memoirs*, Vol. II, p. 388).

Picton's letters in the National Library of Wales:

NLW MS 5416E Sixty-two letters to Lewis Flanagan (which constitute the majority of those collected by Edward Edwards).
NLW MS21687E Twelve letters to Joseph Marryat, MP.
NLW MS 16704E Two letters: to Major-General Browning and to the General Officers of the Third Division.
NLW MS 18428E Seven letters from Thomas Picton and one from William Garrow to Captain Chambers, Picton's aide-de-camp.
NLW MS 14005E Three letters from Picton to John Reese Stokes.
Schedule of Picton Family Documents.
No. 40 Sir Thomas Picton's will, dated London, 9 June 1815.
No. 96 Letter to his brother Edward.

B. *Other material in the National Library of Wales:*

NLW MS 1409E History of the Family of Picton compiled and written by George Lewis, Haverfordwest, July 1868.
NLW MS 11091E Pembrokeshire Papers: including 'Another Affair of Honour', on the duel between Picton and Thomas Hassall (but see

the more reliable account of Glyn Picton listed in Published Sources (2A).

2. PUBLISHED SOURCES

A. *General:*

My two most important sources are:

Myatt, Frederick. *Peninsular General, Sir Thomas Picton 1758–1815,* David & Charles, Newton Abbot, 1980.
Robinson, H.B. *Memoirs of Lieutenant-General Sir Thomas Picton,* in two volumes, Richard Bentley, London, 1836.

I also made frequent use of the *Annual Register, The Times* and the *Dictionary of National Biography.*
The following two articles provided useful genealogical and biographical material: Glyn Picton, 'General Sir Thomas Picton and the Pictons of Pembrokeshire', *The Pembrokeshire Historian,* Vol. I, 1959, pp. 41–59; B.P. Swann, 'Sir Thomas Picton: Some Unpublished Facts about his Career and Relations' *Dyfed Family History Journal/Cymdeithas Hanes Teuluoedd Dyfed,* I, No.6, 1984, pp. 172–5.

B. *On the Trinidad Years and the London Trials:*

The most detailed account of the Trinidad years is provided in Part III of V.S. Naipaul's *The Loss of El Dorado,* André Deutsch, London, 1969. A full report of the trial is found in T.J. Howells, *A Complete Collection of State Trials,* Vol. XXX, Longman, London, 1822. See also *The Trial of Governor Picton for inflicting the Torture on Luisa Calderon,* Derwick & Clarke, London, 1806, and the more accessible but excerpted version of 'The Trial of Thomas Picton' in *State Trials; The Public Conscience,* Vol. II, edited by Donald Thomas, Routledge & Kegan Paul, London, 1977, pp. 169–244.

The following offer highly partisan accounts:

Draper, E.A. *An Address to the British Public, on the Cause of Brigadier-General Picton,* D. Jacques, London, 1806.
Fullarton, W. *A Statement, Letters, and Documents, Respecting the Affairs of Trinidad,* B. McMillan, London, 1804.
McCallum, P.F. *Travels in Trinidad,* John Arden, Liverpool, 1805.
Picton, Thomas. *Letter Addressed to the Right Honourable Lord Hobart,* Shury and Lloyd, London, 1804.
— *Evidence Taken at Port of Spain in the Case of Luisa Calderón, with a Letter Addressed to Sir Samuel Hood,* J. Budd, London, 1806.

C. On the Campaigns in Europe Against Napoleon, 1809–15:

The following are the accounts of soldiers from which I have quoted with some frequency:

Anon (an officer of the 81st Regiment). *Letters From Flushing,* Richard Phillips, London, 1809.

Donaldson, J. *The Eventful Life of a Soldier,* William Tait, Edinburgh, 1827.

Grattan, William. *Adventures of the Connaught Rangers, from 1808 to 1814,* two volumes, Colburn, London, 1847.

Gronow, R.H. (ed. J. Grego) *Reminiscences and Recollections of Captain Gronow,* Nimmo, London, 1889. See also the abridged version with an introduction by John Raymond, Bodley Head, London, 1964; and *Captain Gronow: His Reminiscences of Regency and Victorian Life 1810–1860,* edited by C. Hibbert, Kyle Cathie, London, 1991.

Harris (ed. Curling, H.) *Recollections of Rifleman Harris,* Peter Davies, London, 1928.

Kincaid, J. *Adventures in the Rifle Brigade,* Peter Davies, London, 1929.

Lawrence, W. (ed. G.N. Bankes) *The Autobiography of Sergeant William Lawrence,* Sampson Low, London, 1886.

MacCarthy, J. *Recollections of the Storming of the Castle of Badajos,* Egerton's Military Library, London, 1836.

Marbot, Baron de. *Mémoires du général Baron de Marbot,* Plon, Paris, 1891.

Simmons, George (ed. W. Verner). *A British Rifleman,* A. and C. Black, London, 1899.

Stanhope, P.H. 5th Earl. *Notes of Conversations with the Duke of Wellington 1831–51,* John Murray, London, 1888.

Wellington, Duke of. *Supplementary Despatches. Correspondence, and Memoranda of Field Marshal Arthur Duke of Wellington, K.G.* Edited by his son the Duke of Wellington, Vols I–XI, John Murray, London, 1858–64.

— (ed. J. Gurwood). *General Orders of the Duke of Wellington,* 1809–1815, Clewes, London, 1837.

— (ed. J. Gurwood). *Selections from the Despatches and General Orders of Field Marshall the Duke of Wellington,* John Murray, London, 1842.

Wheeler, W. (ed. B.H. Liddell Hart). *Letters of Private Wheeler, 1809–1828,* Michael Joseph, London, 1951.

D. Background:

Araújo e Silva, Alberto. *The Battle of Buçaco,* Busaco Military Museum, no date.

Azcarate, Pablo de. *Wellington y España,* Espasa-Calpe, Madrid, 1960.

Becerra, Emilio. *Ciudad Rodrigo en la Guerra de la Independencia,* Patronato de la Casa Municipal de Cultura: Ciudad Rodrigo, 1988.

Beattie, J.M. 'Garrow for the Defence', *History Today,* February, 1991, pp. 49–53.

— *Crime and the Courts of England, 1660–1800,* Oxford University Press, 1986.

Becke, Major A.F. *Napoleon and Waterloo,* Kegan Paul, London, 1936.

Bell, George. *Rough Notes by an Old Soldier*, Day, London, 1867.

Birkett, Lord. *The New Newgate Calendar*, The Folio Society, London, 1960.

Bond, G.C. *The Grand Expedition*, University of Georgia: Athens, Ga., 1979.

Bragge, William. *Peninsular Portrait (1811–1814)*, Oxford University Press, London 1973.

Brereton, Bridget. *A History of Modern Trinidad 1783–1962*, Heinemann, Port of Spain, 1981.

Brett-James, A. *The Hundred Days*, Macmillan, London, 1964.

Brown, Ivor. *London: An Illustrated History*, Studio Vista, London, 1965.

Bryant, Arthur. *Years of Victory*, The Reprint Society, London, 1944.

Carmichael, Gertrude. *The History of the West Indian Islands of Trinidad and Tobago* 1498–1900, Alvin Redman, London, 1961.

Cassels, S.A.C. (ed.) *Peninsular Portrait 1811–1814. The Letters* of *Captain William Bragge, Third (King's Own) Dragoons*, Oxford University Press, London, 1963.

Chambers, G.L. *Busaco*, S. Sonnenschein, London, 1910.

Cole, G.D.H. *The Life of William Cobbett*, Collins, London, 1927.

Coleridge, N.H. *Six Months in the West Indies*, John Murray, London, 1825.

Costello, E. *Adventures of a Soldier*, Colburn, London, 1852.

Craufurd, A.H. *General Craufurd and his Light Division*, Griffith, Farran, Okeden & Welsh, London, 1891.

Esdaile, Charles J. *The Duke of Wellington and the Command of the Spanish Army 1812–1814*, McMillan, Basingstoke, 1990.

— 'Latin America and the Anglo–Spanish Alliance against Napoleon, 1808–1814', *Bulletin of Hispanic Studies*, Vol. LXIX, 1992, pp. 55–70.

Ford, Franklin L. *Europe 1780–1830*, Longman, London, second edition 1989.

Fraser, W. *Words on Wellington*, John Nimmo, London, 1900.

Furneaux, Robin. *William Wilberforce*, Hamish Hamilton, London, 1974.

Geggus, David. 'The Cost of Pitt's Caribbean Campaigns, 1793–1798', *The Historical Journal*, Vol. XXVI, 1983, pp. 699–706.

Gil Novales, Alberto. 'Images of Wellington and Britain in Spain after 1815'; the second Wellington Lecture, University of Southampton, 1990.

Hibbert, C. *London, the Biography of a City*, Longman, London, 1969.

Horward, D.D. *Napoleón y la península ibérica: Ciudad Rodrigo y Almeida, dos asedios análogos*, Diputación Provincial, Salamanca, 1984.

Howarth, David. *Waterloo: The Official Guide of the Waterloo Committee*, Pitkin Pictorials, Andover, 1980.

Lewis, W.S. *Three Tours Through London in the Years 1748, 1776, 1797*, Westport, Greenwood, 1941.

Lloyd, Thomas. *The Lost Houses of Wales*, Save Britain's Heritage, London, second edition, 1989.

Longford, Elizabeth. *Wellington: The Years of the Sword*, Weidenfeld & Nicolson, 1969.

Madariaga, Salvador. *Bolívar*, Hollis & Carter, London, 1952.

Mallet, Captain F. *Descriptive Account of the Island of Trinidad* [with map, made 1797], W. Fadden, London, 1802.

Maxwell, W. *Life of Wellington*, S. Low, London, 1883.

Myatt, Frederick. *British Sieges of the Peninsular War*, Spellmount Ltd, Tunbridge Wells, Hippocrene Books Inc., New York, 1987.

Napier, Sir William F.P. *History of the War in the Peninsula and the South of France 1807–1814*, six volumes, Cavendish, London, 1886.

Peters, C.H.J. *Flushing Throughout the Ages*, Library of the Gemeente Archief, Vlissingen, no date.

Plumb, J.H. *England in the Eighteenth Century*, Penguin, Harmondsworth, 1950.

Robertson, W.S. *The Life of Miranda*, Cooper Square, New York, 1959.

Robinson, T.G. *Los sitios de Badajoz*, Ayuntamiento de Badajoz, 1990.

Rudé, George. *The Eighteenth Century, 1715–1815*, Collier–MacMillan, London, 1965.

Schaumann, A.L.F., Translated by A.M. Ludovici, *On the Road with Wellington*, Heinemann, London, 1924.

Sherer, M. *Recollections of the Peninsula*, Longman, London, 1823.

Sherwig, John M. *Guineas and Gunpowder, British Foreign Aid in the Wars with France 1793–1815*, Harvard University Press, Cambridge Mass., 1969.

Siborne, William. *The Waterloo Campaign, 1815*, Fourth Edition, Archibald Constable and Co., London, 1895.

Sugget, Richard. *John Nash. Architect in Wales/Pensaer yng Nghymru*, Royal Commission on the Ancient and Historical Monuments of Wales, Aberystwyth, 1995.

Weller, J. *Wellington at Waterloo*, Longman, London, 1967.

INDEX